I Am Her Daughter

The Healing Path to a Woman's Power

By Licia Berry

I Am Her Daughter: *The Healing Path to a Woman's Power*

Cover Design: Marjorie Schoelles
Cover Image and Inside Title Page:
Mother One, First Mother, collage
Copyright © 2007 Licia Berry

Goddess Image:
Ahset, The Queen Returns, mixed media on masonite
Copyright © 2016 Licia Berry

Interior Book Design: Around the Writer's Table

ISBN-13: 978-0692718360

ISBN-10: 0692718362

for Roz ♥

I Am Her Daughter

*The Healing Path
to a Woman's Power*

(originally titled *I Am My Own Daughter*)

By Licia Berry

*May you feel
Her embrace.*

Licia Berry

Table of Contents

Dedication

I dedicate this book to all my mothers
    . . . to the girl who became my birth mother, who was
silenced before I was born.
    . . . to the girl who knew she was really my mother and
claimed me as her own.
    . . . to the many women who have stepped forward to
mother me when I could not mother myself.

And to the Shining Daughters in all of us, the hope for all
humanity.

Foreword

And in the end, we were all just humans, drunk on the idea that love, only love, could heal our brokenness.

— Christopher Poindexter

We are all broken and in need of healing. In our brokenness, we live only partial lives, always falling short of the full expression of the power and potential that Source has placed in us. Though each of us is unique in the small details of how we are wounded and how those wounds play out in our lives, we have much in common regarding the nature of those wounds and, therefore, in the path that we might take toward healing.

This book is a tale of one woman's experience and every woman's journey on that healing path. It contains profound and powerful wisdom, deep reassurance, and vibrant hope. At its very core, this book is a prayer.

For many of us, especially women, the first wound—the Mother Wound—is the one that shapes our lives. It is a wound to every part of our being—physical, mental, emotional and spiritual—and it must be healed at all of these levels. It is a wound so profound that its healing can only be accomplished with the Divine Healer, the Divine Mother.

If you are a woman or if you love a woman in today's world, much of your life has been defined by the archetype of the Divine Mother as woman perfected. Ancient societies envisioned gods and goddesses who each served as an archetype or crowning example of a human characteristic. The Mother archetype is the stuff of myth and legend, the center of many religious traditions, a major thread in our social fabric, and the topic of more therapy sessions than most of us can imagine. Some of our most ancient images of women are those of the pregnant mother, full of the promise of bringing forth new life. Though the style of these images has changed over the centuries, their essence remains the same.

Before we are born into our earthly bodies, we reside in the embrace of the universe. We are whole, safe, and loved unconditionally. The Divine Mother smiles on us, delighting in our very being. In the womb, we are cradled in that same kind of embrace. We are entwined with the physical life source of our mother's body, perfectly nurtured. Then, from the moment that the umbilical cord is cut, we begin our quest to feel that perfect embrace once again.

As infants and young children, we are taught to expect this perfect, unconditional mother love from the woman who holds this position in our lives, either through nature or nurture. As adolescent girls, we are taught that our highest and best purpose on Earth is to be such a mother. We can be other things, too, of course, but no calling is considered as sacred as this one. Becoming a mother is the female equivalent of the hero's journey.

Many among us have earthly, flesh-and-blood mothers who do a remarkable job of embodying the Divine Mother's unconditional acceptance, deep compassion, and profound understanding. Though they may not do it perfectly, these true mothers bestow enough of that Divine Mother's essence to equip their daughters with a sense that they are worthy of being loved, that they are fundamentally good, and that their lives hold value and meaning. Armed with this conviction, those who bear no Mother Wound step into life better equipped to live into their own power.

But there are others—too many others—for whom the reflection of divine mothering is clouded, broken, or downright absent. Such an absence creates a primal wound, one that we can spend our lives trying to heal. This book is about that healing process. It is a testimony to possibility.

In more than three decades of working with survivors of trauma and persons with substance use disorders, I have seen the impact that the Mother Wound has on every aspect of a daughter's life. Without the basic assurance of being loved and lovable, these daughters can spend their lives trying to earn their right to space and place in the world. They may struggle mightily to attain the love and acceptance that is their birthright, knocking again and again at the door of a heart that will not or cannot be opened to them.

To be sure, unmothered men also carry a deep wound, but they do not struggle with the pain and confusion of being expected to emulate someone whom they have never known, to give what they have never received, to create a feeling that they have never felt. In a world where we are on a quest for wholeness, connection, and personal power, we seek again the original experience of wholeness and connection and, for unmothered daughters, the quest may fall far short.

For these wounded daughters, every important relationship and life circumstance is mistakenly viewed as a chance to be reassured and comforted. No perfect mother waits for us at work, in our social connections, or in our intimate relationships. All of our striving and sacrifice for others, all of our achievements and accolades will not bring us the deep conviction that we matter when we carry the wound of not feeling lovable to the person who was supposed to love us first and best.

In order to heal, the unmothered daughter must recognize that no earthly relationship has the power to fill the hole that is her first and deepest wound. Only the act of reclaiming relationship with the Divine Feminine has that power. To heal our primal wound, we must turn to the Prime Source.

The good news is that this return to original light and love is not an impossible task. With any journey, having a detailed map and a skilled guide can make all the difference. This book is that map, and Licia Berry is the guide that I have trusted for my own journey. Licia tells her own story as a wounded daughter with courage and clarity, holding nothing back. In revealing her own deep pain, she connects with others who have experienced their own profound grief, loss, and emptiness. In revealing her own healing process, she connects with the people that those wounded daughters yearn to be.

When we are able, like Licia, to proudly state, "I Am Her Daughter," we reclaim the relationship that has been waiting for us forever. It is a relationship that we forgot when we were hurt by those who were supposed to mother us, a relationship that we could not see in the darkness of our pain. It is a relationship that we were told did not exist and that we were forced to deny when we caught glimpses of it.

This book is for all of us. It is part prayer, part testimony, part spiritual teaching. But most importantly, this book shows the healing path to that joyful reunion, that precious reconnection with our original Mother, the one whose perfect love for us allows us to finally and completely love ourselves. And, being loved, to live fully in our own power.

Gail Dixon, M.A. CAC, CPP
Tallahassee, Florida
March 2016

Introduction

In December 2003, two days before Christmas, my husband, two young sons (ages six and nine at that time), and I began a decade-long spiritual journey to heal our core wounds—rather, the core wounds of my husband and me, which were impacting our children and our marriage.

For some time, I tried to ignore subtle messages that something was out of balance in our marriage and family. We owned a beautiful home, a 1916 farmhouse on two acres of rolling land with historic oaks and heirloom rose gardens in Asheville, North Carolina, a highly desirable mountain town dubbed the "Paris of the South." My husband Peter worked for a well-known corporation and had just received a promotion, increasing his hours to even more time away from us each week. I had consulting work with non-profit agencies geared toward strengths-based family services, a harbinger of things to come. Our two sons, Jess and Aidan, attended public school, where I was the PTO president for two years, and Peter was an active volunteer when he could squeeze it in. We grew organic fruits and vegetables on our land, had a delightful community of friends, and enjoyed the stately beauty of our life's dream. From the outside, it looked really good, and in many ways it was.

Then, in 2002, a strange, nameless sadness crept into my heart like a fog. It was subtle at first, relatively easy to overpass; my life was busy, after all. Eventually, the fog grew dense. Its tendrils curled around every facet of my psyche, reaching and settling into the corners of my soul. Driving home from work one afternoon, I felt baffled as I considered each of the many reasons to be happy and grateful in my life: I was healthy, my children were healthy, my husband was healthy; we had a beautiful home and we loved each other. I was blessed beyond compare. Why then, did I want to grip the steering wheel of my Volvo station wagon with my hands and sob?

I felt a tremendous sense of loss, and I did not know why.

In September 2003, the signals that a change was coming became more urgent. The imbalance in our lives became more apparent and acute, and I was highly motivated to understand why. I had been developing mindfulness and energy practices to hone my intuition, and I heard a simple message: **Let Go.** But let go of what?

Pete was caught up in the status of his job, chasing down a dream of success that never quite seemed to materialize. We were losing him. We loved our home and land, but it took so much work to maintain it. We spent every available moment working on the gardens or the house or the yard. We had lost touch with each other. We had dreamed of having family time together at this home place, but the reality was that something *always* needed to be done. Our sweet children expressed their disappointment in different ways, but Pete and I were so caught up in the maintenance of the "dream" that we kept pushing along.

And things were not right with Pete and the kids. On weekdays, Peter got home so late that he might catch dinner with us, but he found the boys' childlike presence at the table to be distracting and noisy, and would go eat elsewhere in disgust. Then he would veg out in front of the television, often falling asleep on the couch and not coming to bed with me. The weekends were like trying to put a fourth wheel on a tricycle; integrating him into the close, workable unit of the kids and me was difficult and ungainly. The boys barely knew Peter. They sought his love and acceptance but were afraid of his judgment. What unconscious ancestral patterns were expressing through him? What would they learn about being men in the world from this kind of father? It made my heart sad, and I frequently felt I had to stand between him and the boys in order to protect their child hearts from his impatience and criticism. I was losing respect for the man I loved, and it was taking a toll on our marriage.

Seeking answers, I attended a workshop in October 2003, designed to increase devotion in one's calling. One of the activities asked the question, **"If you are standing at a crossroads, what is written on the signs?"**

I imagined myself standing at this crossroads, as requested. The vision I clearly saw seared into my brain. My heart fell. In my vision, two signs were at these crossroads. One said, "Peter." The other read, "My True Path." In an effort to span the growing gap between my husband and me, I had been trying to live two lives. Now the gap was becoming too wide to bridge. I was at the point where I felt I had to choose between my correct life and greater actualization *or* my precious beloved.

You see, Peter and I had been together since we met in August 1986, really together. We both felt that lightning bolt of recognition and purpose when we "recognized" each other the first time we met. We quickly put down our learned defenses and stopped playing the mind games that frequently accompany dating, because it was not just the two of us in the relationship. There were Three: *each of us and something bigger than us.* From the beginning of our relationship, we felt that a higher power was working through us to teach us about the power of love and healing. We were soul mates, best friends, and cohorts in some grander scheme. We were supposed to be together for life.

Then years later, there I was facing a difficult choice, one I had not wanted to acknowledge but now must. The night of the workshop, I made the choice to plunge forward. I shared with Pete what I had seen in my crossroads vision; it was very hard to do. He was shocked, blown away, and very angry at first. As I shared my concerns and that my truest desire was that we stay together, he softened. Our hearts started talking. To this day, I am grateful he could see that I was not attacking him, but sharing my grief that we were moving apart in our relationship.

We realized that we needed to reexamine our priorities, and we remembered a profound awareness that *love is all that matters.* Together, we made a pact to expose what was driving us apart. For the next several weeks, we rose early every morning and worked the mindfulness and energy practices I had developed. We saw where we had become blind to what was important. We let go, one by one, of the things that impeded our clarity, little things at first, like the number of hours of volunteer time at the school. When the stakes got higher, we were led to release bigger things. Four weeks into our inquiry and practices, Peter felt guided to release his job. We let go of aspects of our lives, a process of continual surrender. With each release, we grew freer. In the still of the morning on November 9, 2003, we were guided to let go of our home.

Our house in winter, Asheville, NC, 1999

That guidance to release our home was the biggest challenge for me and revealed the fantasy to which I was clinging.

When I was a little girl, I sought solace in the midst of chaos through the television set. One of the evening shows I watched was "The Waltons,"a drama centered on a close family living in a white farmhouse in the mountains. This television show gave me respite from the extreme dysfunction of my family of origin; I felt that I crawled into the set with this TV family, where I could pretend I belonged and was loved and cared for. In my heart, a dream of my someday family began to grow; my HOME would be safe, warm, loving, and close like the Waltons' home.

Over the years, I completely forgot this childhood landmark and sanctuary, not realizing that I was unconsciously driven to recreate the family and home I had been privy to through "The Waltons." When we first drove up to the "white house on the hill" with our real estate agent, I felt recognition and warmth. As we walked around the inside of the old house and later stepped out onto the porch to overlook the land, something opened inside of me that I could not name, yet it was powerful. The emotional decision to buy the house was made. I felt myself latch on and became bonded with the property, but I was clueless that our house in Asheville resembled the Waltons' house on TV. When the time later came to let it go in order to save my family, it triggered my core wound. Thus, began my healing. It was not until later that I understood the depth of what I had been seeking in the arms of this house and what it represented.

Our home sold to the first person I told about it the very next day; it never went on the market. We sold our possessions, opening our home for four straight weeks to friends and the public who heard about our story. This was hard to do for me; I felt I was opening my own body to strangers and allowing them to pick through my history. Oh, my things, my stuff, my attachments. I had to practice releasing and breathing every step of the way, reminding myself that *with every letting go I was gaining my family*. I had lots of emotion at this time that I squashed inside of myself, but it came out later when I finally gave myself the space to feel.

Word quickly got around Asheville that this family was making a bizarre, radical change in their lives. The vision of where we were being led started to take shape. One morning, we saw a vision of the four of us standing hand-in-hand on a cliff, dressed in burlap sacks. Another morning, we saw all of us in an RV on a road, illuminated by bright sunshine. RV? We had never set foot in an RV! But Pete and I were accustomed now, in our morning practice, to being presented with something we thought was not doable and learning that we could do it once we surrendered. Letting go made space for the impossible to become possible. We eventually saw that we were going to learn how to be a family in a different way than we had before.

By December 23, 2003, our house and possessions were sold/given away, and we were free. Going down the driveway that cold December night with our few worldly possessions and each other, we flew through the dark and the flurrying snow, away from what we knew. We traveled through the night into an uncertain future. A mere six weeks had passed from that powerful morning when we realized we were letting go of everything, and here we were, completely unfettered. It was as if heaven and earth had moved to support us in our urgent quest to stay together and heal our family. We had each other, and that is all we knew.

Our family is now on the other side of our epic, years-long odyssey, and I feel I can begin to write about this incredibly tender time in our family history. Now, my vision is twenty/twenty. I can see the wisdom, as well as the developmental stages of the years we were on the road. Together and individually, we faced the issues in ourselves that created the imbalance in our marriage and family, and I found the vulnerability in me that had contributed so much to my own dysfunction.

Berry Family, Patagonia Lake, Arizona, 2005

Berry Family San Luis Obispo California, 2008

This book is the culmination of the lessons I learned *about myself* on our family journey, where we learned to identify our core wounds and realized how much they impact everything we do and see and believe. As a result of the decision we made to release the cultural "American Dream" and come back into coherence with greater consciousness, I discovered *my* core wound, the **Mother Wound**. And I learned this wound was not only mine.

Second only to the wound sustained by the notion of our perceived separation from God, the Mother Wound is characterized by *longing and grief associated with not being mothered in ways that make us feel seen, cherished, loved, and wisely mentored.* The lack of deep mothering robs us of feeling self-reliant, self-trusting, self-loving, sexually actualized, powerful, and confident in the world.

Many books have been written about being unmothered. Some of the best mothers had the worst: many brilliant healers were the most unmothered, a strange dichotomy. Perhaps we are impelled by our yearning and pain to be the best mothers because we know what it feels like to harbor that wound. We reach out to help others feel the love we did not feel from our mothers.

For me, the Mother Wound has been the most scarring, even more painful than my recovery from sexual assault and abuse at the hands of family members (as shared in my 2012 memoir *Soul Compost – Transforming Adversity into Spiritual Growth*). While the resilience and ability to make good medicine from bad medicine served me well in dealing with my Father Wound, they were utterly required in healing my Mother Wound. My relationship with my biological mother is complex and multi-faceted, as many relationships with mother are. The more I learned about my pain, the more I saw it colored everything in my life, driving me to make choices that took me away from my center, . . . and the more I understood that this is a universal pain.

My yearning for a mother took me on a spiritual journey that sent me straight into the arms of the best possible mother I could wish for, my ideal Mother, something I experience both within and as a primary component of the larger universe. I differentiate mother with a lowercase "m" as human and Mother with a capital "M" as reference to the archetypal mother. You will learn more in these pages as I share my personal pilgrimage.

This book is offered in multiple stages and voices; I offer an examination of the Mother Wound personally, individually, and culturally, sharing my direct experiences, mystical occurrences, and miraculous healings. I also speak as a practitioner, offering a path of healing that I have greatly benefitted from personally as well as having had great success in facilitating my mentees (clients) and students toward their healing. I want to remind everyone that I am not a psychotherapist, but rely on my own healing as well as training in multiple holistic modalities to support others in their healing. You will see case studies of women in my practice who gave me permission to share their own healing with you, and you will discover practical ways to find Her for yourself.

The book is offered in three parts: Part One, "History," is a linear journey through my life framed by the Mother Wound, essential for my credibility later in the book. Part Two, "Herstory," continues the journey, but from a healing and resolution perspective, decidedly feminine and non-linear. Part Three, "Her Voice," is the sharing of Great Mother's teachings to me for my own healing as well as to offer the world. It chronicles my years of learning how to mother myself and is a guide to navigating sometimes painful territory that many fear to enter. I have been greatly rewarded for diving deeply into this territory, facing the pain with the intent to heal, and finding the greatest, unimaginable joy behind the hurt. You will journey with me as my awareness grew and deepened.

At times, the book touches on a seemingly broad range of topics that to a logical or left-brain thinker may appear unrelated. However, as you will soon see, the Mother Wound is vast and foundational, and impacts many, many things.

In my earnest quest to heal and remember that I am a child of the universe, I have experienced things that are not easily explained in a left-brain culture—mystical, magical things. I will share them here with you, even though you may not believe them. I assure you that everything I write here is the truth. I have found in my fifty years that true healing is a window into the profound Great Mystery. I know from experience that the Mother Wound can indeed be healed. It takes honesty, courage, faith and trust, but most of all, love.

This book is an offering, a song from my heart, soul, and spirit. To whom? Or to what? It is an offering to the woman who birthed me but could not mother me. It is an offering to the women (and men) who actually did mother me. It is an offering to the daughters in each of us, hungry to be loved. And it is an offering to Great Mother, the archetypal Mother energy that is the ground of all being, the One who holds us through it all.

Licia Berry
Easter, April 2015
USA

Part One
History

Dear One,

I trust that you are aware that I am here holding you at all times, within and without. The very ground of existence, that which you and all life spring from, I am the essence of goodness and giving, ever-present. So ever-present that you can forget I am here.

Let me hold you. Feel me cradling you. I am your Mother, and you are my child. No matter what your unique life has brought you, no matter how unworthy you may feel, you are and will always be my child. Let me in.

The protective shell you have built around your heart prevents you from feeling the exquisite nature of creation's love for you. You are part of this creation. Not separate from it. You are part of All That Is.

My arms are open wide.

Great Mother
through Licia Berry
July 15, 2010

Chapter 1: What is Mother?

This is How You Transform Lead into Gold
Collage © 2011 Licia Berry (book cover image for
Soul Compost)

Someone I loved once gave me a box full of darkness. It took me years to understand that this, too, was a gift.

— Mary Oliver

The little girl stumbles through the dark woods, her hair tangled, her face and clothes dirty. She sometimes calls out, but hearing no one, continues her search. She sometimes stops to cry, but not for long. She cannot afford such a luxury, as her survival depends on her successful quest. She is hungry—for answers and for love. She wants to know what is so awful about her that her mother is absent, why her mother does not want her.

She seeks high and low, under branches and in caves, peering into the dark for the face of her mother. *Where is she?* she wonders. She examines the faces of the animals, scrutinizes the odd, chiseled features in the tree bark, and studies the flower blooms. Her quest takes her to crushing boulders and foots of mountains, to cliffs and deserts and waterfalls. She gazes into the sky and surveys the clouds. Is she there? *Where is my mother?*

This girl is a wild child, a daughter of the woods and the trees and the dirt. Nature has no agenda. No manipulations, no games, no back-stabbings, no hurting her heart. She feels safe with the unconditional acceptance of the forest, although she wishes for the warmth of a human hug or the light of a mother's smile upon her. She feels a sense of belonging here, and Nature guides her wisely—but she still feels the ache of being an unmothered daughter.

~ ~ ~

I understood I was worthy when I was young. I felt the Lionheart inside my chest and saw the world through the eyes of God. I remember my childhood after age two very vividly, and recall the wisdom and the grace that seemed to reside

I found the outside to be the safe place. There, I found acceptance and permission to be who I was. Nature did not take anything from me that I did not want to give freely. I looked up at the big sky and expressed my admiration of its endless blue, its vastness, its height. I sat under the trees and felt the loving arms of their branches providing shade, and ate of the fruit they gave, taking their offering into my body. The dirt under my bare feet felt of velvet between my toes, soft and supportive. I was a child of Nature, and my Child Heart took refuge there when no safety could be found elsewhere.

In my interviews and work with hundreds of clients in my practice, I have heard over and over again how Nature is a friendly escape for people who have tumultuous home lives. While most children of previous generations seemed to have some relationship with the outdoors and a good feeling for Nature, for those who did not feel safe in their homes, *Nature actually became their surrogate parent*, the one place they felt accepted and "cared for."

Women in my practice describe retreating to tree branches to sit and talk with the birds about the difficulties with their parents, or walking in the woods and feeling the comfort of the eyes of the forest on them. I remember looking up and confiding in the stars at night. What drives us innately to seek comfort and love in the outdoors? How do we know so early that the arms of Nature are the safest place to be?

What will happen to the young people now who do not play outside, who do not know another outlet besides video games and television to fill their unmet needs, to soothe their unparented hearts?

I was a wild, nut-brown girl, my long, tangled hair and dirty, bare feet a testament to my sunup-to-sundown ritual of spending the day outdoors. The country is a fabulous place to grow up. Resistant to taking baths (but really reluctant to getting naked and near water if "The Husband" or "The Wife" were involved), I avoided going into the four walls of the house within me but which the adults around me apparently could not see. I remember being shocked when I was treated as an annoyance, stupid, or, at worst, a piece of property. I understood innately that I came from a "parent" somewhere else and recall looking up at the sky at age four and asking if I could please come home.

But stay I must. My life would be a twisting, turning journey through a challenging landscape of sexual, physical, emotional and mental abuses in my family of origin and a culture of shaming of women in the Bible Belt of the southern U.S. As I write now, I see that my path has prepared me perfectly to be forced to learn self-love, self-valuing, self-parenting.

It has pushed me to find and define my own relationship with my spirituality and forged a strong bond within me to the forces of good in the universe.

It has lit a fire in me to be a voice in the wilderness, to stand on the mountaintops and pulse a steady drumbeat that speaks the truth: beyond a shadow of a doubt, we are worthy of love.

It has compelled me to find my Mother.

Is this a fantasy? How often do we hear of a cherished daughter? It seems so rare in a world that values sons, that auctions off daughters to be wed with the highest dowry, or even sees baby girls as bad fortune and kills them.

Yet, there are some who know that a daughter is to be cherished; we hear about the occasional parents who raised their daughter to believe in herself, to know she was loved, to feel her place and value in the world.

The cherished daughter

And we know this in our bodies, in our hearts and souls. I believe that we know, at some level, that each of us is precious and should be cherished. We know this as children, and so it comes as a shock when some of us are not cherished. We feel the affront to our inner awareness and slowly come to believe that we are not so precious after all.

According to Nicholas Kristof and Sheryl WuDunn, two Pulitzer Prize-winning reporters for the *New York Times* and the authors of the book *Half the Sky*, violence against women is causing gender imbalances in many developing countries. The current global sex ratio is thought to be one hundred seven males to every ninety-three females, the largest gap since records have been kept, according to women's advocate and activist Gloria Steinem in her speech at the Wisdom Sharing Retreat at Ghost Ranch, Abiquiú, New Mexico, in 2014.

The World Health Organization writes in the report entitled "Understanding and addressing violence against women" that, "Violence against women comprises a wide range of acts—from verbal harassment and other forms of emotional abuse, to daily physical or sexual abuse. At the far end of the spectrum is femicide: the murder of a woman or girl."

The pain of a mother's rejection is an unparalleled anguish that can barely be described. It threatens to tear the very fabric of one's being apart. At a basic, cellular level, we wonder, *That which made me now rejects me. What is wrong with me?* We have the potential to carry a deep, unquenchable need to "fix" ourselves because surely there must be something very, very bad about us. Motherless children carry the unquantifiable pain: the pain of separation from our maker, our earthly origination point.

The illness that derives from this pain creates more of it.

In an age of patriarchy (lasting more than five thousand years), women have been given a message that the feminine is unimportant, dismissible, dirty, evil, expendable. Violence and oppression of women comprise a core wound that underscores all of the other problems in the world—from poverty to war to destruction of the environment, and hostility toward those who are different. Women and girls do not know their value, do not know the preciousness and sacredness of their bodies and their psyches, do not know their resilience, do not know that being a woman is a special gift. *How on Earth can a woman know how to be a good mother unless she is herself mothered by a woman who values herself as a woman?*

As poet Adrienne Rich said, "The woman I needed to call my mother was silenced before I was born." Motherless women are an epidemic, and it is a sociological issue as well as a personal psychological and spiritual issue. The world needs mothers who value themselves as women to turn this grand ship around before humanity destroys itself. As with all change, we must begin with ourselves. This book is a call to be responsible for ourselves so we can be responsible to one another as women.

Over the years, I have studied with interest the photographs of mothers and daughters. I have studied their faces, scanning them for the same emotional features I see on pictures of myself as a little girl, or of my own biological mother. There are no photographs of us together in this sort of portrait. I do not remember ever being with her in this kind of closeness.

What is the magic ingredient that cements the bond between the two females in the pictures? I notice a nakedness, an honesty, and an attentiveness in the faces of the mothers. The mother seems caring, warm, available, *connected* to her daughter. The daughter looks safe, calm, secure in that love, as if she is held by an invisible force field that surrounds her, and *she knows it*. Is this what a cherished daughter looks like?

What does that feel like?

I really wanted to know. In my efforts to understand and to *feel* that kind of mothering in my life, I have combed the world for examples of ideal mothering. There are many out there, plenty of genuinely caring examples of healthy relationships between mothers and daughters.

Allowing Myself to be a Daughter

Happy are they who still love something they loved in the nursery: They have not been broken in two by time; they are not two persons, but one, and they have saved not only their souls but their lives.

— G.K. Chesterton

I have accepted my role as mother, both inner and outer. However, being a mom to my sons has been easy, compared to being a mom to my inner children. I have been pegged as a mom by many friends since middle school, seeming to draw their troubles out of them by simply being in their presence, which continues to this day. People sense something about me, a kind of loving presence that comes through me and that impels them to show me where they hurt, their "owies" safe in my care. I used to resent this because I needed mothering so much myself. It was especially challenging during the times that they projected their own "mommy stuff" onto me, and I did not know how to work with their projection to help them transform the presence of their own biological mothers rambling around in their psyches. My job then was to fill the role of the mother they needed so desperately, and I guided them to release their poor parenting like a helium balloon is released into the air. One would think that more than thirty-five years of parenting others' inner children would make parenting myself a cinch.

Not so. How easy it is to see the beauty and light of another in comparison to the self! My challenge became loving myself as much as I poured love into others. That fearless and compassionate Mama Bear that is apparently innate for me, that compels me to be present to people's pain and to help draw it from them as poison from a wound, seemed to disappear like smoke when it was me who needed my love. So I asked for help.

Everyone has a mother; we were all born of a body and that makes us a child of a biological mother, but not everyone is *mothered*. **The ideal mother is what I needed to teach me how to mother myself.**

Does the ideal mother exist? In human beings, we know there is no perfect mother because **there is no perfect**. There is no perfect love in an imperfect world. We know that mothers run the gamut on the scale of good mothering. *Yet, there is some standard for good mothering because we ache for it when the need is not met. If ideal mothering does not exist, where does this ideal, this ache come from?*

My answer to this question became potent in my years of healing the Mother Wound. The archetypal love that we seek has been called many names since the dawn of humanity, but they can all be summed up in the name Great Mother; scrawled on rocks and cave walls, images of a giant mother figure permeates prehistory. She existed in our collective human psyche then, and she does now.

But who or what is Great Mother? "Great Mother" is my name for the love from which we come. "Great Mother" is my name for the ground of all being, the most basic relationship that we have with the universe. I experience Her as my ideal mother: kind, allowing, accepting, guiding, soft, embracing, nurturing, honest, insightful, powerful, responsible, wise, trustworthy, and as ancient as the universe itself. She is a model in my mind and heart, as well as a knowing in my body. She exists to me. There is no question. Whether she is a figment of my conjuring, as an aspect of my own psyche, an energy in this universe, or an actual deity (or all of the above) does not

matter to me. I feel Her energy when I put my attention on Her, and Her energy changes me for the better. As far as I am concerned, She is as real as I am.

I found the children within me to be very, very hungry for mother love, and this demanded the best kind of mothering that I could find. My need for the perfect mother is what brought the Divine Feminine, or Great Mother, forward into my consciousness. I urgently requested her, and She answered.

The Venus of Willendorf
circa 28,000–25,000 BCE

Letting Ourselves be Daughters

From Merriam Webster dictionary:

daughter

noun daugh·ter \ˈdȯ-tər, ˈdä-\
1a: a female child or offspring, especially of human parents
 b: a female adopted child
 c: a female descendant
2: a woman or girl associated with or thought of as a child of something (as a country, race, or religion)

Growing up with less-than-ideal mothers can make it challenging to allow ourselves to be daughters, to be little girls who need to be mothered. A result of the forced early maturation that must occur to survive childhood in a dysfunctional home, we become little "adults" and leave the needy child behind. We must feel a measure of control in our otherwise out-of-control lives, so we grow our intellect and suppress our emotions, becoming "grownups in little bodies," in essence raising ourselves.

Ollie, one of my clients, shared her experience while in my mentoring program as she healed the Mother Wound

"I've been thinking about the phrase, 'I am my own daughter,' and although the power if it brought me to tears, I am having a heck of a time trying to wrap my brain around it. Though maybe I'm not supposed to. We've been learning to be our own mothers and can be pretty easy and empowering to do so, but how can I be my own daughter? You would think that it's just the opposite. Maybe my experience as a daughter, which was not totally horrible but not totally safe, has me wondering what it is supposed to be like to be a daughter. Maybe I feel like I have no frame of reference. I probably knew what other people wanted me to be, but who was I, really? I had my share of emotional troubles when I was young, became a sarcastic and angry teenager, and started trying to fix my own mother as an adult. But what is it really like to be a daughter? It is hard. It is emotionally demanding. For me, it has been a place where I needed to build walls. Can I be vulnerable enough to be a daughter? To know I am truly safe and accepted for who I am? Is this an ideal anybody really achieves? I am ready to have this experience and be who I need to be to find this out. It is time."

The longing for our mothers is real, natural, and everlasting, no matter our age. As long as we are women, we are daughters.

My longing for a mother drove me to look far and wide over my lifetime. For years, I sought a woman in a physical form who would suitably fill the role of mother. Running into disappointment and failure as I relied on women to mother me who were themselves unmothered, I began to search on a different playing field. Because I had found no mother on Earth who could mother me the way I wanted and needed to be mothered, my yearning for a mother took me on a spiritual journey that sent me straight into the arms of the best possible Mother I could wish for.

She brings unconditional acceptance, deep compassion, profound understanding. We all deserve to be mothered with this kind of love. The Divine Feminine is a vast array of faces of female symbolism over the hundreds of thousands of years that humanity has recorded their stories. The archetypal Great Mother, the Prime Source, the womb from which All Things emerged, is the definitive mothering energy that I desperately grasped for, and found.

That is the gift that came from the box full of darkness, a painful path that led to the most precious realization of all—that I am indeed loved and mothered.

> **The woman I needed to call my mother was silenced before I was born.**
>
> — Adrienne Rich

From Merriam Webster dictionary:

moth·er

noun \\ˈmə-t͟hər\\

1a: a female parent

b *(1)*: a woman in authority; *specifically*: the superior of a religious community of women *(2)*: an old or elderly woman

2: source, origin <necessity is the *mother* of invention>

3: maternal tenderness or affection

Perhaps because I innately understood that I came from something larger than I could see on Earth, I saw my birth parents as "The Wife" and "The Husband" instead of as my mother and father. I did not connect with them as parental figures.

My relationship with my birth mother was difficult, tenuous. I acknowledged her as the female authority in my life early on; my heartache when she rejected or abused me was hard to bear. It is natural for any child of abuse to wonder what they have done, to wonder what is so awful about themselves, that their original source of nourishment and wellbeing are rejecting or abusive to them.

I recall at age four studying the behavior of my birth parents as if I were an anthropologist studying a foreign culture. Perhaps this was a survival mechanism; to distance myself in this way was a way to live through the traumas and increase my intellectual understanding of the situation, something that I used later to explain the way I separated from my family of origin.

While my studies were, on one hand, interesting and provided fodder for my life as I recorded how NOT to parent for my someday children, the process was painful for their fragile, human daughter, the object/subject of their unconsciousness. As each incident after incident of sexual assault and emotional/mental/verbal violence occurred, little parts of me experienced soul death.

I have felt unmothered for most of my life, a state of being that I define as growing up without the knowing that you are unconditionally loved by your mother. It is a feeling of being an orphan, even though the woman who birthed you may still be alive and walking on the planet. It is a sorrowful sensation of being incomplete, of not being enough. It is a feeling of being a rudderless ship, unmoored and drifting, constantly in search of home. Being worthy becomes the question. *There must be*

something very wrong with me that my mother rejects me. Am I awful? When the question is answered by the absence of love in our mother, our worst fear is confirmed. We decide we are truly unworthy of love.

This chipping away of our resilient nature in an environment that does not value us causes us to become bereft of love and to continue to pass down the culture of violence toward children. And women.

The Inner Child

Caring for your inner child has a powerful and surprisingly quick result: Do it and the child heals.
— **Martha Beck**

In indigenous medicine (something I have practiced for many years), it is understood that all of the ages we have ever been are living inside of us. I have a five-year-old self, a seventeen-year-old self, a thirty-nine-year-old self, a five-minutes-ago self. Our psyche is the containment of everything we have ever experienced. My personal practice has been greatly enriched by working with parts of me at every age and stage.

I first heard the concept of "inner child" in the late 1980s, early in my therapeutic recovery as I learned about childhood abuse. My wonderful therapist at the time introduced the concept in a session and I remember a funny feeling coming over me; I became aware of a presence as if from somewhere far away, as if I were hearing a familiar voice calling me from over a distant horizon. I had a strange sense of coming home. I learned that my heart was broken early in my life, creating splintered aspects of myself that could later be identified as "inner children."

I was conflicted about the concept of having an inner child. I had left her behind such a long time ago that, at first, I did not even identify with her. I could not even believe that I had been a child, a baby, an infant. It took physical proof, actually finding and poring over old photographs, for me to even begin to grasp that I had ever been a baby.

Licia as an infant, 1965

I have an excellent memory of things that happened to me as a child, all the way back to age two, but I have identified with myself as an adult throughout my life. I learned through therapy that I saw myself this way because I was "adult-ized," forced to grow up very early emotionally and mentally, older than my years long before I was meant to be. Being a child in my family home was too dangerous. Why would I even want to entertain the idea of a part of me being a little, defenseless young me? Identifying with her was far too risky. I understand now why some people scoff at "inner child work." It took many years for me to overcome my objections even to this simple concept.

As I began to interact with this little stranger, I uncovered a profound source of wisdom, creativity, and joy that had been missing from my life. I began to understand that everything in our lives goes back to our experiences growing up. ***The quality of our lives as adults is in every way bound to the love we felt as children.***

Later in my life, I began to understand that my body had learned to protect the soft, innocent child by putting her away, deep into my psyche. Fighting for my inner child has been a long battle! While my previous time in therapy had been primarily talking about my memories and understanding the intellectual concepts of abuse, alcoholism, dysfunction, denial, and projection, the inner work deepened and actual change occurred when I began to inter-act with my inner child.

Licia, age 5, who later became my Shero

It was a hard time to be an adult once I gave my inner child permission to speak! She had needed attention for a long time, and although my therapist was a kind and loving surrogate mom, I never allowed her to mother me completely because my inner child was so wounded and mistrustful, reluctant to accept love from a woman or a man. It took some time for me to allow this child within me to exist, to acknowledge her, and to give her permission to occupy space inside my conscious life. I had learned to hate her for her vulnerability, to mistrust her weakness.

I have noticed over the years of working with my inner child that she will show up at an age that I can handle, *in tandem with my readiness to "raise" her at that age.* The first time I interacted with her, she was five years old and very vocal. I was a public school art teacher at the time and surrounded by children every day, so knew how to interact and be kind with children her age, but the fact that this child was ME made me want to be unkind, dismissive, angry at her. The fact that this child was ME created incredible discomfort. Being faced with my fragility and innocence, my very child-like-ness, was challenging.

I call the first years that I worked closely with my inner child the "Barbie Years." I broke the bank, buying dolls and clothes to play with, some remaining in their boxes (so I could sell them later to collectors, I reasoned), but many being liberated from their pink prisons and lovingly bathed, dressed, and displayed in my home. My dear husband remained supportive despite the dolls in the living room and my frequent trips to Toys R Us. The dolls were actually a good marker for me of where I was in my healing process; in those early years, playing was about all I could do to reach my inner child.

At other stages, different tools entered the picture; coloring, scribbling with crayons, throwing clay, and spending time in nature, laying on the ground and looking at the sky were helpful. Additionally, I would allow my inner child to tantrum by doing rage release work (also shared in detail in *Soul Compost*). All of these were ways of reaching her and making it safe for her to express her wounded heart. It was important that I do things that she liked to do in order to gain her trust. The years of being tough and suppressing my inner child were over. I allowed her to be in my consciousness without being berated, abused, or shoved into a dark closet. She was free. And she wanted to be heard.

~ ~ ~

When your inner child wants to tell you something, it is a good idea to listen. Our inner children, like real-world children, do not like to be ignored. They have a habit of hanging around until we pay attention to them. If we don't, they gain our attention in another way. If we keep ignoring them, they eventually sadly turn away and learn that we cannot be trusted.

I know about this one. Even after the Barbie Years, I have moments of turning away from my inner child. Perhaps I am too busy, or I do not want to entertain another sordid memory from my past. But if that inner child's voice is making an attempt to tell me an awful experience, it is because I need to heal it. Otherwise, it would not come up. I know, it gets old hearing more stories of your childhood. You wonder where it will end. Well, **we are never done when it comes to loving ourselves unconditionally**; we can always learn better how to do that.

Our inner child is how we learn. She is our exalted (and uniquely qualified) teacher. She will show and tell us how to love her. We must make it a priority to listen with an open heart. The result is that we get the benefit of our own self-care.

The loved inner child equals a loved adult. We see adults all the time who do not love themselves, people who self-judge, criticize, berate. Emotionally, they are frozen in time. Because they are children on the inside, they may blame others for their problems. Taking responsibility for their lives may be very threatening. Navigating the world as a mature, wise adult may be impossible for them. Their inner children are burdened with life as an adult. It is unfair to expect a child to know how to live life as an adult without having been taught how to grow up properly.

The sad truth is that we hold ourselves in contempt if we were not taught to cherish ourselves when we were young. It is easy to know when someone was taught to love themselves; they are easy to be around, take good care of themselves without extremes, are gentle on themselves. These people are few on this planet in comparison to the total number of children who have grown into adulthood.

I know many, many people who march onward, cajoling themselves to "act like adults," imagining that they leave behind their needy inner child. However, we can never leave our inner children behind, because they are US. When we force our inner children to act like adults, without healing and loving them into maturity, they are "play-acting" adulthood. They are informed by the adults who parented them. Either they mimic what they saw modeled to them, and therefore repeat many of the mistakes they experienced in their actual childhood, or they try to do the opposite of what they experienced, creating imbalance in the other direction. When they act from their wounding, the adult they are trying to be is not whole; the wounds in the psyche can never be escaped.

Then there are those who make war on parts of themselves. When we forcibly and violently suppress any part of ourselves, that part will rise up and create havoc in our lives, sabotaging us in the successes we attempt to achieve.

Who will raise these adult children? For that matter, what does an adult who has successfully integrated their inner child look like? It becomes a question of maturity of body, mind, and emotion.

What is maturity to me?

- Knowing myself; continuing on a never-ending quest to know myself, including my shortcomings as well as my strengths.
- Loving myself exactly as I am; recognizing the perfection of my life, while also recognizing the perfection of my desire to improve it.
- Improving and growing myself; accepting that I will never be finished; I will always be a work-in-progress.
- Always checking inwardly first, cultivating self-reflection and insight.
- Taking responsibility for my life and choices.
- Acknowledging that my needs are my responsibility to fulfill.
- Doing what needs to be done.

- Being fully alive, seeing life as a gift.
- Being fully present. When going into the past to retrieve or heal a part of self, a large part of myself is firmly in the present to wisely observe and facilitate this process.
- Reaching out to others for help when I cannot do for myself.
- Being willing to receive and accept help and love from others.
- Caring for people without having to take care of them.
- Giving generously for the sheer joy of it, without expectation of return.
- Keeping good boundaries when needed; keeping myself wisely safe.
- Being in integrity; the inside and outside match up.
- Being committed to inner work when things are not going well.
- Seeing others and All Creation as a reflection of self.
- Appreciating diversity; letting others be who they are. Live and let live.
- Being willing to be wrong, and saying, "I'm sorry," with a sincere heart.
- Knowing I do not have all the answers; being willing to ask questions.
- Not taking things personally, but as opportunities to grow.
- Taking the high road; always striving to be my best, biggest, most expanded self.
- Forgiving myself when I am unable to be my best, biggest, most expanded self.
- Being utterly protective of children, no matter what.

Obviously, I hold a high standard for myself, and I do hold it for others. This list comes from a stringent search for people I could respect and trust. When I realized that I trusted someone, I observed them in an attempt to understand why I felt safe with them. The qualities I identified became this list.

Then came the work to "grow parts of myself up" into that model. I deeply desire to be a wise and mature person in this world, adding to the love and safety of it, rather than being a force of destruction.

Save and Protect the Children

The last item on my list—*Being utterly protective of children, no matter what*—is important, especially for this book. It came to my attention some time ago that children are fresh into this world from the Great Beyond, whatever name you give it; I think of us all coming from the Womb of Creation, our Origination Point, or Source. Children are new, not yet inculcated into culture, imprinted with the limitations of language and the rules of earthly existence. I believe that children carry the original expression of the outpouring of generosity, acceptance, and love that created this universe, until they learn otherwise.

Children carry a knowing that we should all be observant of, even reverent of. Children are our teachers, reminders of what we came from. They are here to evolve us, to grow the frontier of consciousness—a brilliant design, the biological imperative! We are programmed to continue life, and each new life that comes through us will evolve us into more expanded beings if we allow the process to unfold as it is meant to.

I do not advocate that we put children in a position of little gods and goddesses; that is simply another way of imposing our will upon them. We are charged with guiding them and protecting them with our lives, so it is our duty (and part of the original design) to watch and learn from them as the truth-tellers that they are. They are here to grow us, after all—if we will let them.

What is the role of adults, then? Our job is to provide guidance to children about how to live in a three-dimensional world, to show them ways to thrive in a physical body, but to give them room to discover things for themselves as much as possible. To allow them to be who they came to be, not to impose upon them our own ideas of who they should be. To invite them into our hearts as little gurus, while never forgetting that we are the adults. To keep them safe, to take good care of them, and—by all means—to show them that they are loved.

Yes, for all their worldliness and wisdom, children should be loved unconditionally.

Children need to be mothered. Mothers are our ground of being, our "home base." Mothers reflect us, in their eyes and in their arms. We know the world through our mothers—our safety, our worthiness, our belonging. I cannot think of anything worse than being unmothered.

Every manner of horror can befall us, but if we are mothered, we have the innate resilience to bounce back from whatever we may encounter in our lives. An inherent strength and buoyancy comes from knowing you are loved by the one who made you. It is my wish that every child experience the miracle of a mother's love.

Unfortunately, child abuse is rampant. According to the Office on Child Abuse and Neglect, reported or discovered cases of neglect and physical/sexual abuse touch a tremendous number of children: 62.8 percent for neglect (which occurs in many forms) and over 25 percent for physical/sexual abuses. The number of cases has grown despite attempts to educate the public. We perpetuate our wounding when we have not healed the wounds inflicted upon us.

Children are small, vulnerable, innocent, trusting. Unscrupulous, unhealed adults can and do manipulate and force children to do things that rob children of their innocence and trust. Quite the opposite of holding children up as reminders of our sacredness to be cherished and protected, many adults break children into little pieces, scatter them like the four winds, leaving them to grow into fractured, unhealed adult children—and the cycle continues.

It isn't just the extreme, obvious abuses that do this; we also break children down in little, more subtle ways, ways we do not typically identify as abusive.

For example, I worked as a public school art instructor and saw what our current educational institution does to children. Where, in my early years as an art teacher, my students' right brain and left brain were harmoniously utilized to learn and grow, other school subjects tended to shut the right brain down. Imagination, intuition, the understanding of symbol and image-based language, a sense of meaning, a sense of being an included part of a whole are all right-brain functions. Instead, an imbalanced left-brain approach of black-and-white thinking, accomplishing goals, achieving a grade, jumping through hoops for approval, and being labeled as insufficient if you do not make the mark is how we show children they are to survive in this world. By creating a left-brain culture from the age of four years old, we virtually ensure that children grow up feeling disconnected, insufficient, driven to consume, with a sense of longing for something they cannot even name (unless they receive different messages from the adults at home). How many people do you know who yearn for a sense of belonging, purpose, unconditional love?

Unconditional love is missing in so many of our lives. While it is often talked about, I do not see many folks living it. Is unconditional love such a high ideal, that it is impossible to attain in a physical world with limitations and boundaries?

But I have experienced it, a sense of being loved no matter what, through my relationship with my husband and children. So I know it exists, and I know that it is possible. It feels wonderful to be in a field of unconditional love, so safe, like permission to exist on the planet. In a field of unconditional love, anything is possible—healing, growth, achievement, extraordinary joy. I want everyone to feel that. It is something we can strive to cultivate within ourselves if we cannot find it outside of ourselves (yet).

Being utterly protective of children, no matter what also applies to our inner children, the parts inside of ourselves that are seeking wholeness, to be embraced. We do not want to repeat with our inner children the ways we may have been abused when we were children!

We Are Each Other's Daughters

In 2014, I attended a retreat in New Mexico that featured Gloria Steinem, Alice Walker, and Dr. Hyun Kun Chung, the kind of women I aspire to be. I realized there that these women are my mothers, that all of the three hundred and fifty women in attendance are daughters, and that *we as women constantly mother each other*.

This explained my years of relationships with women being so painful. I had been looking for my mother all along, but from a fractured perspective of woundedness. I had attracted women, over and over again, who hurt me the ways my mother did. I had involved myself in situations in which the abuse was replayed and my heart was broken again and again. As a result, I had not mothered other women very well. In my desperation to find mother in other women who were in an unhealed state, I drew my mother's face again and again, . . . and then treated other women in some of the ways she treated me (thankfully not all)—dismissive, unfeeling, withdrawn. Now, from a healed and truly mothered perspective, I can see that every woman on the planet is my daughter and that I am equipped to mother them exquisitely, if I am being conscious.

Doesn't every interaction with another woman touch us at a level that is hard to logically explain? Doesn't another woman's kindness, looking upon us with appreciative eyes and a gentle, supportive manner nourish us at a deep level? And when another woman says an unkind word, betrays us, it cuts us to the bone?

My worst hurts have come at the hands of women, and that's saying a lot from a woman who has recovered from multiple sexual assaults and attempted murder. There was something baser about the harms that men did to me, something animal and not quite to the heart, that I could somehow recover from, even forgive. But the hurts passed onto me by my mother and other women in my family, those were truly wounds of the heart.

Over the years, I observed that the things that we do to each other as women are the most impactful in our lives. This is because I had experienced my greatest hurt and feelings of disappointment by the actions/words of women. *We truly are mothering one another, and when we betray each other, we reinforce wounds we may have received when we felt a break with our own mother.*

This is one of the reasons to learn to parent the inner child: because we must do better. We are all parenting one another, and for women, we are mothering each other and being each other's daughters. We must be responsible for ourselves so we can be responsible to one another as women. When we mother ourselves, we are good mothers to the rest of the world's daughters.

~ ~ ~

At the risk of being perceived as a self-righteous, self-important, militant, woman-centric fanatic, I feel that mothering is the most vital work in the world. Every woman's primary relationship is with her mother. Our mothers grew us in their bodies, giving them central importance in our awareness of our connectivity with All Creation. Through our connections with our mothers, we understand that we belong to the Earth and to one another. We understand that there is no separation.

If we care about the human species and about our planet, then we know that the issues we face today are because we do not feel that we belong to the Earth and to one another. Excess use of resources without thought of consequences, discrimination against people who do not fit our framework, competition for what we perceive as limited—all of these are symptoms of a lack of belonging. No one causes us to feel that we belong more than our mothers do. We must reexamine how women are treated because it is an indication of the consciousness of a culture; nothing is more important than correcting the imbalance that has resulted in the near extinction of feminine principles on this planet.

After more than five thousand years of patriarchy, we are in a dire, critical situation in which there is suggestion that the human species may not survive another four generations. The efforts to bring us back from the brink have helped us become aware of the problem, but have created a polarization that fractures the attempted progress and even sometimes causes regression. The work to midwife our species into the future must be done now.

Progress has been made, make no mistake, but the backlash that has come in response threatens to throw us into the dark ages. We must remain steady in our devotion to ensure the survival of the species.

A Quieter Voice

In writing this book, I was repeatedly guided to "go to the waters." The waters of my womb, the waters of feeling, the waters of memory. A different process than logically plotting out a manuscript or preparing a "best seller," this offering would be written from the heart, from the belly, from Her voice. To care-take it like a treasured child, like the daughter that it truly is. The waters of the Atlantic unlocked this mystery for me, and I was finally ready to birth this book.

This book is written for the woman who is seeking to remember her sacredness. She may not have learned it from her mother, and she certainly did not learn it from her culture . . . but she knows. . . . deep inside she hears the call, . . . and she is answering. Rebelling against the culture that disdains her, daring to fight for what she knows in her heart is right, she is seeking to learn of her sacredness and determined to own it for herself.

It begins with the woman's personal experience with her mother, then with the culture. Ultimately, from inner claiming of the archetypal Great Mother and raising ourselves as our own sacred daughter, we then move outward into revolutionizing the world.

I feel a strong connection with other women who also have an emptiness inside them; I seem to attract women who had been unmothered and are seeking permission to take up their space on the planet and make their mark. After decades of devotion to my own healing, I became a practitioner who helps women connect with their worthiness. My note-taking as a young girl about HOW NOT TO be a mother came in handy, but the best training about HOW TO be a mother was the return to that innate sense of the bigger, divine parent I had as a child. Here was the complete acceptance and non-judgment, the unconditional love for which I was so thirsty. As I learned later, the mother I really needed was the ideal mother. I found her in many faces of Great Mother.

When I found this love again, I was back in the universe where I belonged, a universe that wanted me and within which I am a part. Great Mother scooped me up. I was no longer on the sidelines, wishing that I could be included in the games. She wiped my tears and said:

"I am with you. You are Mothered. I've been here all along. So go live your life like it matters."

Then She set me down to play.

Invocation of the Great Mother Within

By Licia Berry, 2008
*Debuted at "Loving Your Inner Feminine" Women's Retreat at
Ghost Ranch, New Mexico*

Great Mother,
The One who holds all of creation in her tender embrace
The One whose body is millions of stars through all the universes
The One who is the yin, the other half, the completion of the
equation
The feminine face of All That Is
The One who loves no matter what

Great Mother,
I call upon you now.
As the earth turns and evolves,
As humanity continues in its waking up to love,
And as my own life expands and becomes,
I want you now.

Many times have I denied you in my life,
Many times turned away from your sweet love.
In my own incompleteness, I rejected your invitation into
wholeness,
Thinking I could take care of myself alone,
Projecting onto you that you abandoned me,
When what is true is that
I abandoned myself.

In your eyes, I see the love for humanity,
In your gaze, the warm smile of understanding and acceptance.
I know that you see me before you,
Your shining daughter,
And then, reflected in you, I see myself.

Great Mother,
You hold me, you allow and encourage me to be who
I truly am—
The wild child, the playful and innocent maiden, the sexual
priestess, the powerful creator, the wisewoman, the Great
Mystery.

In all of your expressions, you give me full permission to explore
all of mine, and to love them regardless.

You love me unconditionally.
In your quiet strength, you watch and smile.
You kiss my cheek and I sleep as my soul rests on your bosom.
I trust in your heartbeat as I walk the earth,
Forever safe,
Forever safe,
Forever safe.
You will never leave me,
And so I can finally rest, knowing, in your arms.

Great Mother,
Knowing that you are me,
My wisest, deepest, most loving, discerning self,
Knowing I reside within the womb of my greatest creator,
I invite you now, consciously, into my life.
I choose to love myself the way that you love me.
I ask for your guidance and your Light.
I ask of you to mother me in the ways that I need it the most,
And, with joy, I choose now to take refuge in your love.

AHO
Blessed Be

Chapter 2: The Fish Daughter –
0 to 12 Years

Sea Twins
Collage © 2008 Licia Berry

I sat at the dinette to write, looking through the RV window at the Gulf of Mexico, just feet away. It was summer of 2004, six months into our family odyssey. I watched as my husband and sons enjoyed the waves, playing with abandon in the warm waters off Padre Island National Seashore in Texas. My heart ached. I used to love the water, too. When did the water become my enemy?

Growing up on the Outer Banks, I had loved the ocean. I felt I belonged to it. In conceiving of my birth, I imagined that I was a little, silvery fish in the surf, scooped up by my father and brought to my human mother's arms as a prize.

The Atlantic was my mother. I knew this as surely as I felt her primordial waves calling me, pulling and drawing me back home. The salt water was the amniotic fluid of my youth. The ocean's memory of me held me, told me stories, reminded me of my sisters and brothers across the waters of the world. When her waters touched my toes, my face, my belly, no matter how long I had been away, she knew who I was. She said, "Daughter, my daughter." She never forgot me.

As I think about it now, I came to the ocean open-armed as a young child because it mothered me in a way. The waters of my youth were a respite of feminine energy. Swimming was an expression of my body asking to be carried and lifted into love. The ocean held me as if to a mother's bosom.

Now, here I was, age thirty-nine, confronted by the immense waters where I could not escape them, beckoning me into the waters of my memory in order to find my way home again.

Mistrust of the Feminine

My human mother, my birth mother was a mere eighteen years old when I was born. At sixteen, she had come as a vacationer to the Outer Banks and met my father, an island boy whose European ancestors had washed ashore in the 1600s and married into the native population. The Ocracoke village dance was the beginning of my story.

What made her fall for the rough, local, young man she met? An upper-middle-class city girl, she was the daughter of a successful mortgage banker. The boy who would become my father was an unlikely prospect. What seemed a summer beach vacation romance lingered and bloomed into a first love. They visited one another, she returning with her family for beach vacations, he driving the four hours to Charlotte for the weekends. When she turned seventeen, they got in a car with her sister and brother and crossed the border into South Carolina, where it was legal to marry. They returned to her parents' house that night a wedded couple. She had been accepted to university and had plans to go in the fall. When she came into the house with a ring on and nonchalantly announced that she was married, all hell broke loose. Her parents forbade her to continue to live in the house and sent her and my father packing that night. They were not welcome; since they had made this adult decision, they would need to fend for themselves. My mother did not make it to the university. I was born ten months later.

My mother's feminine presence looked like the movie stars of the era. She was dark-eyed, dark-haired, olive-skinned, exotic to a simple beach boy. I can only imagine how he saw her the first time—a Sophia Loren right there on Ocracoke Island. Attraction must be magnetic, two polar opposites irresistibly brought together as if by fate. Romance is initiated by completion of a circuit, positive charge drawn to negative charge, the joining of molecules through the oldest law of physics.

She had a flair for drama, having been in the performing arts in high school. Photographs of her reveal her need for the camera eye to be on her, and her response when it actually was. It was as if she needed documentation to be sure she existed. As I remember from an adult perspective, the anticipated movie camera was always around the corner and she was always ready for the fame that would surely come eventually.

When I was born in April 1965, they had made a home in a little house on Hatteras that belonged to his parents, who were willing to support the new couple. He worked at the gas station his father owned, while she stayed home with me. She was among strangers in a rural fishing village with a baby and not even out of her teens. I can only imagine her fear and loneliness for her family and environment that she had known. I imagine her worrying over the changing of her lovely, petite figure. I imagine her questions and fears about having a baby so soon, not wanting it, even entertaining secret thoughts of getting rid of the child. I imagine my father finding out and forbidding it. They have never talked about this time, as if it is covered in a haze of secrets, shame, confusion, or grief. What happened while I was forming in those dark waters of her young womb, swirling around in the memory of the ancestral mothers before her?

A healer I spoke to during my forties when I had a health scare told me I had pre-birth work to do. She said that, starting at my second month in utero, perhaps when it was confirmed she was pregnant, my biological mother was thinking thoughts about whether she wanted me or not. Forming in the emotional environment of her womb that ranged from ambivalence to actively wanting to expel me, my embryonic cells collated with an understanding that I was coming into an unsafe place, perhaps one that wanted to harm me. My molecules carried a message of protection, and, armoring myself, I came into the world anyway. My fear that I was not wanted helped form my spine, my organs, my tissues. Defense against the mother who grew me inside of her helped me survive. This protective stance made me strong enough to live through all that happened after I emerged from that womb too. What was perceived as independence and stubbornness in my young personality was actually a survival attitude that bore me through until it was safe for me to examine my childhood.

The open heart required to write this story is challenging all of my defenses; I have to pause periodically to soften and re-open my heart center. My heart has been well-defended in my life, but it did not happen in the womb. When I emerged, I still had the innocent heart of the Buddha. I observed and felt and lived, even though I apparently died inside in little ways. My young mother, still a child herself, did not know the kindness that was needed to help me be safe with her. She dressed me as if I was her dolly and threw me away when she had had enough playtime. My infant heart learned there was something not safe about her, something wild and unpredictable.

When I was in high school, she used to tell the story at her dinner parties (at which lots of alcohol was consumed) of me at seven months old, crying on the floor, and of her dismay and frustration at my cries, so much so that she "punted" me "like a football." She would gesture with her hands to indicate how my baby body turned end over end, arcing through the air, and landed with a thud on the floor; she would laugh with flair like she was performing on stage for an audience as she told this story. So did the rest of us at the dinner table. It was amusing, like a cartoon in my mind, to think of a baby kicked by a big foot and sailing through the air. Though, by age two, my heart had been broken, I did not put it together that the flying baby was me until many years later.

My parents moved us back to Charlotte (where she grew up) when I was two and my mother was pregnant with my sister. I have clear memory of our rental duplex on Greenwood Cliff and the early sexual abuses that occurred. My father worked as a mechanic at Sears, my mother was at home with my sister and me, and we were very poor. There are stories of us not having enough to eat and relishing Sunday dinners at my grandparents' house.

We moved next to a rental house on Harding Place, a short distance away from the duplex. The house was laid out in an open-square format, with a living room that spread across the front of the house, opening into the dining room and the kitchen at the back, circling into a den which circled again into a hall that had doors to the two bedrooms and bathroom, eventually ending up back at the front of the house into the living room. This circular layout and the hardwood floors enabled me to run around the house and slide in the hallway in my footie pajamas. I loved the speed I could attain and the freedom as I surfed the slick surface of the worn wooden floor.

I wrestled with the nature of reality in this place. I felt such darkness around us there, and wondered, at the tender age of four, if I was insane. The halls seemed haunted with specters, perched high in the corners near the ceiling during the day and coming down to roam the house at dark. I recall sensing frightening presences at night and making the trip down the dark hall to my parents' room, asking to come into bed. When they refused, I lay on the floor next to their bed, watching the feet of the ghosts as I curled up in a ball. Who knows if these hauntings were creations of my mind? We often had unsettling influences in the house, such as my father's love of "Iron Man" by Black Sabbath. That album was on so often I learned the words and can sing them to this day.

There was also the frequent use of a Ouija Board. My mother and her family explored speaking with the realm beyond with this tool. While harmless to some, it became, in my dramatic and highly sensitive family, an instrument of harm. "Spirits" told them things that would happen, which preyed on their alcoholic states of mind, including that my aunt would be killed in the shower "Psycho" style (she did not shower for many weeks) and that a painting of a Spanish lady was haunted by an evil spirit and needed to be destroyed by fire (they did). While I cannot comment on the veracity of these insights, I can say they made for a terrifying environment as a young, feeling child.

At four, I attended a Methodist preschool. I am uncertain why my parents enrolled me there since they were not religious in any way. Perhaps it was to get me out from underfoot while my mother attended to my baby sister's needs. I was a curious child and asked lots of questions, so possibly, they saw that I was intelligent and needed structure beyond the home environment. I loved going to school, loved the atmosphere of learning, except when my teachers talked about God.

This Creation Story was centered on a male deity who touched with his finger and made things occur. Pretty powerful fellow. Nowhere in the Creation Story was the presence of a Mother, or a female face, until Eve was "made from Adam's rib" and then made the dratted decision to learn about the world through the Tree of Knowledge. The expulsion from the Garden of Eden and the blame of Eve was a clear message to me. God could do some pretty neat things (like the making of the world) and some punitive, violent things—and He did not like curious women. Since the suffering of the world was all Eve's fault, clearly, females who sought answers were troublemakers.

I had already been having direct experiences of what I understood was God. The first that I can remember is at age two in my sandbox. MY personal encounters with Spirit were very loving and kind; I felt safe and warm. But the God that my teachers talked about had a wild side. Their God unpredictably lashed out and smote people. He was a judging God, and if you did not measure up, you were punished, sometimes forever. I could not relate to that God.

Could it be that there were two different ones? I wondered. I LOVED my God; I loved the feeling I had when I connected with God. It was so good, so pure, so sweet.

I started to worry that I might be wrong on a day when my teacher talked about how sinners go to hell. She pointed out that we were all sinners, everyone in that room included. I looked around the circle at the other children in my class. These kids were sinners? I thought they were my friends, not bad people who needed to be punished. Then I realized she was talking about me, too.

I had gotten the message at home quite a bit that I was a bad girl, whether it was said consciously or implied by my parents' behavior toward me, especially my mother's. Perhaps it was true. Perhaps I was a bad girl after all.

I internalized this message. All young children are little sponges, absorbing the information they are given every moment of every day. I have learned in my neuroscience studies that a brain built on a foundation of negative experiences is likely to recreate them. The way we think is based on the messages we were given as children; the way we think about the world, each other, our connection to these, and how we fit into them stems from our earliest learning. If our brain is hardwired with a foundation of neural pathways built from negative messages, it is likely to reinforce those messages by repeating them. The most insidious way that early programming can affect us is in the ways we think about ourselves.

Young children's brains build neural pathways based on their experiences and thoughts that will uphold them the rest of their lives. The voice we use to speak to the children becomes their inner voice later in life. It is important that children are given the most positive and loving environment that we can possibly manage to provide. If we tell them they are wonderful, loved, and inherently good, this is what they believe about themselves. If we tell them that they are bad, wrong, stupid, or other negative concepts, this is what they will integrate into their impressionable minds.

What kind of structure builds a brain that functions in the positive? A brain that has been built on a solid foundation of loving, supportive, life-affirming messages and experiences is a brain that is self-reinforcing toward wellbeing, self-actualization, and a happier life.

My mother believed I was evil when I was young. As an adult, of course, I know that a child is not evil, but I carried that projection most of my life. I hoped it was true that "Yes, Jesus Loves Me," like we sang in preschool. I hoped Jesus could look into my heart and see that I was good and that I was a little lamb in his flock. I believed I would be taken care of, even though things at home did not necessarily back that up. I believed, if all else failed, that I had God.

The concept of evil that is taught in Christian preschool is that women are the bad guys.

I imagined my mother as Eve, and to this day, still dream of serpents, which has become my subconscious symbol for her—a menacing black snake, a creature of dark waters, a water moccasin.

One day recently, I was doing some work to reclaim Inner Tribe™ members (something you will learn about in later chapters of this book), parts of myself that I had disowned in childhood, and I found a Dark Self. I wrote in my journal:

> This Dark Self is the accumulation of all the things I don't like about myself. . . . I had her heaped in with the wounding that I ascribe to my childhood. I'm given to understand that most of us, even those not dealing with significant trauma, disown the Dark Self because we are afraid that it is the true self. . . . but it is just a part of the self, part of who we are.
>
> My Higher Voice says, *"Own your darkness. Make peace with the things you've disowned. Embrace the power that you've suppressed."*
>
> I set the intention in my usual way, asking for the help of All Creation to embrace my darkness and heal the chasm/wound that I pushed my Dark Self into . . . backfilling from the inside out with unconditional love.

I watch as a large earthen hole begins to fill with "lit up" soil, lifting any remnants, little pockets of darkness up into the light, to the surface. I am determined that nothing will remain buried. The pockets poof into nothingness as they are exposed to the light, becoming one with my wholeness. Except for one.

In my left field of vision, on the left side of the hole, is a black snake. It is getting buried under the "lit up" soil, covered up where it can remain under the surface. No more burying! I must embrace this part of me, whatever it is . . . but I am terrified to do that. This black snake is the common symbol in my dreams of my mother, a frightening and unpredictable water moccasin. I lift it out with my mind, will it to the surface by reasserting my intention to embrace ALL of myself. It comes up to the ground where I can see it; I am afraid it will strike out and bite me. I once again reassert my intention to embrace it, and suddenly the snake is in my arms. I just know that any second it will strike, but what it does instead is flick out its tongue and "kiss" around my mouth.

So surprised, I notice I now hold the snake in my arms like I would hold a reclining baby—there is so much love here. The snake dissolves into nothingness, and at the same time, I hear myself say, "I love you, Mama." I sense a connection between me and my mother that feels very young. There is forgiveness. The tears come. And then I feel a splitting, sudden pain in the left side of my sex organs . . . my left ovary, Fallopian tube, into the uterus, and expanding up into my hip. This is an area where I have felt constricted and stuck. The pain clears and my left hip relaxes. My inquiring mind asks what just happened, and my Higher Voice says I just released tension that I'd been carrying in my body for a long time, since I was 3 years old.

Oh. My mother first told me I was evil when I was 3 years old.

I am so grateful that I have done the work I have done and found wonderful resources to help me unlock the falsehoods I have carried. There is no such thing as an evil baby.

I have asked myself the question: Is there such a thing as evil? I have always associated evil with unconsciousness, with separation from the heart. Willful causing of pain falls under that definition. My mother was evil by that definition; my inner children are afraid of her. My Child Heart clung to the belief that I was evil because it was beyond terrifying to think that my mother was the evil one. Even though I recognized her in the movie characters of the Red Queen in *Alice in Wonderland* and the Wicked Witch in *The Wizard of Oz*, I feared it was really me who was evil to the core.

The Child Heart

As Angeles Arrien says in *The Four Fold Way*, "Many native cultures believe that the heart is the bridge between Father Sky and Mother Earth. For these traditions, the 'four-chambered heart,' the source for sustaining emotional and spiritual health, is described as being full, open, clear, and strong. These traditions feel that it is important to check the condition of the four-chambered heart daily, asking: 'Am I full-hearted, open-hearted, clear-hearted, and strong-hearted?'"

I have realized over the years, since I started recovery work at age twenty-one, that the wounded heart is really my main concern. There are many wounds in this thing called life, to be sure, but the ones that cut the deepest are those that penetrate the core of our being. The heart is the first functional organ in vertebrate embryos and, in the human, beats spontaneously by week four of development. Everything else comes after the heart. The center of the universe and the center of our existence, the heart—the Great Processor—emanates pulses that signify we are alive.

My Child Heart defended early in my life so I have a very young baby in my core who needs comfort, nourishment, and love. If love does not come from those who raise us, we will seek it from other places. I recognized the feeling of love in Nature.

Perhaps this is why, in coming back to Hatteras as a girl, to the land that was my home place, I would cry when it was time to leave, hiding in the bathroom. My young mind did not understand, and I certainly did not have the words, but it was because I was leaving my True Mother.

In Which I Grapple with Jesus

My conception of Jesus was that he was a nice man we studied in a book called the Bible. I had no model for him in my life to truly understand who he was until I "met" Fred Rogers on PBS children's programming on television. When I got home from preschool, I watched *Sesame Street* and my favorite, *Mister Rogers Neighborhood*. Mister Rogers was kind, gentle, and sane. He felt safe, a refuge in my day. He reminded me of what I thought Jesus would be like if he was a real person.

That's right. I could not believe Jesus was a real person; jaded by age five, I had reasoned that Jesus was make-believe, just like the characters in the Neighborhood of Make-Believe on Mister Rogers. Perhaps because I could not find a living example of him in my daily life, I relegated him to fairy tale or fiction. Or perhaps that kindness and caring for others seemed impossible.

I love this quote from Fred Rogers:

> *The child is in me still and sometimes*
> *not so still.*

It warms my heart that he acknowledged the presence of the inner child, as well as the **unrest** of the inner child. His loving, inclusive attitude is one that I have worked to emulate toward myself. He is a kind of internalized role model that I was fortunate to have been exposed to.

I continued kindergarten at the same Methodist church where I attended preschool the year before. That year, I had a teacher who seemed on the surface all sweetness and light, like the stereotypical mid-western housewife with apron and apple pie in the oven. But her dark eyes held a different truth. I later discovered that she carried a deep, subversive streak of judgment and hatred for women. I can only imagine that she hated herself for being a woman because she bought into the religious notion that women were the downfall of man. When I felt her eyes on me, I sensed her disdain. Like all children, I was a bright and smart little girl, full of God's presence, and yet I felt when she looked at me that she saw a piece of trash. The self-loathing simmered behind her eyes, so much so that it seemed that she could not see the devotion that I held in my heart.

Breaking Up with Jesus

My grandfather (my mother's father) also had an interesting relationship with Jesus. My grandfather was a handsome, intelligent man who carried incredible pain and never healed it. His intellect became a weapon along with his anger, and he dispensed abuse in the form of words and alcoholic rages, including becoming physically violent. He drank to incredible excess, I imagine drowning the pain with his gin and tonics and Old Fashioneds.

One of his frequent ranting targets was Christianity. In addition to ridiculing belief in the religion, he judged any kind of devotion as ridiculous pursuit. He criticized from his chair at the head of the family table where he held court, the mindlessness of faith and the stupidity of believing that God was part of human beings' lives.

I shrunk before his penetrative eyes; they seemed to bore into me with relentless intensity, unflinchingly critical. When he drank to excess, he seemed to weigh and measure anyone his eyes lit upon, revealing a mechanistic, deductive thought process, like taking apart a clock to see how it worked. When he was not completely drunk, he could be sweet and caring at times, but I often found him judgmental. He seemed to decide who a person was before even knowing them. It did not matter what you said or what evidence to the contrary you presented to challenge his thoughts; if he decided it, it was done. Under that condemning, laser-like gaze, I wondered what was wrong with me. I felt like a butterfly pithed in my center against a display board, helpless under the curious and detached observation of a collector with his magnifying glass. Which leg would he pull off next?

I was very confused and concerned. Here was the grand patriarch of my family, almost spitting with disdain about Christianity and God the Father. I wanted to share with him the goodness I had directly experienced with what I thought was God, but I was afraid to contradict him.

My actual father made an inappropriate relationship between a father and daughter, causing me to lose confidence in my voice and invoking doubts about God the Father in my mind, too. My kindergarten teacher was an echo of what I had already encountered at home in my mother—that I was evil. Who could I believe?

Nowhere did I see a positive model for relationship with God. With this confirmation in my only other safe haven of school, I had to begin to believe them. If my mother and my teacher both saw me as evil, surely I must be.

This was the year that the church, no longer a refuge, broke my soul, turning me away from Christianity just as surely as the sexual predation by the men in my family turned me away from my body. Experiencing God as love, I could not find it in my elders. Years and years of wandering the wilderness as I found truth have helped me heal this now, but as a discerning adult looking back, I believe that "Christianity" injured me worse in some ways than they did.

Music is Love

I began playing piano, a gift given to me by my father's parents on my sixth birthday, when we moved to Goldsboro, North Carolina, out into the country. My father had been transferred in his job with the Sears auto department. We lived for four years in a simple, brick house surrounded by acres of open land in the form of tobacco fields and farms. I played outside a lot there, but when I was inside, I enjoyed composing made-up songs on the piano. Something about music calmed my spirit.

I remember feeling swept up in the passion of imaginary stories as my little hands flew up and down the keys. My mother arranged lessons for me when I was in first grade, and I performed at a couple of elementary recitals, but my preference, by far, was to create my own music and play by ear the songs I heard on our little stereo. The songs I made up were mostly sweet and simple while the chaos of our family life raged on, although one song of note was a long, torrid affair about a young girl trapped in a tower over a crashing sea, amidst a raging storm, a metaphor describing my home. I found the piano to be a refuge after losing the church.

Once, at my maternal grandparent's house, I was playing a song that I had composed when my grandmother's brother, my Uncle Ernie, came to sit next to me on the piano bench. Uncle Ernie was a kind, loving man of gentle nature. His voice, like his manner, was soft and measured. His face was open as he listened to my song, receiving it and seemingly feeling my innocent heart.

When I completed the song, he turned to me and expressed how beautiful it was. He smiled and said to me, "You are very special." He was so genuine; I was afraid of this naked appreciation. The mirror of my beauty and goodness was too much to accept, and I knew he must be wrong, that he was mistaken. I downcast my eyes and stammered a "thank you," but rejected his kindness and saw him through the eyes of my grandfather, judging him as weak and emasculated like Jesus, judging the face of love as too good for me and therefore not to be accepted. I stood up and walked away from the piano. I did not play for him again.

Jesus became my metaphor for the child within me that had been crucified. They were one and the same. Rejecting kindness or compliments as "a mistake" (surely they could not see how awful I was), I would wander the wilderness for much of my life, looking for that purity again, in myself and in the world.

Not until I was an adult could I recognize that my relationship with Jesus (and therefore the goodness and innocence in my own heart) had been broken to the point that I could not accept unconditional love when it was freely offered.

I could not recognize Jesus in the form of my kind Uncle Ernie even when he was standing right in front of me.

I Become What She Sees

Goldsboro was a phase in my life in which I became the projection of my mother, allowed myself to be molded by the environmental culture of my home.

Have you ever noticed that? That when others see you in a particular way, you seem to become what they see? This can work positively or negatively for us. Sometimes I rise to my truest self when others expect it of me and see the best in me. Other times, I find that I fall into the dark hole of another's worst view of who I am, and somehow struggle to pull myself out of it, even if it is not true for me.

It seems we contribute to creating each other, doesn't it? This means we need to really see each other in our best possible light, especially children.

We lived in Goldsboro while I was in first through fourth grades, a truly formative time in a child's life. I remember Nature being my greatest ally as I became the product of my upbringing; Nature was a reminder of the truth beyond this life. My relationship with the trees and earth and sky were nourishing to me, a balm for my soul and a calm in the storm.

as much as I could, preferring the wind pulling on my hair to my mother's painful yanks as she combed through my tangles. One day, in her frustration, she cut off all of my hair.

A metaphorical significance of the cutting of hair goes far back in historical context. In Japanese feudal society, dishonor came with the cutting off of the samurai topknot or women's meticulous long hair. Shearing of the head in slavery

Licia, First Grade

was a stealing of identity and power by someone overseeing the breaking of the will of the slave. The wrapping, trapping, or shaving of hair in religious cultures reveals our deepest knowing . . . hair represents freedom. To this day, cutting our hair remains a symbol of a dramatic break with the past, a line between "what was before" and "what is to come."

My mother symbolically announced a new chapter in my life through the shearing of my locks, heralding a kind of dramatic, life-altering change.

Fierce Spirit

My first-grade year turned out to be a transformative and tumultuous time for me. While on one hand, I had a stable environment in the educational system, on the other, my home life was getting wilder by the month. I began to feel like two different girls—the good, smart girl at school and the wild, unsupervised girl at home. Looking back, my awareness that children need to feel the safety of structure around them came from this dichotomy.

My parents began drinking to excess this year, inviting people I did not know to our house and partying with loud music late into the night. In the morning, I sometimes had to get ready for school and wait for the bus on our country highway by myself. I developed a more independent streak, rebelling in little ways, such as sneaking out in the early morning to watch TV, eating spoonsful of ice cream from the freezer, or taking my bike out onto the road in front of our house to get down to the convenience store to buy candy without my mother knowing. Later, I would come to know this part of myself as strong and determined, the one who developed a protective stance because the unimaginable happened.

"The Most Forbidden Thing"

From a short story in *Blue-eyed Indian – Stories the Land Told Me*

I awoke to the red/orange cigarette light floating eerily in the darkness. Sometimes I thought it was a ghost with one red eye, but the light bobbed up and down from waist to mouth level, so that must not be it. Maybe our family dog coming in to check on me? You know how animals get that funny glint in their eyes at night. Oh, this was one eye; last time I looked at the dog, it still had two. Could it be an angel coming to protect me in the utter blackness of the house?

My heart pounded so fast. It was my pattern to close my eyes and freeze when I saw things in my room at night. I reasoned that if I stayed still, it would be like I was not there at all. Maybe if I stayed invisible and paralyzed under the covers, they would go away. This time, though, the red/orange light kept coming.

It seemed a cruel thing for the entire house to be pitch black in the night. What if I or my little sister, who slept like the dead in the next bed, awoke in the night to go to the bathroom, or god forbid, need a drink of water. My parents did not respond to those requests; they were almost always so drunk that my mother was passed out in bed, and the father prowling around in the night like a nocturnal predator looking for his next meal.

I did not like how my father became when he was drunk. He got mean, grumpy, sloppy, and touched me in ways that made me scared and uncomfortable, and deep-down angry at him. My mother became sad, and cried and cried and cried. She had a silly dramatic character to begin with, but when she drank alcohol, her drama became so big as to encompass her entire being. It felt to me like the house would fill with my mother's tears and the entire family would drown, swirling around in the dark salty water with the living room furniture and the dog.

I lay in my single bed with the maple leaf carved in the darkly stained headboard. I couldn't see it but I knew it was there, having traced the outline of it many times with my finger. It was a beacon to me sometimes, that leaf. It reminded me of being outside with my friends, the trees. I thought of how nature was such a place of solace and safety. It was always there. It didn't want anything from me. It gave to me instead of taking away from me. It was a place of ease. Sometimes I would try to get lost out in the woods down the dirt road from my home. I would turn this way and that, trying to confuse my infallible sense of direction—but I always found my way back home. Isn't it a Canada goose that has the incredible homing instinct? Like the ones my father hunted with his buddies back on the Outer Banks?

As the red/orange light continued its approach, I felt my little heart trying to escape my seven-year-old chest. My breath became very shallow, coming in short little pants. I did not cry out because I knew no one would come, that there was no one who would protect me. The light came to the side of my bed. I felt my body turned to the right, then lifted, and a blackness blacker than the dark house engulfed me; I remembered no more.

~ ~ ~

The independent, tomboyish girl that I was became a dominant character in our family, frequently labeled the "storyteller," "liar," "sneak," "bad," or "selfish." It was a very confusing time for me. My central identity at home as a scapegoat conflicted with my identity at school. I was the straight-A student who was a "problem child" at home. In my mind, I felt so unsettled, on edge when I was at home and at peace at school. One day, for show and tell, the two worlds merged.

Storyteller, from the short story "Liar"

It all started with some costume jewelry, a pair of fake crystal prism earrings. I don't even remember where I got them now. But at age seven, I was captivated by them.

They were clip-ons, and I wore them with everything. Tearing around outside by day in my shorts, playing in the dirt, riding my hippity hop like a race horse, and talking to the trees, I was a wild girl who wore the earrings for a touch of elegance I did not see in myself, but rather in my mother.

My mother was an elegant, beautiful visage. She looked Indian to me with her long hair in ponytails on either side of her brown face. A petite and shapely woman, she had the ideal figure, the one all the men wanted. She caught stares in public and the attention of men outside of my father. I wanted to look like her so much, but I didn't. I was the sturdier body of my father's side—tree trunk legs, thick neck, and barrel chest. Strong, resilient. Perhaps like my Outer Banks ancestors, my body was made for battling salty waves of the Atlantic, hauling survivors out of sinking ships.

My mother was indeed physically lovely, but always looked haunted to me. Looking back now, I cannot tell if it was because she was reliving some childhood trauma, anticipating a hand or an unkind word ever ready to strike her down, or if she truly was living a haunted existence out in the country with only my sister and me (and the garden) for company while my father was at work all day.

I don't think of her as happy; I don't remember her surrendering to laughter or mirth, except when she drank at night and danced wildly, spinning around the den. She was usually serious and dramatic, and struck me as being someone who always thought she was on camera; she would turn her head cocked at an attractive angle, or wave her arm in a slow, exaggerated way. I unconsciously mimicked her until I was old enough to realize there was no camera. Quieter during the day, her emotional demons came whipping out at night after the happy buzz devolved into dark despair. Her black eyes peered from inside her skull as if something fearful was just coming around the corner. Something wicked this way comes.

My school in Goldsboro was called Belfast Elementary. My new first-grade teacher, Mrs. Mooney, had replaced the original teacher in my first-grade class. I loved Mrs. Mooney; she did not wear tent-like polka dot dresses and horn-rimmed glasses hanging around her neck on a chain. She was young, cute, and kind, and she smiled at me. She was not frowny and old and stodgy like our previous one.

She seemed stable enough, an authority figure I thought I could trust. Like my mother, she was a brunette of slight build. In my mind, she became a kind of "other mother," one who actually interacted with me, took an interest in what I did and said. She praised me for my good works in school. I could pretend that she and my mother were two sides of the same person, my daytime mom and my nighttime mom. They were very different people.

I took the "crystal" earrings to school for show and tell one morning; there, I concocted an elaborate tale of how I had come into possession of this magical treasure. I don't remember much of the story except that it involved a long journey in unknown lands with a giant wolf as my companion. My beloved Mrs. Mooney, my trusted mother at school, ratted me out. My mother later confronted me to relay that Mrs. Mooney said I "was quite the storyteller."

My reputation at home for being unreliable took a turn for the worse. When it was revealed to my parents that this seven-year-old had "a good imagination," it became the ideal cover-up for the sexual abuse going on in my house.

I became the liar who made up stories about being visited in her room at night and being afraid of what might get me in the dark. How perfect.

~ ~ ~

The split that occurred in my psyche that year essentially mirrored the acting out of my parents. I learned as an adult that the independent girl, whom I later called "Fierce," was my internalized masculine role model, patterned after my father. In my mind, I became a "boy" to survive his advances. Alternately, in response to my mother's girly/victim/seductive role modeling, I decided I wanted to be a Playboy bunny.

I talked to my mother about the light that wandered the halls at night, but she said it was a ghost. I later learned that she witnessed some of my sexual abuse and became jealous of me. She began to treat me as a rival instead of her seven-year-old daughter. I realize now that I was groomed for the sexual abuse; my father gave me his *Penthouse* and *Playboy* magazines to look at, and my mother, . . . where was my mother? Hiding from the truth of what was occurring. And because she didn't believe me, I thought that these things that were happening to me must be my fault, that there was something terribly wrong with me. I wondered, *What did I DO that she hates me so much? Why am I so awful?*

In second grade, I gained weight. I was still a diligent student in school, but there were certain things I could not wrap my head around. For example, I had difficulty learning how to tell time. Later in the year, I had no problem with it; was it a developmental issue? I remember sitting at my desk and wondering why I could not get my brain to work! The feeling of that year is hazy. I do not remember much of second grade, except for my newfound love of the Waltons. Home life was more of the same: wild parties, loud music, drugs and alcohol, and a new twist, . . . The Husband's and The Wife's infidelities.

I believe that my parents' alcoholism started in earnest then. There was a partying culture in the early 1970s anyway, and their parties devolved into sex, drugs, and rock n' roll with regularity. The environment in my house, which was already unstable and scary at times, took on a free-for-all quality, an "anything goes" air that seemed congruent with the hippie culture of the times. My mother's affair with her best friend's husband took betrayal to a whole new level. I was not told that these affairs were going on, but could feel them acutely. The feeling I remember at that time was of hanging out in a void, with nothing to grab onto, nowhere to stand, nothing to hold me.

This is the same time I began to be afraid of the water at a deep level, my beloved ocean lost to me. The sexual abuse, paired with the lack of boundaries or protection, was terrifying, and the vast, unpredictable ocean was too much for my vulnerable psyche. I had no one. It was as if I lived among young people with no responsibilities, as if they were in college and not married with two children (and a third soon on the way). It was 1973.

Third grade saw me coming back together after a year of wandering the void, integrated of a sort. "Fierce" more stridently became my internal image. I started to be physically active again, becoming one of the fastest runners, playing tandem jump rope, and pretending to know karate, beating up the boys who chased me, through my HI-YAH! chops. I began to feel more powerful, but through violence and activity, like an over-achieving boy. I was still smart and did well in school, but when asked what I wanted to be when I grew up I still said "a Playboy bunny." I became indoctrinated in the dominant culture this year.

My inner masculine, patterned after my father, became how I related to people who were kind or receptive; I saw them as weak, vulnerable, powerless. Establishing dominance was important to a girl who had her power stolen. The masculine I internalized seemed the best way to be safe; the only other way to remain in some sense of power was to be the girl who *wanted* to be objectified and strut my stuff, like the ladies in my father's magazines. The seductive, vampiric, feminine model of my mother actually complemented my internalized masculine. She mostly left me alone.

I was obsessed with ghost stories in third and fourth grades, roaming the library shelves for new books and re-checking the same ones I had read before if I was out of luck. I pored over the tales of woe and tragedy, enjoying the spine-tingling awe of the supernatural, now so familiar to me, although, the "ghosts" that haunted our house were not the paranormal kind.

Fourth grade came along and so did the separation between my real self and the self I played in the world. Pictures of me that year show a girl who is very aware of how she looks, posing seductively for the camera while I feed my new baby brother in his high chair. I finished the year out at Belfast and then our family packed up to move to Wilmington, North Carolina. A new chapter in my short life began.

Nature Gives Me a Spine

Wilmington was an old southern river town, and in 1975, rife with racial tension. Where I had not experienced much in the way of black kids in my old school or in the country, here, the simmering conflict was a presence that could not be ignored. In our neighborhood, I was shocked when my little sister and I were assailed by a girl and two boys, black and about my age, who followed us home while we strolled on the sidewalk from a friend's house. I turned to grapple with them while I told my sister to run; she did, our house being right within reach. The kids let me go when they realized I was so close to home. It set a tone, though, to have this experience so soon after we moved in. I became afraid of the kids with dark skin and learned mistrust of this cultural "other."

The presence of Nature was also pervasive, even though we lived in town on Grace Street in a neighborhood of older homes. We were surrounded by magnolias, oaks, other hardwoods, and azaleas. After the open countryside and tobacco fields of my former landscape, the trees here were awe-inspiring. There was something about their straightness, the way they reached up from the ground into the sky with no shyness or apology, that I seemed to take subconsciously into myself. I fell in love with the landscape here. It spoke to me in a voice that was related to the voice of Nature I had been experiencing, but there was a new, deeper feeling that I became aware of. Turning eleven years old, I was stepping into the transition of puberty, and the hormones awakening in my system seemed to call to a greater Wise Voice.

I started doing ritual in a way I did not know, yet felt guided from the inside. It began one day when I was exploring the ground under the shrubs in our backyard. I remember a timeless feeling as if the overgrown bushes were an enchanted forest rising above my head as I crouched, and the ground a magical kingdom full of secret intelligence. To my surprise, I happened upon a dead bird, perhaps killed by flying into one of the windows above the hedge line. It was so precious and beautiful, and I picked it up in my hands. I was suddenly overcome with the urge to chant to the sky, asking that the spirit of this bird be helped to find its way home and that the ground accept its body back into the dark earth. It was the first time I facilitated the passing of a being from this world to the others. Later, this happened with some regularity, and I became highly sensitive to the supernatural, something that is in abundance in a historic river town. I was left alone enough that I could explore my new interests, observing Nature and the spirit world with a keen eye, and learning many things about the world of ancient knowledge within.

My school life was a typical southern, inner city experience. Fifth grade was in a beaten inner city school, a dreadful building that could not keep teachers. My fifth-grade year was characterized by multiple, short-term, substitute teachers taking shifts of several weeks at a time, and not learning very much except that I was admired for my ability to run like the wind. I remember the dirt playground and kickball and tag, but not much in terms of good friends. There was a girl who hung out with me a bit, similarly hardy on the exterior, named Rhonda; she talked tough, but she had a good heart. I liked her, and she even invited me to come over, but I was not allowed to go.

Sixth grade was an absolute joy. I moved up to a newer school and was placed in an honors class with other smart kids who were serious about their studies and could mostly behave themselves. I loved my teacher, who took me seriously and treated me like I had a brain. To my delight and thrill, she seemed to "see" me. She respected us enough to tell us when we were not doing our best work and delighted in our brilliance. I reveled in the light of this kind of attention and blossomed socially as well as intellectually. My feminine side, formerly informed by the role model of my mother and the pinup girls, was now internalizing this woman. I was no longer interested in being a Playboy bunny, but now wanted to grow my capacity to learn and expand my intelligence.

My mind explored boundless ideas; I became interested in UFOs and extraterrestrial life, reasoning at age eleven that it was arrogant to presume we were the only "intelligent life" in the universe. I devoured topics at school and got involved with extracurricular projects. I entered a library contest, with the winner announced over the loudspeaker each week. The winner guessed the correct answer to a mystery question; I guessed "roadrunner" for a desert bird. I remember clearly feeling an intuitive hit about it as I wrote my answer down even though I knew nothing about the desert or roadrunners, and knowing I would win. (Interesting that I would wind up living in Arizona as an adult, where the roadrunner is the state bird!) The librarian showed pleasure in giving me the prize and asked me how I knew. I told her that I had just guessed. Being recognized for my good qualities, being SEEN, was a revelation. I understand now that I was hungry for a positive female authority/role model and that she was an ideal teacher for this formative time.

Interestingly, the 1976 presidential election was occurring and our class was assigned the roles of campaigning for our choice for president. There was something about Jimmy Carter that I trusted and latched onto, and I campaigned fervently on his behalf. This was the beginning of my awareness of making effort to elect a leader and of activism toward a larger cause.

The other wonderful thing I worked on was a research project that took weeks to complete; my choice of subject was the deep sea. This choice is interesting considering the dark nature of the bottom of the ocean and the strange creatures that roam those shadowy waters. I was now staying out of the water for the most part, and I have to surmise that I was keeping my distance from the waters inside, too. Feeling emotional was not rewarded in our family home, so keeping on solid intellectual ground was the way I found that I could get positive reinforcement and feel safe. What compelled me to this deep, watery subject matter? How intriguing that I chose to completely lose myself in this dark, watery world for completing a major grade in my class. I learned so much, and loved doing it; I felt at home. It may have been the very thing that prepared me to research and write books and curriculum as an adult.

Accessing emotion became a problem later that I would devote considerable effort to healing. Living in my head, although trained and rewarded by the culture to do so, is an incomplete way of being. The hiding away of our tender heart can separate us from feeling the consequences of our behavior. My mother was less feeling than my father in many ways; she could separate herself from her heart with precision.

Once, I fell from the top of a tall magnolia tree in our front yard. I remember a sickening, melon-thudding sound as my head hit the branches. When I hit the bottom, I landed on the roots of the tree across my spine. I was paralyzed for a few moments then managed to drag myself into the house. My mother, dressed prettily to greet guests for a dinner party she had been preparing for, met me at the door, and blinked blankly at me. What a strange and unexpected visage I must have been to this busy party hostess, standing on the threshold with leaves in my hair, smudged face, and split lip. I stammered out to her what happened. I was pretty beaten up, bloody and scraped, and clearly shaken and somewhat disoriented. She purposefully took me up to the bathroom and put me in the tub with a washcloth on my forehead, directing me to soak and then get into bed when I was done. She left me there alone as I quietly went into shock while the party began downstairs.

Where is My Mother?

Looking back, I am horrified by the fact that I was not taken to the hospital or to receive any medical care whatsoever after this major accident. Knowing what I know now about the brain and head injuries, as well as spinal cord injuries, I could easily have done myself permanent damage as a result of this fall. I seem to be all right, albeit with some neck stiffness in a particular region; I guess it is a good thing that I have a hard head. But what happened in that moment was clear. My mother chose to continue to prepare for her party instead of take care of me.

My awareness now is that she was so checked out, so not-in-her-body, so unfeeling, that she could not connect to me or to my needs as her daughter. Perhaps my being a girl scared her, or reminded her of her own history, or maybe she is just a cold, walled-off person. This event helped me later in my life to understand the extent of unmet needs of my childhood, framing the neglect that my mother perpetrated. For so many years, decades really, I blamed myself for being unlovable. Why would a mother ignore her child's injuries and wellbeing? Surely, it was because I was an awful person. In children's vulnerable moments, it is not unusual for them to wonder whether they are valued by their parents. The dreadful realization that we are not as treasured as other spheres in our parents' lives erodes our self-confidence and impacts us unless we heal. My own healing process extended into my forties. I am happy to report that the child inside can indeed be healed.

Perhaps in my attempts to locate a mother figure, I again looked to the television for support. There I found a prediction of my later life in the innocent guise of Saturday morning cartoons. Sandwiched between ScoobyDoo and Shazam I found the remarkable role model of Isis. The show fed a great hunger for an example of an intelligent and kind woman who became an ancient goddess in moments of need. Her ability to listen to her inner voice while she commanded forces of Nature seemed to reflect my budding shamanic capacity. I pretended I

was her, holding my arms behind me, closing my eyes, and calling out, "Oh, mighty Isis" with my face to the searing sun.

In the absence of my mother's voice, I had ample opportunity to look elsewhere for guidance, in Nature, in teachers, in television. I used every resource at my disposal to find wise counsel, and to learn that I was okay and not some scourge on the Earth. I found Great Mother's voice in ritual, in the ground, in the pulse of life. I found this voice without a name to be kind, patient, consistent, accepting—just what a confused, twelve-year-old girl needed.

My mother was a mystery to me, only seeming to interact when she needed me or when she was angry. Her pretty, dark, seductive physique seemed to grow shadow-like and scary when she spoke critical or unkind words. More times than I may even know, a psychic dagger was inserted into my back, my solar plexus, my belly, and finally my heart. She was mean, spiteful, alternating with brooding and neglectful. When she drank, she danced and laughed, seemingly freed from her usual somber nature, becoming wildly expressive and sexual. I was afraid of her then; her eyes carried the same superiority that my grandfather's expressed, the same judgment. Later in the night, she cried, yelling at my father or us kids if we were unlucky enough to be in their presence. My parents were wasted a lot, more often than in Goldsboro, it seemed. My sister, my brother, and I mostly stayed away from them, hiding in the TV room or upstairs in our rooms.

At the ages of eleven and twelve, I dreamed of being chased by a menacing presence. I awoke myself screaming "NOOOOOO!" in the night. Once again sensing a roaming predator in the halls, standing in the threshold of my bedroom, then hovering over me as I slept, I felt haunted at this house. Once again, the nighttime presence was explained away as the ghost of the house's former owner, Mr. Shrier. I was scared of this unseen, unsettled man who roved our upstairs floor. I wanted him to go away.

Thinking back about my mother from my present place, I can clearly call up my dark fears of her, but now my heart is soft and my eyes are open. I see her and her complex persona and unconsciousness, and I have compassion for her as an ill woman who was trapped in her wounding and her family life. She devastated me, to be sure. But I see her as a woman who was seriously troubled, unable at that time to make the choices necessary to change. I am not making excuses for her behavior, nor her unwillingness when she was later confronted and invited to engage in healing our relationship, but I have found that I have come to such peace in myself that I do not feel trapped in my tortured relationship with her any longer. My needs as a daughter are met by the wonderful inner Mother I have found.

A New Country

Midway through my sixth grade, my father received a promotion and was transferred to Little Rock, Arkansas. I was pulled by my tenuous roots out of the encouraging school environment where I had begun to find my voice. Our house sold quickly and we moved during Christmas break, making our way across the country from North Carolina. I specifically remember the snow on the road in Tennessee and the "bubble" Holiday Inn where we stayed in Little Rock when we arrived late that night, the steam beading on the lit dome over the heated pool. In my mind, I, having been in North Carolina my whole life, felt we were moving to a different country. We may as well have been moving to Africa, as far as I was concerned. I imagined arriving at a village with straw huts and dark-skinned natives dressed in grass skirts, as I had seen in *National Geographic* magazine. We arrived at our new house made of quarried stone and on a little bit of land in an older inner city neighborhood. The sloping yard was larger than most in the area and bordered a cement runoff ditch. On the other side was low-income housing and lots of African-American children yelling at each other. Perhaps my vision was not that far wrong.

I remember a strange, timeless quality while we were at this location. We lived there only seven months, yet it seemed to me we were there for years. The abrupt move from my wonderful class in Wilmington left me sadder than I knew, and the school I was placed in was crowded, racially tense, and confusing to me. The middle school schedule of changing classes was baffling, and I could not seem to understand my math courses. It reminds me of how confused I was in second grade with the telling of time; I just could not get my head around fractions. School was stressful, and home was airless, dark, and slippery. Still thinking something was wrong with me, I sought answers in friends and spirituality, including the Bible. Little Rock was a stressed-out town at this time as racial integration was occurring. I felt it everywhere and did not feel safe.

As I came into puberty, my mother seemed even more distant. I again turned to the television for a female role model in the form of the Bionic Woman. I made collages with her photographs and placed them around our bedroom. I liked that she was sunny, kind, and strong; it was a necessary opposite archetype of my mother, who seemed completely absorbed in her own darkness. I really started to feel her absence in my life here, and when she honed in on the one place I felt nourished and she threatened to take away my TV viewing of *The Bionic Woman* as a punishment, it was as if she wanted me to suffer as she was suffering. I needed her more than ever, but she seemed far away from me, wrapped in her own sorrows about leaving Wilmington.

Middle school girls are notorious for low self-esteem and crises of confidence. Girls of this age are coming into their puberty threshold, and it a very confusing time when she desperately needs a trusted elder to show her how to evolve as a young woman. This threshold is an important juncture in her life, as her navigation through this essential passage will define her as a woman. When I later taught middle schoolers, I paid special attention to giving them positive messages and affirming their intelligence and innate talents. A girl of this age without wise guidance to show her the way finds herself lost on a dark path, at the mercy of whatever comes along.

Chapter 3: The Angry Daughter – 13 to 28 Years

Mother Four
Collage © 2006 Licia Berry

If you bring forth what is within you, what you bring forth will save you. If you do not bring forth what is within you, what you do not bring forth will destroy you.

— **Jesus, in the Gospel of Thomas**

There were several omens in that strange Little Rock life that our family was caught in the grip of some ugly, downward spiral. The kids across the ditch threw rocks at us when we tried to play outside, snakes freely roamed our back yard, the neighborhood was unsafe, and lightning struck the house multiple times, to name a few. The sensation I remember was one of a breathless pause, of waiting for something to happen.

The nameless darkness I felt in our lives manifested in July 1976, after a storm knocked power out in our area. My parents left the windows open overnight because it was so hot, and us kids and my mother camped on the floor of the living room, the coolest room in the house.

Around three a.m., a black man with a gun crossed the threshold of the living room windowsill into our house. I was the closest to him, so he grabbed me by my ponytail, using me as a shield and hostage while he ordered my family around. With one hand, he held the gun to my temple. With the other, he slipped his fingers down into my bathing suit and into my most intimate place. My memory of this event is marked by the odd sensation of how familiar it felt to be touched this way, and how I felt if I cooperated with him, let him do what he wanted, I would be able to save my family.

My sister, age nine, began having difficulty staying in the room and wiggled out of sight under a table. My poor little brother was only four years old at the time and remained frozen and still. My father, who had emerged from the master bedroom, yelled at the man to get out of his house. There was an odd timelessness, as if our home and all of its inhabitants were suspended in super-charged amber.

My mother was silent until the man holding me said he wanted to take me somewhere. I did not know what he meant, but I did know it was bad. My mother screamed, "NO, take me!" and he exchanged hostages.

He raped her at gunpoint. I can only imagine what horror she underwent by taking my place as the intended rape victim.

She told a family member later that she felt it wiped the slate clean between her and me, that this act on her part absolved her of the years of allowing my father to sexually abuse me.

My shock, then rage when hearing this ridiculous philosophy is hard to describe. It felt like being violated all over again, but this time by her. I have difficulty even articulating my feelings about it because it is so preposterous for her to think that she can be free of responsibility for her choices as a mother because she was raped by the intruder who victimized our whole family. My analyst colleagues have remarked that this event was like an externalized manifestation of the dark themes that played out between my parents through their life choices—sex, addiction, violence, predation, evil.

Regardless of her spiritual beliefs or mental rationalizations, my mother has to work it out that her rape has not karmically erased her behavior as a mother who knew her daughter was being sexually abused, did nothing to protect her, and blamed and vilified her daughter for it. She uses this to avoid making amends and as a defense for her current behavior. To this day, she has not chosen to make this right; she has not come to me with sincere apologies or a request for forgiveness. The lack of consciousness is stunning to me, until I remember that she is unconscious.

The man was caught, convicted, and is still in prison. I played a major role in seeing and catching this man, a strange justice for my family to come through the scapegoated "liar who has a warped memory." There is a certain vindication, a mythical quality to the tale of my childhood, whereas it seems as if a circle closes here. I became a woman, or perhaps more accurately, a heroine, through this completion. Had I been preparing myself all along in my aptitude for female superheroes? Was I looking to women of strength because I was called to become one myself?

Suffice it to say, this event began another new chapter in my family's life.

The Shining City

We moved away from Little Rock after the break-in. My father put in for a transfer and our family, fractured into a million tiny pieces, dragged east to Atlanta, Georgia. We struggled to live our lives, each of us in our own way. I began, at age thirteen, my seventh-grade year in a middle school that carried tensions similar to Little Rock, but seemed to have a better way to handle them. My siblings and I went to school and my father to work. My mother was at home; she started therapy for her rape, selecting a psychiatrist who was later imprisoned for operating a child porn ring for fifty years.

A benefit of being back in the Southeast was our proximity to the Outer Banks, where we had been a regular fixture at every conceivable break prior to the move to Little Rock. The drive from Atlanta to Hatteras was thirteen hours, and my father insisted on driving it himself in one day. We had a station wagon and us kids would stretch out in the back and sleep while my mother curled up in the front seat. We would awaken at an early morning hour to the smell of the salt water and a humid breeze.

When we were at the Outer Banks, I was at peace in the environment I was born. The beach was my familiar place, and though I mistrusted the creatures in the water, I had a deep love of the vast ocean. I felt calmed, and the horrors dissolved away at the caress of my home breezes. I felt her, the ocean, as my mother, another voice that was not a voice but called to me nonetheless. The wisdom I felt when I tapped into her was ancient. She told me stories of creatures that evolved beyond her watery embrace and of the kinship between the creatures currently sea-bound and myself. We all came from her, she told me. Truly, she was my real mother.

Yearning for the Wise Mother

After Little Rock, there was a sense of loss, perhaps previously unacknowledged. Now, it was part of our daily respiration, breathing in and breathing out, a palpable grief on the surface of everything, like toxic dust.

My teenage years were full of angst; I was angry and lost, looking for guidance. I wanted love and wisdom, but heartbreak was my state of being. I kept waiting for her to arrive in my life— some wise, kind, accepting, and loving woman— but she did not show up.

My grief poured out when I played music. My

Licia, age 18 at the Outer Banks, North Carolina

saving grace during those years, music thawed my frozen emotions and washed me of the crusty constrictions that would have made me a bitter human being. When I was at the ocean, I felt keenly. I took my little music device with me and cried on the sand, not knowing why. I played a Moody Blues song over and over, called "You Can Never Go Home Anymore." It seemed to speak to my sense of loss. The wind seemed to surround me like a blanket, comforting and wiping away my tears. The blue sky looked down at me and offered condolences, sympathy.

What lost little girl would not want her mother?

There are many mythical tales of girls setting off on a quest, frequently due to being forced to leave. Sometimes this is because of the loss of her parents, or because society has deemed that she is unworthy in some way. *I feel this is a form of initiation for us as women.* Being pushed out of comfort or relationship causes us to seek answers within ourselves, impels us to find the strands of the web woven before us, the paths of wise women. My shamanism was enhanced by this forced walk, a kind of "trail of tears." If we can survive it, we will have gained the wisdom of the ancient ones. We meet many on the trail who offer us bits and pieces of the answers, but for me, I often rejected them because I wanted the wisdom to come from my mother. How often I walked alongside a woman who could give me what I sought, but I felt I was walking alone. One, in particular—my mother's little sister—set the stage for the greatest offering of all.

My Aunt Wendy was eleven years old when I was born and claimed me as "her baby." As Wendy watched me grow, she took me under her wing several times, showing interest in the growth of my mind. She was tall, dark-haired, funny, beautiful, intelligent, observant, caring, and alert to social injustices. The warrior in her inspired me without me even knowing it. However, she was molded by the abuses of her parents and her older siblings, so she also carried the wounded girl energy I was trying to avoid. She was therefore under the radar in my search for a wise mother/guide. Not until much later in my life would I recognize her for who she was.

Wendy Holding Licia, 1965

One of my favorite memories of Wendy is when she sat with me when I was age fourteen in the giant, vaulted living room of my grandparents' house in Charlotte, North Carolina, and she introduced me to the then-popular singing group The 5th Dimension. We repeatedly listened to their rendition of "The Declaration of Independence," a song putting the actual words of our country's declaration of independence from England into music. She sang it with me over and over again until I memorized it. She did not let me leave until I had learned it; it took hours. I remember the song to this day. In times of needing to recite The Declaration, I have sung it to myself to remember it. How extraordinary that she taught me the very thing that would enable me to understand that we sometimes need to break up with our abusive parents! The symbolism of having this declaration drilled into my head is nothing short of apt and miraculous. *The hardest breakup is the one from where we came—our source of life.* I have included the text from The Declaration here, with a suggested filter for you to read it through . . . of separation from the abusive authority that exists for you.

~ ~ ~

The Declaration of Independence: A Transcription

IN CONGRESS, July 4, 1776

The unanimous Declaration of the thirteen united States of America

When in the Course of human events, it becomes necessary for one people to dissolve the political bands which have connected them with another, and to assume among the powers of the earth, the separate and equal station to which the Laws of Nature and of Nature's God entitle them, a decent respect to the opinions of mankind requires that they should declare the causes which impel them to the separation.

We hold these truths to be self-evident, that all men are created equal, that they are endowed by their Creator with certain unalienable Rights, that among these are Life, Liberty and the pursuit of Happiness.—That to secure these rights, Governments are instituted among Men, deriving their just powers from the consent of the governed,—That whenever any Form of Government becomes destructive of these ends, it is the Right of the People to alter or to abolish it, and to institute new Government, laying its foundation on such principles and organizing its powers in such form, as to them shall seem most likely to effect their Safety and Happiness. Prudence, indeed, will dictate that Governments long established should not be changed for light and transient causes; and accordingly all experience hath shewn, that mankind are more disposed to suffer, while evils are sufferable, than to right themselves by abolishing the forms to which they are accustomed. But when a long train of abuses and usurpations, pursuing invariably the same Object evinces a design to reduce them under absolute Despotism, it is their right, it is their duty, to throw off such Government, and to provide new Guards for their future security.

~ ~ ~

Yet another mother who actually reminded me somewhat of Wendy was Lynda Carter's Wonder Woman on television. They even looked something alike and fought on the side of the good on behalf of goddesses, like Isis. Another face of the Divine Feminine coming to my subconscious!

The Crushing, the Seeding, and the Watering

As I grew, recognition that my mother was not the woman who could guide me to maturation, nor to wisdom, also grew. Her way of hiding from truth, her cynical and judging eye, and her mean-spirited criticism all served to push me further away. She no longer could be a mother figure to me, even in my fantasy, but rather, someone to tolerate, to survive, until I could leave home.

I was aware that I had outgrown my mother and that I need not look to her for anything, much as I did not look to my dad for the things a cherished daughter might expect from her father. Loyal to them, though, I did not seek outside help. I have wondered why I did not go to a school counselor or a teacher for guidance. I think it never occurred to me then that what was happening in my house was abuse (a frequent symptom in abusive families). Plus, I needed them.

I was fairly shy and reserved in school, and had little self-confidence except in my intelligence, but even that was shaky. I had no solid ground to stand on inside of myself, and outside of myself, they were all I had. I also did not want to hurt them. They were my parents, but in some ways, they felt like little children, and I felt some responsibility toward them. Yet, they were my authority figures and were destructive in their elder power.

In my late teens, I followed the normal, healthy developmental phase of forming a point of view, exploring my artistry and my will, rebelling against authority in order to separate. This was quickly squashed in my house. My father would raise a fist and set his jaw, threatening violence at the first sign of my dissent. My mother picked on me, making snide comments about my weight, my body, or the way I looked. I absorbed her commentary until I starved myself to gain her womanly approval. She said nothing until I started to disappear. "You're looking frail," she remarked, giving me a sideways glance as she sipped her gin and tonic and stirred the dinner on the stove. I promptly started gaining weight again.

Rape happens in the spirit if not also in the flesh. The sexual boundaries that my father crossed earlier in my life were one kind of soul-stealing, but my mother crossed physical, emotional, mental, spiritual boundaries repeatedly, decimating them to the point that I no longer had any. I was like a corpse left out on the hill for the carrion birds to pick on at their leisure. My body, mind, heart, and spirit were completely open to her penetration when she was so moved. After an attack, I would slowly start to put the pieces back together and try to heal, but my stability was soon dashed again. It took years to reconstruct appropriate boundaries in psychotherapy, all the while my therapists having to remind me that my mother did not live inside me, as it felt.

One day, when I was sixteen, my mother and I argued about my request to go out with my friends. The reins were tight on me, and the reasons that she gave to prevent me from leaving the house and trying to be with other people were flimsy, even ludicrous. We faced off in the kitchen, my sister and brother at the kitchen table. I confronted my mother with an incongruence in her logic, something ridiculous, and she slapped my face. I was shocked momentarily, then, shaking, grabbed her hands. She suddenly looked terrified and trembled like a child. I towered over her, eyeball to eyeball, and using every bit of my control, growled, "Don't ever hit me again."

I quickly left the room, heading upstairs to cry in my bedroom. She followed me to the base of the stairs, looking up with her dark eyes at my tear-stained face. Confused, hurt, reeling, I stammered, "If I am a bitch, it's because you taught me to be!" No longer the child, she was back in her power, and she smiled, evil pouring through her.

Something very important happened in this interchange: my mother became the child through my restraint in not retaliating, physically or verbally. Even though I was taller, stronger, and heavier than her, I did not wield power over her. I learned about myself that I was made of stronger stuff than she was. This was clearly demonstrated in front of my sister and brother, and to my own psyche.

The other important occurrence was that she showed me clearly how fractured she was. Of course, I did not have words for this until much older and after years of study and personal integration. The illnesses revealed in this moment in time included five or six identifiable personality disorders. My mother's sociopathic nature was revealed through my repeating this memory to trusted professionals, where, through reconstruction of my childhood memories, I was given the gift of her diagnosis. This freed me considerably from the awful perception that I was at fault for my childhood.

My mother is wounded deeply by her own mother. She was two years old when her grandmother found her locked in a room with her older sister, dazed, hungry, and with feces all over her. My grandmother, her mother, had left them to their own devices for many hours and was nowhere in sight. This is one of the few stories that surfaced about the mental illness that shaped my mother. Only in sideways, hushed conversation and quickly covered over with a new topic, this kind of revelation to explain the pain that seemed to drive her appeared rarely. When I think of some of the odd scenes that flash across my consciousness as if from long ago—being burned by a hot iron, being held under water—I wonder if they could be real snippets of unconfirmed memories, or if they are even mine. Are they hers?

My mother is still deeply wounded and has not done the work to heal herself so that she can be available to mother her own children. The alcohol she drinks every day is a bridge to some forgetting, and there, she can pretend that the world is as she sees it, reinforcing the illnesses she is afflicted with.

Her kind of predation crushed my sense of direction. I felt very close to the female figure, perhaps a holdover from the *Playboy* magazines or perhaps my love of paper dolls and designing clothes for them. Regardless of the cause, as a teen, I designed fashions and drew them on models. My focus on appearances was an attempt to understand who I was, to see myself from the "outside" via my drawings. Art became a focus from which I thought I might make a career. After the confrontation in the kitchen with my mother, I floundered once again. Would I be like her?

I was so angry at her. Every turn I made, every time I tried to create myself, with every building block, she tore it down. My self-determination was decimated. It was not about wanting to be loved by her anymore—that was a ridiculous, childlike dream. Now, it was just trying to have permission to exist, to become my own person, to stay alive.

A girl is meant to express herself, just like a boy. The culture rewards males for having ideas and opinions, for testing things, and striking out on their own. Self-determination seems to be the birthright of boys and men, but girls are also meant to self-determine. We have yang energy, too, and it seeks to make its mark on the world through our creative acts, no matter what they might be. It could be through our work, our art, our children. We get to decide how to express our yang energy, if we have nurturing and encouraging parents. If we are strong, we can survive the oppression of our yang energy until we get into a more encouraging environment, where we can flourish and grow. This is what I want to say to all women: *you have a right to express and to create in your own way!*

Leaving Home

I made it to college by some miracle. I can barely remember preparing to leave home. I got to the University of Georgia in Athens with tremendous relief, then promptly played out some of the patterns of my childhood, such as sexual predation (I was date-raped my first weekend there) and betrayal by people I trusted.

I learned a lot through mistakes and trial and error, things I would have learned in my home environment had I had safety, room, and permission to try things out. My parents were so locked down in themselves it was too much to have an uppity girl to challenge them, and I went wild at school. I tried drugs and drank alcohol (dampening my intuitive receptivity), explored sexuality, dropped a couple of classes, and explored screwing up as a human being. These are the trials we must undergo to become who we are, but it is best to do these things at home, in a safe environment where the consequences are less damaging. The scars when we strike out to become adults and fail are hard to heal. It can be challenging to transform the self-image we create once we are out in the world, on our own. We must forgive ourselves for not knowing how to be successful adults if we have not had that modeled for us.

My father asked my mother for a divorce as soon as I left home. Perhaps my presence was a glue that held my family together. This is often the case for scapegoats/sexual abuse victims.

After the divorce, my mother called me periodically at night, drunk out of her mind. She cried pitifully to me about her loneliness. I offered advice as best an eighteen- or nineteen-year-old girl can. She said in awed tones, "You're so wise." Now I was wise. How very funny. Her request was that I come home, that I placate her and help her. I remember huddling under the bedside lamp in my dorm room, feeling utterly at a loss to understand how this woman who seemed to need me so much was the same woman compelled to drive me into the abyss as a girl.

I stayed in school, thank goodness. After two years in Athens (thank you, Pell Grants), I managed to transfer to Atlanta to a program at Georgia State University that combined my calling to art with education. I guess I was getting serious about my major and wanted to start again at a different school. (This occurred at the same time my mother took my siblings and moved away from Atlanta to North Carolina due to her budding relationship with a new man.) My parents had apparently fallen off the side of the Earth by this point. Mother never called or checked on me. My father was holed up at Lake Lanier, partying with the bros. I was on my own.

Back in the Shining City, I attempted to leave the victim persona behind me in Athens. I cut my hair, sporting a manly style with just a shade of bangs to hide behind, and wore androgynous clothing from the second-hand stores. I strived to be a responsible adult, taking a full load of classes on my student loans and grants, as well as working almost full time to pay my rent. I can see now that I "became a man" in my attempt to take ahold of my life, to start over, but it seemed I could never get ahead. I could not afford to eat and barely slept. I went out at night to dance the rage out of my body, where others bought me drinks, perhaps my primary source of calories. I am very fortunate that I lived through this time. There were several opportunities for me to remove myself from the Earth, but somehow I stayed.

I did not realize the extent of support that was being extended to me until a July day after my junior year when I distinctly heard a disembodied voice in my car say, **"Licia, if you keep this up, you're going to be dead by the time you are twenty-five."** I had four years left.

The Sun Comes Out

After hearing the voice in the car, I had a profound spiritual experience. Something about the randomness of this warning seemed to indicate that I was cared about. By whom, I did not know. I had lost my regular connection with Nature and with myself, working three jobs and putting myself through school full time, a brutal pace for a sensitive young woman. I had to survive, so the quieter, more sensitive parts of myself were put on the back burner. But the voice reminded me of something I used to know, that there was a presence of caring in my life, even if I could not see it or remember it.

My heart cracked open. I started sleeping, eating, avoiding the clubs, the sex, the alcohol and drugs. My sensation was as a nun or monk, my life more prayerful just in making choices to take care of myself. I felt scrubbed clean. Three weeks later, I met Peter.

In *Soul Compost*, I describe how my life utterly changed as a result of meeting this person who embodied the closest thing to unconditional love that I had ever experienced, so I will not repeat it here. However, what I have not written before is that *Peter expressed the love of Great Mother and literally nourished me back to myself.* My light came back after years of wandering in darkness.

Revisiting Family

Peter and I fell in love instantly, embracing each other as if we had known one another for a long time. It was not long before I met Peter's parents; initially, it seemed that I might be safe with these new parent figures. They didn't seem to be alcoholic or sexually inappropriate, which was a welcome change for parent figures. Overjoyed, I looked to them as a fresh start with family, with hopes and dreams of loving, accepting guidance, support, and wisdom.

My second meeting with Peter's mother occurred at their house. After a nice brunch on the enclosed back porch, she shared with me very intimately about her struggles with her own mother. She told me, much to my great shock, that she suffered as a daughter, having a knife held to her throat by her mom who was diagnosed as schizophrenic and was hospitalized. My experience as a young woman of twenty-one did not prepare me for this unsolicited confession at a second meeting from my elder parent figure. It frightened me, and I did not know what to say. However, something seemed oddly familiar about the lack of boundaries being shown. I went into a kind of defensive posture with her, behavior that later would become routine when she spoke with me because of her tendency to over-step appropriate limits.

At that meeting, I met Peter's father for the first time. Peter was named after his father, a tradition carried on by many old, Southern families. I met him hopefully, wanting to gain his favor as Peter's beloved. To my dismay, my failure to impress was cemented due to my old clunker of an automobile leaking a little pool of oil onto their pristine Dunwoody driveway. Peter's father expressed his disdain and irritation about having to clean it up to its previous condition.

Already, I feared I had somehow screwed up with his parents, and my old childhood beliefs about myself were reactivated after a few years of a little relief. These dynamics were an indication of what was to come.

I was completing my last year of a five-year degree in Art Education and would soon enter my final semesters of student teaching. My life looked pretty good on the surface; I was excelling in my program at school, was living with the love of my life and future husband, and had already been noticed by the city school system, with which I hoped to get a job upon my graduation. I was respected by my teachers and felt on track to create a future for myself. It seemed my life was finally becoming my own.

But I could not celebrate my successes, no matter how many A's I received on my school projects. I was thrilled when a respected teacher gave me compliments or encouragement, but I felt I did not deserve them. Under the surface of my hopeful life, something was wrong.

Things came to a head when my new husband and I chose to live in a little cottage on his parents' property. Being in a family environment, complete with parental figures, made me feel unsafe, stirring up my childhood wounding. I noticed that I slept a lot and ate for comfort rather than for health. I was very depressed, and I did not know why. I found myself feeling judged and criticized constantly by Peter's parents, but being polite and not accustomed to speaking up for myself, I absorbed it. I assumed all responsibility for conflicts with his parents because I already believed that I was bad, that I was at fault.

The in-my-face presence of this family dynamic, which was so very close to my own family of origin, was too much to bear. My depression deepened, and I cried when I was not sleeping. I gained weight. Suicidal thoughts started to creep in. I wanted to die. Why? I had everything that a young woman could want in her life. I decided to enter therapy and began to ask around for a recommendation.

My introduction to my inner child began in 1989, simultaneous to cutting off all of my hair for a third time. I was blessed to be led to a woman who was completing her supervised hours, having finished her schooling. She was kind and a very good listener. I remember the feeling, when I first sat in her office, of being almost giddy that someone wanted to hear about my life and my feelings. It seemed too good to be true! My elation soon wore off, though. I began the difficult work of deconstructing my childhood. As we continued into the true work of therapy, the hard feelings began to surface. When I shared with her some of the experiences I had with my biological parents, it was she who carefully but directly said to me that what I had experienced was abuse.

Thus began a two-plus-year journey into my understanding of what happened to me as a child, my initial dive headfirst into my recovery and healing process. She wisely shared that *we tend to work on the easier of the parents first* when I elected to heal from my father's sexual advances. My Mother Wound was too much to deal with at the time. Over the next two years, I had therapy every week with my trusted therapist, and group therapy and body work two times per month each.

I was truly in the thick of it while trying to maintain my career path and living in proximity to Peter's family. I projected my pain onto them, blending my mother and father with his parents. It was a difficult time to honor my feelings while also wanting to take care of them. My pain was so clouding my vision that I could not see that they thought they helped by psychoanalyzing me and my family of origin. I found the act of their diagnosis judgmental and superior, and I began to see the dysfunction in their own family dynamics, turning the judgment back on them with my newfound therapy skills.

During that time, the situation with Peter's parents became too confusing and emotionally charged and interfered with my recovery. Asking for space from them so I could get clarity about what was mine and what was theirs, I activated wounding from their own lives and became what I was in my own family: the bad guy.

We moved away from their property in shame and sadness. My husband, although still supportive, became angry at me for my unraveling. I once again felt on my own.

We survived this challenging period, however, through the miracle of a larger love that bound us together, regardless of the frightening things I discovered about my life and the ways they had molded me. Peter shared with me that he worried he would come home to find me dead. It was a tremendous strain on him for me to remain in the process of healing myself. I gave him permission to leave our marriage, realizing that I had to commit to my personal process even if it meant losing him. I think, looking back now, that the larger love that held me (and held us) gave me the strength to continue to dig, cry, transform, and put myself back together.

Once I began to understand what I was dealing with, I threw myself into my recovery with all of myself. It was a hard, hard two years. I had to come to terms with being a childhood victim of incest, emotional and physical abuse from both parents, and had to suffer the feelings of rage and despair that come along with this knowing.

It was quite a surprise to me when my therapist suggested I had an inner child living inside of me. What? Childhood was over (thank god), and it was time for me to be a grown up. My therapist pointed out that I would not be able to fully grow up until I went back and re-parented the lost inner child who so desperately needed parenting. So began my uneasy journey with Little Licia.

When I met her, she was age four. She was very sad and looked hollow. It is hard now to remember her being like this, as she is so vibrant and alive and full of energy! But then, her shoulders sloped, and her back was stooped; she looked down at the floor. She could barely believe that I could even see her. When she realized that I was looking at her, she looked up. It took only a moment before she smiled a little bit. But it was a sad smile. This was the beginning of her telling me her story, and the beginning of my learning how to be a mother to my own inner daughter.

In the summer of 1990, we went west for a much-needed, three-week road trip. Afforded a lengthy vacation due to my job as a public school art teacher, we ventured further west than I had ever been, to the Four Corners states of New Mexico, Colorado, Utah, and Arizona. There was something freeing to me about being out of the Southeast, as if the open desert landscape and the giant blue sky gave me permission to be. I felt safe. When we came south over the White Mountains into southern Arizona and then the Tucson area one sunset evening, I saw a new life spread out before us, and I fell in love with it. I could see the possibility of a new beginning, away from our southern family pasts.

When we returned to Atlanta, I became invigorated, as if a heavy water had been drained off me after the breath of fresh air the west provided. Perhaps the dry desert air cleared out some emotional weight and I began to see a possible new life for me.

That fall of 1990, I began training for the annual July 4th Peachtree Road Race, a 10K race run in the dog days of summer. Running on Atlanta's streets, I felt power in my body for the first time in my life. Two years later, I completed the race, proving to myself that I could do it. I felt I could leave Atlanta victorious. So much pain had transpired here, along with so much growth. We saved our meager funds, packed a truck, and headed west in 1992, toward our new life.

Chapter 4: Belly, Memory, and Light – 28 to 42 Years

Mother One, First Mother
Collage © 2007 Licia Berry

The Southwest was a revelation. We began again in the fresh, unfamiliar town of Tucson with a radically different landscape. We went everywhere in the state, roving the mountain roads and the desert paths with glee, two young people striking out away from their family history. It was marvelous.

Arizona's craggy peaks, the severe landscape, the aridity, and the spiky plants led me to believe that the area held a masculine presence. I realized later that I saw through a lens determined by what I was willing to see at the time. In actuality, the feminine spirit first touched me in Arizona. I did not know its name, but I recognize now the calling of that spirit to me across the lands. The desert beckoned to me like the ocean did when I was a girl.

I also had a powerful vision—something that happened often to me over my life, but not all were so powerful that they stayed present in my mind thereafter.

In the vision, I am in southern Arizona (the area around Tucson, where I lived at the time), but I am looking across the lands to the immediate east and north, into northern New Mexico. Across the miles of mountains, I see a large figure rising from the high desert floor. It is an elder native woman with long, white hair, dressed in an earth-colored robe. She is as tall as the sky. She is standing in the land area of northern New Mexico and southern Colorado, but I sense she comes from a time when they did not have those names. She is turned to the south, her face toward me in southern Arizona, holding her arms out at her sides as if in beseeching prayer. She is looking at me, beckoning me to her land.

I did not understand the importance of this vision until much later, after many experiences. For now, I focused on creating our new life in Arizona.

My intention to start over was reflected in my new position with the State of Arizona's Division of Developmental Disabilities as a Living Skills Trainer. My education background qualified me to guide children with brain disorders (and their families) in creating some independence in their lives. I felt uncomfortable without a background in special needs, but received training along the way. My supervisor was a wonderful, encouraging woman who became a good friend to me during our stay in Tucson. She would become even more important to me years later; she would be my advocate when I doubted my work with spiritual mechanics and women's leadership.

On my twenty-ninth birthday, I went for a hike in the Catalina Mountains. It was a tradition for me to do something by myself on my birthday to honor the anniversary of my arrival on the planet. I hiked for several hours up the range, coming to a flat rock outcropping that looked out on the city of Tucson and the valley floor beyond. I laid down to rest in the sun, closing my eyes. I suddenly heard and felt the flapping of giant wings maybe thirty feet over me. I opened my eyes right away and looked for the bird that should have been well within my vision, but nothing was there. I learned soon after that I was carrying my first son.

Another Chink in the Armor

My pregnancy was a dream. I felt beautiful and more connected to myself. My spiritual nature seemed restored. I felt flow and grace again. I felt an archetypal mother energy inhabit my body. It was old, deep, powerful. I was giddy as I felt it flow through me. However, it soon brought me back to my mother.

In Atlanta, when I had been in a very vulnerable state near the start of therapy, I had called my mother one night to gain her support. This is a big no-no, known by children of alcoholics; I should have called her during the day when she had not had anything to drink yet. But I felt like a little girl who wanted her mommy, and I incorrectly rationalized that she had grown and matured in the years that had passed.

In my need, I asked her to hear very hard things about my sexual abuse, praying she would show up like the mother I really needed at the time. She responded harshly, calling me crazy and a liar (an old refrain), and she denied the sexual abuse, saying, "Your memory always has been warped." I thought this odd after all the times she had remarked on my wisdom and the uncanny accuracy of my memories when I supported her during her divorce.

I was devastated and spent the subsequent three years in limited contact with her. Here I was, pregnant for the first time, and no clue how to live this "motherhood thing."

Jess was born without my mother being there, a difficult and disempowering "medical menu" kind of birth. If I had known then what I know now about the incredible initiation that birth is for a woman, I would have sought wise council and an alternative to the medicalized version of "delivery."

I prohibited my mother from coming for his birth, aware that she would want to drink and I would not feel safe. She still had the same knack for making everything *about her* as she did when I was a kid living at home. The very act of fending her off activated old trauma for me, but something wise inside of me told me to protect the experience of Jess's birth by telling her to stay away until I was ready for her to come. Jess was working on me before he was even born.

The remarkable soul that came through me in the form of my son is a healer and shaman. I believe that the Spirit Bird I encountered on my birthday hike was his great spirit entering my body. He is of those mountains, just as surely as his little body was formed by the air, earth, fire, and water of the desert. My vulnerable inner child fell in love with him, my first baby. My inner mother was a mess.

Having no idea how to be a good mom except for my preparatory reading and years of therapy, I slid into a darkness that eclipsed my joy at being a mother. I had a case of postpartum depression that left me wondering if he and Peter would be better off without me. I left for mini-trips when Peter was home, leaving pumped breast milk for my precious baby. I contemplated suicide.

I wonder how many cases of postpartum depression can be linked back to inadequate or abusive mothering? How often does becoming a mother ourselves crack wide open the chasm that is the Mother Wound?

I was disheartened that my old wounding seemed to be rearing its head again. I had made a decision that, in therapy, I would go through the horror of my childhood so I would not pass on what I had experienced to my someday children, if I ever allowed myself to have any. I determined that "the buck stops here" and dug in for a second round of therapy work.

She Comes

I began therapy again when it became clear that I was unable to heal myself. Jess's presence alone was calling forward my unresolved issues with my mother, and I remembered my Atlanta therapist's remark that *we start with the easy parent first*. It seemed it was now time to dive in to the dark waters of my Mother Wound. I found an excellent female therapist who carried an air of elder wise woman, something I sorely needed.

My little shaman baby seemed to look right into me at the depths of my hurt. Sometimes, I would cry under his penetrating gaze and pray that I would not pass on this pain to my child.

My therapist, Peter, and I discussed inviting my mother to Tucson to meet Jess in the months after he was born. She arrived and I felt such conflicting emotions. She treated my little son with such care, kindness, and responsibility, yet could not see that she had hurt me as her daughter to such a degree that I could barely remain in my body while around her. She had gone to school to be a massage therapist, and she practiced on Jess, who loved receiving the massaging. When she massaged me that trip, she had a weird look on her face the entire time. I felt squirrely, young, and afraid under her hands, despite my age. I was aware of her hands on my thighs, a place on my body that she had consistently judged when I was a kid. Her hands almost felt like my father's did.

My therapist asked me questions after the visit: did my mother sexually abuse me as a child? Did she collaborate in sexual abuse with my father? This line of questioning was too much to consider at the time. The dreams I interpreted in the therapy office included a Frankenstein monster and a vampire, both chasing me and threatening to take something from me. It became clear later that the dumb monster assembled of corpses represented my father, and the blood sucking, seductive predator was my mother. What did they want to take from me? At a deep level in my psyche, these two people were the worst kind of no-good. After rigorous discussion and torturous healing in myself, I decided not to invite either of them back into my life in any serious way.

This decision seemed to open the flow of my spirit back to me, like breath to the lungs. I found myself drawn to healer women and sought training in several subtle energy modalities. I manifested a case of hives during this trial that rivaled anything I had seen. Making the choice to go inward, I healed my porous skin with love, skills, and determination. It was as if the pain that had flushed up and resulted in a healing crisis was moving out through me, my sensitive nervous system processing so much data as to be overwhelmed. Once I was clear in conscience that I was making the best decision for myself (and therefore my new little family), the situation resolved. The ground under my feet was a friend again, and I could sense the intelligence of the wind, the mountains, the saguaro cacti guarding the hills. My shamanic leanings re-awoke and I found myself at sacred sites of the Pueblo Indians that still roamed this land, if in spirit. I came home to myself.

A happy time in my life occurred as my intuition started to expand. The women I drew to me were wise and mysterious, even a little witchy. I made good friends with females for the first time in my life during what became a kind of renaissance of my soul. My little healer was getting older and talking up a storm. He frequently named the very thing I was thinking about, and sometimes it seemed someone much, much wiser than a two-year-old was looking through his empathic eyes. Who was this remarkable soul? My heart jumped when he said, "Mama, I want to go downtown" in the most drippy southern drawl I had ever heard. He grew up in Arizona (where most folks are from the Midwest or native), and his dad and I had no southern accent. Where the heck did that voice come from? Later, I would understand that he was pointing us back home to the Southeast, to our origins.

Soon after Jess's surprise southern performance, I began seeing the image of a little blonde girl in my mind, lovely ringlets of long hair and an angelic smile. I mentioned to Peter that we might consider having a second child before Jess got too old to enjoy one and assumed this little apparition was the spirit of my coming daughter hanging around. Her presence got more insistent, and one day, I saw her behind me in the bathroom mirror, floating above my right shoulder. I talked to Peter again, this time more insistent. We conceived right away and the visitations stopped.

At this same time, we were exploring relocating to a new town. Tucson had been good to us for almost five years, but we were itching for a change.

We elected to go on a road trip of a few months to look at new locations. Our house sold quickly, and we left our careers and the sunny Arizona desert behind. I was five months pregnant and felt different than I did during the first pregnancy. This time, I felt diminished, as if the baby was using my body to form itself. (I recognize that this is the case with all babies in utero, but I was unaware of this feeling in my prior pregnancy. Quite the opposite, I felt Jess gave to my body rather than taking away from it!) I needed to eat a lot of protein during the second pregnancy to keep my stability. We traveled the Midwest, Northeast, and then down to North Carolina before we settled on Asheville, in the Blue Ridge Mountains. Asheville was a place on our radar to check because Peter's sister and her husband lived there. It greeted us mysteriously with mist and grey skies, a stark contrast to our sunny Tucson.

We moved into a rental house and settled in to see if our new town felt like a good fit, planning not to buy for a year and allowing the twenty thousand dollars from the sale of our Tucson home to mature in savings. I found a nurse midwife to attend me, wanting to avoid the disempowerment of my birth experience with Jess. I learned so much from this wise woman, who trusted the ancient rite of birth. She encouraged me to trust my body too, to pay attention to the subtle rhythm and flow of my pregnancy.

The land of these mountains called me in a way I had never experienced, through my belly. I walked barefoot in the mud and danced to tribal music. A feeling, sweeter than molasses and as slow and dark, came into me. I was in reverie, held by something ancient and good.

I met several women who played in a more earth-centered playground as well as participated in a women's circle, and I deepened relations with my feminine side, becoming more at ease with women. I was sexual, a priestess, a fertile goddess of old, and I was so happy in myself.

I went for my seven-month checkup, and because the baby was getting big (I apparently grow large children), it was suggested that I have an ultrasound. To my great surprise, I was having another son.

During my freshman year of college in Athens Georgia, I had met a cheeky, eccentric woman from the United Kingdom, a fellow student. We befriended one another, and eventually, I learned that she was a palm reader and intuitive. She called me out as a very intuitive person too, and I felt a certain kinship with her. She had a funny, mischievous side that was entertaining to be around. She read my palm one day, and said much of the typical fare. The thing that I remember, though, was her looking at the lines etched in the outer side of my hands and saying, "You will have two children, a boy and then a girl." I remember feeling the congruence of that with what I had always thought to be true of my someday-maybe-future. I knew it would be true.

In Tucson, when I became pregnant with my second child, the little blonde girl with the long ringlets stopped showing up, and so it made sense that I was now carrying her. A friend had suggested a psychic, a highly accurate elder woman in a Latin community in south Tucson. She pronounced that I was indeed carrying a girl. I had been relating to this child in my belly completely as a daughter.

When we found out he was a boy, I was stunned. How could I have been so wrong? I felt certain that this was my daughter. I had even named her and started planning what kinds of daughter/mother activities we would engage in together. Deep inside, though, I was afraid of having a daughter. What if I was terrible to her as my mother was to me? All the healing and inner work I had done had helped me become a better person and mother, but I felt broken, damaged, unable to overcome my conditioning when it came to raising a daughter well. How would I measure up, I worried?

I went through a short period of grief as I adjusted to this new vision of my life. I prayed over my belly every day that this baby would not misinterpret my grief as some sign that he was unwanted. In my mind, I took this as a sign that I did not deserve a daughter because I had not healed enough, was therefore unworthy.

Premature Forgiveness

When a man seeks obstacles to measure his strength,
he goes towards the North.
If he needs rest and tranquility, he turns to the South.
To learn of his future he sets off for the West
And he returns to the East to discover his origins.
But for the longest of voyages he travels motionless,
inside himself.

— Uman

We had moved from Tucson back to the Southeast because something called us there. I thought perhaps it was to work things out with my family of origin. Since they lived in the vicinity, I assumed that this was part of the great plan. However, *change in a relationship requires willingness on the part of all parties concerned.* I had done so much inner work that I had grown bigger than my previous hurts. I felt stronger than I ever had and so extended the hand of healing to my parents. They had not changed, though. I learned this the hard way.

After much discussion (and concern/skepticism on Peter's part), I invited my mother to attend me at Aidan's birth. I told her clearly that I had conditions and specific needs, such as no drinking, being fully available to me, Peter, and Jess, and no drama; and asked if she could meet them while she was there with us. She agreed, yet arrived with a suitcase full of wine and fancy going-out clothes. She planned to see a man who currently lived in Asheville that she had dallied with back in Goldsboro when I was a child. We did the best we could to withstand her visit, but I hung on to the baby past the due date. I could not relax; I did not feel safe with her because nothing had changed. She was still selfish in meeting her desires and unable to be there for me on my most important day. She departed, then later told me on the phone how disappointed she was that I had not given birth, that she had been left "empty-handed."

I had some work to do to relax my body again after my mother's visit. How amazing that we can clamp up and refuse to do something as powerfully natural as giving birth because we do not feel safe! As Aidan's due date had passed, my midwife expressed concern about his size and my desire to give birth at home. Like Jess, Aidan was almost ten pounds and we were nearly two weeks past his due date. I desperately wanted to avoid the medical experience I had giving birth to Jess. I wanted to take my power back in this powerful ritual that millions and millions of women had done before me.

One afternoon, I uncharacteristically had the house to myself for a little while. I sat in the rocking chair, thinking about the possibility of having to go to the hospital. I cried, so sad for this possibility. I rocked some more, then cried some more, a kind of letting go process that helped me come to terms with whatever needed to happen to have a safe birth. Wave after wave of tightness left my body as I wept. By the end of this process, my body had relaxed.

Aidan arrived in a beautiful birth a few days after my mother left. I called my sister to come, and she and Peter took care of me (and of Jess) while I had a short, four-hour labor and gave birth in the water at home, naturally. My newest boy had arrived.

We Try (and Try) Again

Forgiveness is the fragrance that the violet sheds on the heel that has crushed it.

— Mark Twain

Aidan gave us a run for our money. He was a bright, beautiful Buddha-like child, with a huge grin and a laugh that melted us. But he was an insatiable nurser and had night issues, unable to sleep through until he was three years old. My sleep deprivation took a toll on my brain and the constant nursing wore me down. Perhaps this is why I made the same mistaken choices with my mother.

I repeatedly set up meetings with her, inviting her to our newly purchased home or dragging my children with me to her place. I was clear as usual about my requests to feel safe: no drinking, no smoking in the house or around my children, and a request that she cease pretending that the sexual abuse did not happen. As usual, she was unwilling to meet these requests. It made her angry that I asked for these things, citing that I was cramping her lifestyle and trying to control her. I asked her to come to therapy with me so we could converse about it in a place that I felt safe. Again, this was too much.

I was a daughter who wanted a mother, and now I was a mother too, raising my children as consciously as I knew how. Stepping back into the arms of my childhood dysfunctions did not seem a healthy course of action after so much effort to heal so that I could be a good mom. But I kept trying. I know now that the little girl inside of me was asking for a mother for herself, and I mistakenly hoped my mother would miraculously come through.

My husband finally set a limit with me. After years of watching me struggle to make my relationship with my mother healthy and inviting more hurt and broken heartedness into our lives, he asked me to seriously consider whether I would ever get what I wanted from her. So I started to let go.

Back in the flow, letting go: this was my new mantra as a mother of two young children who wanted to live joyfully. We had great times in our wonderful yard and played together under the great oaks. I grew bigger than my hopes for my mother and me, and found love in the Earth, the sky, in my children's laughter or discoveries. It was sweet and innocent living as a mom to those two delightful boys. Peter became more involved in his work, and the boys and I missed him, but we were a happy trio, for the most part. The river that flowed like molasses that I had felt prior to re-engaging with my mother was coming back. I saw a pattern. Every time I tried to get mothered by her, I stepped out of the flow of goodness in my life. In addition, every time I let go of any expectation that she could give me what I wanted, I stepped back in.

I was learning some wisdom.

Running into the Arms

Around the year 2000, I started having experiences that led me to wonder if I was channeling an ancient tongue. It started as a sensation in my belly, a fullness, a kind of odd awareness that I had a big cauldron inside and the lid was getting ready to pop off. Then I dreamed about a language that came up from my belly into my throat, another kind of pressure when I awoke. My body was doing something new and interesting. It seemed to be giving way to some kind of information. Then came the dream with a giant book, pages and pages full of symbols that were lit as if from within by a golden light. Again, I awoke with a strange pressure in my throat, as if something were bumping up against the larynx and trying to come out.

Soon after this, I met a fellow and talked with him about singing and old indigenous beliefs that the world was sung into being. I shared about my recent bewildering experiences, and he said, quite simply, "Sounds like you'd better start singing." I did!

It was weird and embarrassing at first, but I made sure not to do it in front of anyone. I opened my mouth, and sounds came out that seemed like a cross between Russian and a Middle Eastern language. It was quite beautiful. After I got used to it, songs started forming, and I was able to sing them around other people.

Then the songs became regular channeling experiences, where a body of information would "download" as if from a larger source into my consciousness. I began understanding things I had not studied, like mechanics of the universe and the workings of Nature. One day, I leaned against one of the great oaks on our property and saw in my mind's eye the same golden symbols moving up the tree from the Earth that I had seen in my dream of the giant book, the language of light.

I had visions of large pillars of light coming out of the Earth and reaching to the heavens, forming a grid around the entire planet. I was given to understand that the wisdom of the Earth was coming to the surface because more of us were awakening. The larger pillars of light appeared to form as a result of a trio of smaller pillars of light. (I later realized that each small pillar was the light of a single person who carried awakened feminine energy.) Forming a triangle, each trio held the larger form, a kind of "portal," for the large pillar of light to emerge from the Earth and shoot to the heavens.

In addition, each woman in the trio, sitting at her point in the triangle, could rotate and create another triangle with two other women, forming a new trio and opening another portal for the wisdom to pass through. The language coming through my body called this "Trebalikyeh," or "Triangles of Light." This was very exciting to me. I felt as if I was seeing a great transformation occurring in fast-motion. Who knew how long this would actually take? It was thrilling to feel part of this process of ancient wisdom coming up from the Earth through women.

From 2000 through 2003, I had extraordinary growth and deepening understanding of the Earth as an intelligent source of wisdom. As I deepened, it became harder to play in the culture of commercialism and capitalism. My home and my family seemed the most important things to me, and I let the need for having pretty things go, although I had never been much of a lady of finery.

My children and I drove across the country a few times, camping in the Black Hills of South Dakota or in the desert on our way to California. Having boys was easy for me, it turned out. I did not have to teach a girl how to be lady-like, and it's a good thing, since I did not really know how. I realized that my mother focused completely on her appearance and had not taught me how to apply the skills of make-up or hair, or how to behave in a lady-like manner. I felt obtuse around fancy people and especially women who had carefully constructed their faces and physical appearance. I knew from my experience with my mother that a woman could be pretty on the surface but be dark and stormy underneath, so I learned not to trust the machine of "beauty."

My mother continued to be a conundrum to me. I was in bliss, learning about spirit and the Earth, and feeling such connection with the greater intelligence that I barely missed her. But, occasionally, I felt my old longing reactivate. She was busy living her life and, since she did not call or visit, seemingly had no concern for me or her grandchildren. When I asked when she would come to visit, she told me that she was "doing her own thing," or alternately scared to drive the four hours to our house. As a mother of young children, I sometimes felt abandoned by her, but then remembered the woman I wanted did not exist.

I kept the door open to the possibility that she was evolving, but each time I reached out to try again with her, I was disappointed that she had not changed at all. Every time I felt the old anger, I worked hard inside myself to forgive her. In doing so, I realized that I had already forgiven her for the past; however, the anger was new. Her neglect was a present-day issue. It was not an old hurt, but a fresh wounding every interaction we had.

In 2003, my bliss in my spiritual awakening was divergent from my relationship with my husband. He was becoming someone different, no longer the man I knew. In addition to the corporate culture he was asked to buy into at work, he seemed to be slipping into some automatic dynamics with our children. His own childhood had left marks on him, and he had not healed his relationship with his parents. His behavior with our sons, now ages nine and six, showed me how deeply wounded he was.

My relationship with his parents was uncomfortable, and my husband's unresolved pain made it even more challenging to be with them. I saw their treatment of him at the time as quite different than when he was a child, but his wounding was alive and well. This was especially evident when they were disrespectful to me. Peter was unable to stand up for me in the face of their beliefs and judgments; I felt my husband de-evolve into a mute little boy when they spoke unkindly to me.

Unfortunately, my issues with his parents colored our relationship with them. They seemed to form some ideas about me, as well as about our family, that were inaccurate. I had worked hard on limiting my exposure to toxic beliefs that other people had about me. Years of therapy and insight had helped me reform my picture of myself. The old picture was one I had inherited from my mother, and it was wrong, far from the truth of me. I learned that I was a good person, intelligent, strong, and with a loving heart.

Keeping this discovered truth in my mind was the necessary work of being sane, kind, and a good wife and mom. I had to guard against people who did not see me for who I was. I could not afford to entertain the negative projections of others. Too much was at stake. For my husband, my beloved and life partner, to allow his family to disrespect me was becoming beyond my capacity to overlook. Years of withstanding their judgments began to weigh on me, and it eroded my sense of safety with my husband. We were growing apart.

Things came to a head when Pete's parents were scheduled to come for visit, but called to say they wanted to arrive several days earlier than planned. I had plans that I could not change and their early arrival would disrupt our family's schedule, so we told them it would not work for us if they came early. They were upset, citing that they had contributed to the down payment for the house, and that we were family, so they should be able to come when they wanted. The controlling dynamic that held my husband hostage was exposed, in ugly, unflattering light. His inability to stand up to his parents was tied to their expectations about their limitless access to us and their judgments if we had an opinion that differed from theirs.

It was a painful awareness for Peter to see his parents this clearly. What we did not know at the time was that their behavior predicted a theme for our forthcoming family odyssey.

Escape from Prison

As I wrote in the introduction, the fateful day came in October 2003 when I attended a workshop about following my calling and I distinctly saw impending tragedy for our family. The choice was clear: let go of everything or allow my precious family to fall apart.

So we left the American Dream, others' notions about success, obligation and expectation, and a harmful ancestral lineage. We began what would be a life-changing journey and an invitation into a very different way of life. We would be shown that we had been trapped in many boxes, living confined by cultural beliefs in our families, our society, and the world of patriarchal values.

We began, ironically, by pointing south to Florida to Peter's parents' house outside of Panama City. The Christmas holiday was a convenient time to get together and it was a chance to see them before we began the road trip. It was stressful to be with them, and after such a big change, we needed some peace, so we cut it short to head to our first place of rest, Cape San Blas, Florida.

The Cape on St. Joseph's Peninsula is an approximately six-mile stretch of protected beach in a state park. It was a natural and quiet place for us to recover from the tremendous change we had all been through, and in such short order. Serving as a kind of "womb" for our family, the Cape held us while we went through our shock at what we had done by leaving our lives to go on this spiritual odyssey. The notion that we might be crazy surfaced a few times, but all we had to do was think about what we might have lost if we had continued on our prior path. This was the sanest thing we had ever done.

The Cape provided white sandy beaches (the Gulf was beautiful, but it was too cold to swim in late December), maritime forest, wildlife, and campers for our thirst for adventure and fun. We had important work to do as a family though, so we began each day with a family meeting to set the tone. We were not on an extended vacation; this was no pleasure trip. We embarked on an intentional healing journey that would last for many years to come, and it was crucial to keep this in the forefront of our minds.

For four months, we hovered around this sweet place. It remains one of my favorite spots to retreat. We came to life and started establishing a new rhythm, traveling farther south to springs and rivers, bending around the "armpit" of Florida. The presence of water was a constant in every place we were guided to go. We remained connected to the Gulf of Mexico for almost a year, traveling north to where we had started in Florida, then west to Texas. Our adventures were many and magical.

It is important to note that one of the primary strategies we learned together was to listen to the larger intelligence, by whatever name you call it. We needed help to heal our family and we knew we could rely on Spirit to guide us to greater truth, beauty, and strength. Surrender in the higher perspective was essential for us to proceed; the culture did not reward listening to a higher perspective. We had to retrain ourselves to come back home to our centers.

We found that when we surrendered our egoic ideas of how things should be, a truer, more meaningful path revealed itself to us. We asked each day in our family meeting for guidance. All four of us received information that was useful and we heeded what we "heard." Some days the guidance was about heading to a new location ("head west tomorrow"), sometimes it was about things to keep an eye out for that day, but often the guidance was about unconscious patterns in our family that needed to be addressed. The four of us created a kind of energetic "pyramid" by sitting in a square with our intention above, centered in Spirit; we began calling our family meetings Pyramid Meetings. One of the primary lessons in sitting in this configuration was equality. The boys each held a corner of this structure and reflected how we treated their point of view. This was a tremendous healing for them and a huge change in trajectory, based on where our family had been headed. I hope they never know the kind of life they would have had if we had not made this fundamental shift in our family dynamic.

We headed west after an overnight stop in Houston, guided toward Padre Island National Seashore. We were in the middle of the Texas wildflower country with fields of bluebells and Indian paintbrush all around us when the tire on the tow dolly exploded. We broke down on the outskirts of a tiny town called Yoakum and happened to be less than a mile away from a lovely city RV park. We parked the rig and had a wonderful two-week stay in this little town while we waited for the replacement parts to arrive. We had close-up interactions with nighthawks, horses, flowers of every variety, and fun locals at a dance. We would have experienced none of these things if we not followed the guidance to trust that we were being taken care of.

This proved itself over and over again. We would receive some surprising instruction and follow it with some skepticism, only to have it bear fruit and reward beyond imagining. I feel that it is not that we are special; really, it was that we were willing to let go and get back in the flow of life's greater intelligence, and let it take us. Releasing our need for control put us in the hands of life, and I have learned that the Big Intelligence is WAAAAYYYY smarter than I am. It treats me better, too, than I often treat myself.

The connection to the land that we experienced was profound, as well. Each place had its own flavor, much like personalities. Inevitably, we were guided to places we had judged in our previous life as inferior or stupid (like Florida or Texas) and, every time, our prior judgments were proven wrong. The people, the places, the adventures, all pointed to the deeper truth: our minds were prisons if we did not keep them open.

Padre Island

Padre Island National Seashore is the longest undeveloped barrier island in the world. The national seashore is seventy miles long, more than ten times the protected beach/lands than where we started at Cape San Blas. We were guided there in the usual mysterious way, our family sensing the place and not knowing the name. It came through the lips of an elderly woman who wound up becoming a surrogate mother to me, for a time. The place was wild and rough, a shoreline that attracts refugees from Mexico and floating trash from all the world's seas.

The beach was not as pretty as our Florida haven but no less magical. All manner of sea turtles migrate there to lay their eggs in the sand, returning to the place they themselves hatched. The surrounding area was a fisherman's paradise, a boon to Pete, who loves to fish. The park consisted of a campground, ranger station, gift shop and museum, and miles of sand that could be camped on for no cost other than the park's entrance fee. This attracted a wide range of visitors to

the seashore, which felt more like the Wild West sometimes than a serene seascape. Dune buggies, motorcycles, vehicles of all kinds could speed down the beach with no limitation. I was nervous a lot because there were not enough rangers to monitor such a large area.

One day, we spoke with a ranger who suggested after hearing our story that we serve as campground hosts. The advantages of this arrangement were a free campsite, electricity, water and sewer hookups (you would not believe the luxuries you are so grateful for when you are on the road for so long!), and a protected beachfront view without having to park on bare sand. I liked it. Taking the kids off the raceway of the unprotected beach made me breathe a little easier. We started our stint as volunteer hosts in April 2004 and stayed there for six months. It was hot, humid and sticky, and irritating at times; but a body of work started to emerge while we were there that would begin to heal my Mother Wound.

It had not escaped my notice that the trip thus far had been centered on the Gulf of Mexico. I wondered if we had been guided to travel that way for Peter, who had special associations with the Gulf from his childhood. Different from my beloved Atlantic, the Gulf was gentler, softer, kinder water. It was friendly to those who partook of it, taking less risk to interact with it. It was an ideal place for a woman who was scared of the water to try to make friends again. We feel fortunate that we were guided to center on this body of water and to thoroughly enjoy it prior to the BP oil spill in 2010 that rendered so much of the Gulf coastline unapproachable.

I also found it interesting that the name of the island was Padre, father in Spanish. Conveniently, the Laguna Madre (Mother Lagoon) was right next door. We were sandwiched on a slender sand spit between the Lagoon of the Mother and Mother Gulf. How very interesting.

> Characteristics of Laguna Madre and many more on the surrounding land prompted The Nature Conservancy in 1998 to designate it a high-priority conservation area.... The Laguna Madre is a rarity: one of perhaps six hypersaline (i.e., saltier than the ocean) lagoons in the world. It is perhaps one of the most overlooked natural wonders in North America. If one stands on its shore and simply gazes at it, the Laguna has no obvious physical attributes to distinguish from any other body of water in the world. **To be appreciated, the Laguna's unseen side, the life hidden under its surface, must be studied and revealed.** (Note: the emphasis here is mine.)
>
> — *from "The Laguna Madre" on the Padre Island National Seashore website, National Park Service*

The presence of Mother seemed all around us, from the hyper-fertile bed of life in the lagoon and the fertile warmth of the Gulf to the sea turtles, a symbol of ancient feminine wisdom, and the water in the air, the pervasive humidity that created a sensation of walking though and breathing warm soup. Water seemed to be the medium through which I was being agitated.

I was miserable there. Not only was the climate a challenge for me, but I felt a strange, internal pressure building. I felt old, yucky feelings come to the surface, things I had not felt since I was young. I began having body memories and emotional rememberings that were challenging my ability to stay centered in our task to heal our family.

Sitting inside at the RV window, watching my children play with such joyful abandon, I remembered the ease with which I gave myself to Her, Mama Ocean. I wondered why the ocean became so threatening to me later, and if my relationship with it could be repaired. I was guided to delve into my past for answers.

In the early mornings, I got up to write as the sun rose over the Gulf, and new information emerged about my fear of the water.

Fear of the Water

Journal Entry, 5-11-2004, on the Berry Family Journey

Pete just saw a shark from our dinette window. . . . It was in two feet of water, cruising just in front of our RV site in the same place where the kids and Pete were playing for the last several days. Yikes! In terms of inspiration for some writing, this plays into my fear of living water, and how this began to happen.

My fear of it, distance from it. The dark, murky, unpredictability of it. Dangerous. Volatile. It takes what it wants. Unmerciful. Merciless. Don't know what is in there. Under the surface, there are scary things that will bite you. You cannot see what is in there.

My relationship with the sea started early. Family from Hatteras for generations. Instead of blood, seawater in my veins, . . . I identified so strongly with the romantic notion of my ancestors having washed ashore from a shipwreck onto this little sand spit, thirty miles off the mainland. What fortune, what damnation to have landed there. Marrying into the

Indians, strength and sickness required to survive in the isolation of Hatteras Island.

I uttered one of my earliest words when my family's Jeep crested the drive-over at Hatteras. My view of the expanse of blue ocean over the dunes and dashboard of the car resulted in an awe-inspired "OSSSHHH." This is a word that I continue to use when I talk about Her.

When I was a young girl, I was a mermaid. I played and swam in the sea with abandon. I loved the feel of the cool, salty water, a delicious stinging on my skin. The ocean was my friend; it felt safe and playful. I delighted in the quiet freedom of being buoyed, immersed. It felt old, familiar.

I did not go deep into the ocean because I was not allowed, not until I was older, and only with an adult. I don't remember doing this many times. I do remember the feeling of bobbing over the swells that later became waves as they hit the sandy shoreline. It was neat to feel the water lifting me up so gently, kind of like a slow motion amusement park ride, then deposit my feet back down into the sandy bottom. I don't remember thinking much about what may be lurking on the bottom right around me.

It must have been when I was about 6–7 years old that this began to change for me. My grandfather Wheeler had a sister named Myrtis. I don't remember interacting with her much. It seemed as if she lived somewhere else part of the year with her husband Lacey.

They had a spartan, little white house just down the street from my grandparents. It reminded me of a saltine crackers box. I did not like to go there. There weren't any toys to play with, and the grownups drank and laughed and talked. On the rare occurrence that an adult would talk to me, it was usually not nice. Comments about my "chubbiness" or that I was eating too many appetizers were common.

I was particularly afraid of Aunt Myrtis. She was a big, tall, loud woman with piercing eyes and a mouth full of Ballance teeth. She had the same toughness that all women from Hatteras seem to carry in them, a steely "there you go" attitude that made them seem more like men than women. She had a particular smell, like a cross between mothballs and Listerine. She said cruel things sometimes, and she would grin afterward. It would probably have been a beautiful grin, if there hadn't been such nasty black words still hovering about her mouth. She had big feet and painted her toenails bright colors. I think that she usually wore sandals. Her feet and toes were very present in my vision, maybe because I was so close to them.

One night when we went to visit over there, the grownups did their usual getting drunk and yucking it up. I hovered a bit too near to the cluster in one of my swoops to get some chips and dip when Aunt Myrtis cast her critical eye on me and drew me into her field. I happened to notice her feet and saw a bandage on her big toe. Perhaps out of curiosity or concern, I asked her what had happened to her foot. She then proceeded to tell me that she had been walking in the ocean and a crab had "bitten off" her big toe. She looked right at me and did not smile when she said this. It felt as if the air went out of the room for a moment while she watched me for my reaction. It did not occur to me that if a crab had bitten off her toe she would not have anything to bandage there. I saw the bandage and took it very seriously that she had suffered a grievous injury at the claws of an Atlantic blue crab. I was mortified. And she allowed me to be. She never did say to me, then or later, that she had been kidding.

I had seen plenty of crabs before. Usually we would see them, live and hopping mad in big wooden crates on the docks when the fisherman came in with their loads, their claws up in the air in a menacing but futile gesture of self defense. We ate crabmeat on a regular basis when we came to Hatteras. On rare occasions, I had seen blue crabs in the water on the sound side of the beach and had been warned not to let them get too near me or they would pinch. However, I hadn't thought about crabs as demonic mutilators of humans before. Why did this story grab ahold of me so strongly at this time? What else was occurring in my life that my mind was vulnerable to this kind of story of predation/violence?

I don't know that I can attribute my fear of the water solely to this incident, or if it is a natural occurrence over years as age, more information, and worry take their toll. However, after this horrific information was divulged to me, I began to watch the ocean floor a little more carefully when I went in to swim. If I did see a crab, or accidentally stepped on one, I screamed and ran out of the water. Over time, I began to look for them, knowing that they were there, lurking in the shadows, waiting for my feet to come close enough for them to get a nip. Eventually, I stopped going in the water at all. This fear of crabs pinching me in the murky water seeped into my fear of animate predators that I could not see.

There was such a cost. . . . I mourned the loss of my sweet mother ocean; no longer did I feel the freedom to frolic in her waves. As a teenager, I sat high on the sand and cried. The ocean became a dangerous and unpredictable entity to me, something that actually desired to take something away from me. I felt this loss acutely.

So here I sit, many years later, at the age of 39, camped for several months on the wild seashore of Padre Island, right in the face of the Gulf of Mexico, contemplating the importance and loss of this relationship. I have been given messages for some time that overcoming my fear of the water may be a useful thing to do, but I have not been highly motivated to tackle this fear. My young children have played in the ocean since they were little; I have consciously attempted to prevent my fear of it from leaking into their experience. I want them to feel the same freedom that I did before my idea of the ocean changed. But I think they would love it if I went swimming with them. Maybe I will be able to overcome this fear someday.

What does it all mean? What will happen if I reclaim this part of myself that is so central to me?

~ End of journal entry ~

The family work was happening consistently and we established a "hum" together. We were settling into our new life. The boys were full-fledged volunteers and greeted new campers, educating them about the rattlesnakes and coyotes in the dunes. Since it was summer, kids came to the campground all the time, so they frequently had new friends to play with. Peter was completely preoccupied with fishing, painting a commission he had gotten from the King Ranch, and his duties as volunteer. I was mama and volunteer most of the time, but because I did not do well in the heat, I was inside the rig, enjoying the miracle of air conditioning and writing about the mysterious experiences I was having.

The beach was a mirror for me. Trash washed ashore every day, a strange kind of plunder from the waters. It was our daily task as volunteers to clean up the beach, and we found all manner of syringes, shoes, plastic (all shapes, sizes, and colors), debris from shipwrecks, condoms, children's toys. You name it, we found it (and yes, we wore gloves). We never knew what would wash up. It became a game to see who could find the newest, most unusual thing.

The rangers told us that the refuse came from all over the world, picked up by a current and dumped here on this beach. We found trash printed in Japanese, Spanish, and of course, English. An amusing parallel existed between the offerings from the sea and memories in my body, coming to the surface and bobbing there, landing eventually in my consciousness, asking to be seen and recognized.

Testing My Trust

Something bigger and smarter than me brought things to my awareness in exactly the right timing and in tandem with my ability to handle them. Something guided my process with such care and exquisite handling, like a brain surgeon. But with insistence, too. I felt some urgency as my inner life was mobilized. Slacking off was not an option. Well, it was—I had a choice. But I found that resisting the flow was like trying to push back a wave at the shore. That was a futile effort that took a lot of life force and was not effective for long. Trying to avoid the issues being brought to my attention would not help anybody.

We also learned to trust the larger intelligence in situations that were more pressing than sitting together in our Pyramid Meetings and asking for direction. Sometimes, we faced choices that could be more serious, such as interacting with risk or danger. Often, the lesson was about overcoming fear, realizing that when fear had us in its grip we could not see clearly. Sometimes, concern is warranted, of course, but we often found that there was a difference between genuine discernment and irrational fear.

Frequently, we were shown that our fears were a creation of our minds, and that the larger intelligence had our backs if we would only trust. Being the worrier in the family, I felt the lessons about overcoming fear were mostly for my benefit, and the lesson to trust was mostly for Peter.

An example of being re-educated about fear was in our frequent relocations of rattlesnakes. Not exactly a volunteer job by my way of thinking, but the rangers asked us to do it since they could not be there all of the time, so we did.

The Mississauga rattlesnake is indigenous to the area and common in the sand dunes on this coastline. They were often found in the parking lot of the campground or slithering across the walkways between dunes. One even staked out a nice home under the outdoor showers. And sometimes they were big! A particularly impressive fellow appeared to be over six feet long (we did not touch that one!). Our first interactions were blessedly with smaller ones. To my great relief, they looked nothing like the black water moccasins that represented my mother in my dreams. Once I overcame my fear, I discovered a natural curiosity and appreciation for these snakes, who truly wanted nothing more than to get away from us.

After investigation about the rattlesnake as an animal totem, it made so much sense that there was a steady parade of them during our stay at Padre. (They represent deep transformation and powerful regeneration, rebirth. They also model lessons about boundaries, warning folks to back off if they get too close!) We were developing this wisdom about boundaries in regard to Peter's parents and family, who repeatedly asked us to come visit. We explained we were doing deep transformative healing in our family but this seemed to be ignored or minimized. Peter's parents finally insisted on coming to Padre for a visit, but an impending hurricane in Florida (their home at the time) cut their trip short.

We also got to test our trust when it came to weather! Padre was subject to sudden and powerful storms coming off the Gulf. We experienced several and learned to respect the weather as a boss! A few times, the larger intelligence used the storms to help us with our fear/trust issues. From my journal at that time:

Fear of the Water II, Storms on Padre

Journal Entry, 5-18-04, *written in third person as an experiment to write more freely*

She was given every indication that overcoming her fear of the ocean was of paramount importance to her healing process. Her husband, her therapists, her own inner guidance, all prompted her to move in this direction. Sometimes the attachment that her husband and children had to her loving the water as they did was prohibitive; it was natural to her to resist doing what anyone wanted her to do. However, it was time now.

She had been camping at Padre Island with her family for two and a half weeks. When they were given guidance to go to Padre and camp on the beach, she had been terrified. Any Hatteraser worth their salt would never put an abode right on the beach! All those city folks come down to the island and build their houses right on the water, then the water comes along and pulls them down. It just isn't smart to live where the water can easily get to you. Or so this was how she was taught to believe.

They had weathered two storms when the Gulf broke through the seaweed barrier at the surf and came up on the beach where their motor home was parked. The storms on Padre were violent; wind gusts of up to 60 miles an hour, pelting rain and hail, and massive amounts of lightning that reminded her of strobe lights on speed. The first storm happened during the day; they watched as the rain fell sideways and blew into the RV's closed windows. Then the Gulf started to come ashore.

Little waves at first broke through the seaweed barrier in little rivulets. As the day got longer and the wind and rain did not abate, the waves coming into shore got bigger, and more seawater made it up to the dry bank. As the waves got successively closer, the family panicked and drove off the beach when the water was 50 feet away.

The second storm happened at night, and during high tide. That night there was quite a bit of what looked like heat lightning in the sky all around them. They checked the weather radio on an intuitive hit. Massive severe thunderstorms were headed their way on two sides. Her inner guidance was to stay. Her husband did not question this, surprisingly to her. He was the one who seemed to be conservative when it came to keeping the family and motor home safe; it had been his idea to move during the last storm, even though her guidance then had been to stay. This time, he seemed to trust that they would be all right.

She listened to the beating of her heart. She weighed the guidance against the possibility of the RV being damaged by the storm, or worse, her family getting hurt. The anxiety of making the decision to trust versus what appeared to be a logical choice to leave permeated her being. What in the hell was being asked of her and her family?

Then a voice entered her heart, the way a gentle breeze enters a room. The voice, not audible but a felt presence of love and calm, spoke to her.

"My Daughter, do you believe that I would allow harm to come to you? Your children are safe in my keeping, just as you and Peter are safe in my keeping. Do you not know by now that you are protected? As you have traveled, have you not heard the guidance to move and to stay, and have you not experienced the warmth of extraordinary experiences as a result? I ask this of you to show you that you are held in my arms, that you will never be asked to do more than you are capable of, and to learn to trust me when the stakes appear at their greatest."

When the storm hit in the dark of night, it began with a wailing, moaning, high wind that ripped around the RV like a cat o' nine tails. The motor home shook and rocked. The children, asleep in their makeshift beds, were dead to the noise. The heavy rain began pounding the roof, then flying sideways against the walls of the rig, power-washing the many days' accumulation of sand off the RV in moments. This storm was a big one.

She and her husband, with no recourse now that the storm had begun, decided to try to get some sleep. As she lay there in the darkness that was steadily interrupted by lightning, she became more afraid. What if her guidance had been wrong? The rain came down harder; after a little while of lying in bed, with eyes wide open, she got up to check the sand. The flattened, compact sand that served as the road down the beach was shiny with standing water. Between flashes of lightning, she searched the dark beach for the line of the Gulf of Mexico; where is it? How high has it come up? She thought she saw the Gulf not much higher than when they went to bed a couple of hours ago. She went back to bed because there was nothing else she could do.

At 3 a.m., her husband jumped out of bed. She awoke, alarmed and short of breath, and made her way in the dark down the hallway toward the front of the RV. Her husband was watching through the windows, trying to eye the height of the Gulf on the sand. It was impossible to see because of the hard rain on the windows. His concern made his body tense and straight as he searched vainly for the sight of the water line.

In her adrenaline rush, she grabbed a flashlight and threw open the motor home door. Running out into the maelstrom, the rain stung her arms, face, and legs. She shined the flashlight around on the ground, trying to see her way through her long hair, morphed into wet whips by the strong wind. She made her way against the wind to the front of the RV and shined the light down on the sand. There was standing water right next to the RV, maybe 3 feet away. Was it fresh water or the Gulf? She took a few steps out beyond the front of the RV toward the Gulf, attempting to see the water level. Then immense lightning strikes down the beach on either side of her caused her to instinctively run with amazing speed back into the RV, like a ghost crab speeds sideways into its hole when it sees a seagull. She did not get to see the Gulf at all, not privy to that information. She had gotten a clear message to get back inside.

After this occurrence, she and her husband checked in again with guidance and still received the message to stay put. For the rest of those agonizing dark hours in bed next to her husband, she prayed for help to trust and release fears—fear that the water would come up to the RV, fear that the RV would be picked up by the Gulf and taken out to sea, fear that the sand would saturate with water and would suck the motor home down, groaning, into the earth, with her whole family inside.

Even beyond these fears, there was a deeper, unnamable terror of the water. It was dark, moving, all-powerful. It could not be reasoned or bargained with. It had no conscience. It could do horrible things in an instant flat. It could completely change your world.

She did not get to the bottom of these fears, and exhausted, fell asleep while holding her husband's hand. In her fearful mind, she saw a vision of her and her husband, lying on the bed next to each other, while the water swirled around them and seaweed entangled around their entwined hands.

They awoke to a sweet, early morning sunrise, a light, fresh breeze and blue sky after the rage of the storm. They were in one piece. It was still hard to see from inside the RV where the Gulf had wound up, so she suggested to her husband that they go outside and take a look before the children awoke (who had slept through the entire night!).

When they emerged onto the beach and stood in front of the RV, they saw that the Gulf of Mexico had indeed moved inland, and was now less than twenty-five feet away from their home, all they had in the world. There was evidence in the way of scattered clumps of seaweed that the sea had reached all the way to the dunes on either side of them. However, *the sand under the motor home was untouched.*

She nearly fell to her knees.

They knew that the next high tide was in three hours, and the water was already high, so *they* made the decision to move out to higher ground. They parked in the primitive, paved campground behind the dunes at Padre and, exhausted, slept most of the day while the children played quietly.

~ End of journal entry ~

Water, Water, Everywhere

Why am I afraid of the water? This question plagued me every day. Having the Gulf a few hundred yards from my front door was a persistent, in-my-face presence that made me uneasy, all of the time. Even when I was inside the RV, with the doors closed, the family active and talking, AND the TV or stereo on, the sound of the waves was an unvarying, incessant reminder of the constancy of the sea. It was breaking me down! *"I'm here, Licia. . . . I'm not going away, Licia. . . . You need to deal with me, Licia. . . . "* Always there!

I started to feel as if the water was like my mother—dark, mysterious, hiding dangerous things under the surface. As if the water had eyes, I felt it watching impassively, beckoning me to come close, but ready to strike at any moment. Obviously, I projected my fears onto the water, but even this was instructive. Perhaps my perception of the ocean as a dangerous entity had roots in my childhood experiences with my mother.

An interesting occurrence at this time was the widespread news story about a mother who drowned her children. She strapped them into their car seats and rolled her car into a lake. This story captured my attention in a way that did not make sense to me. It haunted me, would not let me go. I was so fiercely protective of my children that I could not understand how a mother would intentionally kill, much less harm, her babies. Why did this hook me so? What place inside of me could be receptive, alert to this information? And why was I so horrified by it?

Soon after, there was another news story about a mother drowning her children in the bathtub. Why did this seem somehow familiar? Here are two journal entries I wrote at the time.

Fear of the Water III, Swimming

Journal Entry Excerpt, 5-18-04, *written in third person so I can write more freely*

I am petrified. Will she drown me? Will she hold me down under the water again?

These were the words that came to her mind when she felt into the tumult and fear in her belly.

The day that she knew she would try to get in the water, she had a knot in her stomach. She was on edge, irritated. She found herself being less than loving to her family. She knew that this fear was a big one to get through.

She had been talking to a colleague who was a life coach the day before about the block she felt in writing her first book. They had talked about the technical aspects, research that needed to be done to get the process moving again. Somehow, the conversation got onto water. She talked about how her fear of the water was so pervasive in her thoughts.

She felt herself at a breakthrough point in her inner healing, great resistance and agitation in the last weeks since being at Padre. Eventually, the resistance gave way to surrender, a beautiful day on the beach when she gave in to the inner tide that is the flow of life.

Why put so much energy into resistance? Much like most adult human beings had learned to become, it was a fear of feeling. Opening to and making peace with the water meant she was opening to her emotion; once that door was opened, she would feel again. What was she scared to feel? What could be so heinous that she would been driven away from her beloved waters for all these years? And why was just knee deep when she went in the water okay, but no deeper? What happens if the water touches her thighs, her hips, her bottom, her yoni? What feeling is locked up there that the touch of the water will awaken?

She needed to go swimming, not just knee deep either. To immerse herself completely in the ocean, let it carry and buoy her. But this would require trust.

By the time she and her family got to the beach, she was afraid but resigned to getting in the water. There was an inner motivation; she would be a step closer to freedom if she could just do this.

She had her water shoes and three willing escorts. They all made their way out into the shallows. She felt the tingling glee that she used to feel when she was a girl. There was so much ocean to jump into! They moved a little deeper, to knee level. She asked that they stop there for a bit. This was the deepest she had been in the waves in some time, maybe years. There was less seaweed than there had been in previous days, and the waves were calmer. As if the sea were cooperating with her efforts to make friends again with the water.

She felt ready to move deeper to crotch level. She had not allowed the water to touch her yoni in as long as she could remember, except for the two times that her husband had won trips to the Caribbean and she had swam because the water was so clear. Easy to see the beasties in crystal-clear water. But thinking back to those few times, she had not been very present in her body. Her heart had raced, her breathing was labored, and she could not remember much about what she had seen through her snorkel mask.

Now, she felt again into her body. She felt here! She felt a joyous lightness come over her, and she dove, holding her nose, headfirst into a wave. She came up laughing and wiping her long hair out of her eyes. Her husband looked on and smiled; she continued to play and jump and allow the waves to crash over her head. Her children were so excited. They had never seen their mom actually play in the water. It was a good time, and she felt some of her fear move a little out of the forefront.

She did keep an eye out for the beasties, though. About 45 minutes later, she got stung by a jellyfish; nothing major, but enough to give her the heebie-jeebies. She refused the offer to escort her out deeper into the ocean. She made her way back up to the shore and sat in the shallow water, nursing the minor sting.

She debated whether to head out again, and she did for a short while. But her childlike joy had dissipated. She spent the entire time watching for menacing sea creatures. Her son and husband both got stung, as well, so they eventually decided to head home. Later that evening, her husband congratulated her on a job well done. She felt she had made some headway, but that there was much more to do toward releasing her fear of the water.

The next day, she awoke feeling odd pains and sensations in her upper thighs, hips, low back, and belly. She lay in bed, just noticing, and wondered if this was the beginning of the unlocking of the feeling. She made a mental note to watch for anything, any sign of feeling that was different than usual.

Memories in the Belly

Journal Entry Excerpts, 6-1-04, *written in third person so I can write more freely*

The ocean brought it up for her. Whenever she went to the beach, even later as an adult, she would have that funny feeling in her belly and a low-grade discomfort/anxiety. It was as if, at thirty-nine, she was the full-bellied little girl standing with one finger in her mouth, a *feeling of being a little girl with a problem.*

Whenever she was in the water, she had a strange feeling. Even in a wet bathing suit, it could happen; having the water in her suit next to her skin set it off. If she had been swimming with a lover and they had touched her intimately, it happened. Something bad happened in or around the water. Something that made her feel dirty. What was it that did this to her? Was it something in the water that made her feel this way? And what did the mothers that killed their children have to do with her fear of water?

As she refined her healing process, utilizing techniques to lift impediments to her understanding of the truth of what happened, her ego rebelled. She felt her body getting closer to telling her information that she needed to know to move on, but then resistance would come up and stop the process. Her solar plexus had been in spasm for days on end. She told herself to give in, to surrender, and to go with the flow. To let the truth wash over her like the water.

The water and memory, . . . What was the connection?

Since they had been at Padre Island and she had come to the awareness that getting into the water was instrumental to her healing process, almost everything that came out of her mouth was in water language. It was as if the water and her psyche were inseparable.

Intuition and imagination, dreams and the feminine, or yin, energy: these were symbolically associated with water. What was awakening inside of her?

She remembered her childhood so well; and yet there were things hidden, mysteries behind a curtain. She recalled afternoons coming back from the beach, getting washed by an adult to clean up, a hurting belly right around having a nap, and a strange sensation of having something stolen from her that she could not name. Something about a tub, water all around her, seeing her father's face. Her mother coming in and seeing them together. A feeling of misery and despair into the evening until the adults started drinking together (although they had been drinking beer all day at the beach). This time of the evening, she could feel safe because they were entertaining each other. The sun going down was a joyous time because it meant she was free for a time.

Over the years, her family of origin had vacationed at the Outer Banks, alternating between Hatteras village, where her father's family still lived, and Ocracoke Island, the charming village where her mother's family had vacationed for generations. As a teen, she and her father were alone in the Ocracoke inn room and she was seen being fondled, through the window, by her mother and aunt. She didn't remember this instance, but did remember that she came to the door of the room with her father, answering the knocks of her mother and aunt. When he answered the door, or maybe it was her, her mother asked if she was alright, a strange knowing look in her eyes, as if she were performing for the aunt's benefit, movie camera always on.

Why did her mother ask that? Why didn't she immediately accuse the father of what she had witnessed with her own eyes, as well as with the aunt? For that matter, why didn't the aunt say something? And the more important, and the most telling, why did her mother put the pressure on the daughter, the sexually abused, to absolve the situation by answering, "I'm fine"? To somehow, in one short verbal interchange, erase the immensity of what had just happened, what was just seen? This was the pattern in her life; she was given the message consistently that she was responsible for the advances of her father, not him.

~End of journal entries ~

For years, I did not remember my father fondling me that night specifically, but had a vague sensation of something so familiar happening as to escape my notice. My body tells me that I experienced many things I do not have memory of, as in visual confirmation or total recall. I later learned that I was in and out of my body, mostly out, I think. Frequent for abuse victims, the body experiences the abuse but the mind fractures in such a way as to not be present to it, preserving some shred of sanity. This is called Dissociative Disorder, and it is a survival technique for experiencing the unimaginable.

I felt like a detective looking for clues. The question of my fascination with the news stories of mothers who drowned their children was somehow related to the trips of my family of origin to the beach. How did these things connect? How could I love the water and fear it so much at the same time?

The swimming incident was not repeated during that trip at Padre. My one experiment in the Gulf brought up such a wave of memory that I had my hands full for the remainder of the summer. The immersion of my body in the water was like a baptism, opening up my inner waters. The image of ice, of frozen water, its flow and motion arrested, showed up frequently in my art during this period. Engaging with the ocean freed up the frozen water in my belly, and I started feeling again.

My guidance told me that the feeling center in my body was my belly. This coincided with what I had been taught, as well as what I had experienced about the second chakra, the trauma/childhood/sexuality/creativity center in the body. My experience of my second chakra was that it was "blocked" a lot. My helping guidance suggested with frequency that I set the intention to open my second chakra, and I could feel a softening and swirling sensation when it opened back up. This coincided with the flowing and memory that was restored with the thawing of the ice, the frozen feeling. This is why it was not enough to be knee deep in the ocean; I needed to be belly-to-belly with the sea. The waters outside needed to meet the waters on the inside to free my internal process from the impediments to remembering and to remain in the flow. This was more important than I knew at the time.

In September 2004, a category 5 hurricane was forming. It was remarkable that no hurricanes had chased us away in our long stay on the coast. Back in August, in one of our sessions with guidance from larger intelligence, we were given a departure date to head west on September 13. We found ourselves getting more nervous as Hurricane Ivan grew in size and created surge in the Gulf. We had learned to trust the information we were given, but as we watched the water reach higher on the beach, we considered leaving early, ignoring the guidance. We decided this was another opportunity to trust, and the morning of the 13th, we left Padre Island behind, the Gulf all the way up to the dunes.

How apt that I would leave the place that had brought up so much inner water for me while the ocean threatened to take over the land.

The Desert and the Water

We pointed the immense nose of our RV west, landing in northern New Mexico, "land of enchantment." It was a most welcome change from the humid, hot, and watery world of the Gulf. Here we were amongst high desert, mountains, beautiful sky. The arid environment seemed to take pressure off my process, and I started to breathe. Strangely enough, at such a higher elevation than we were used to (the Albuquerque area ranges from five thousand to sixty-seven hundred feet above sea level), I was breathing better than I had in months. My lungs welcomed the dry, clean mountain air.

We stayed in a campground in Bernalillo, north of town on the Rio Grande. The Rio is considered an "exotic river" like the Nile because it flows through the desert, bringing life. The mountains are made of granodiorite, which according to Wikipedia is "a phaneritic texture intrusive igneous rock similar to granite, but containing more plagioclase feldspar than orthoclase feldspar. According to the QAPF [Quartz, Alkali feldspar, Plagioclase, Feldspathoid (Foid)] diagram, granodiorite has a greater than 20% quartz by volume." The area geology contributes to a greater degree of ability to tap into information from subtle sources due to the feldspar and the quartz in the ground and surrounding mountain ranges. There is a high vibration that lends itself to greater psychic power that we all experienced. We were off the charts with our guidance abilities and met such wonderful people as a result of showing up at the right place at the right time. We remained in New Mexico for one and a half years, taking a brief stint as volunteers further south at Lake Patagonia in southern Arizona. It was a very productive time as we enjoyed local residents who feel like soul family; we remain friends to this day.

I enjoyed so much the wide-open landscape, something I had missed since we moved back east from Arizona to North Carolina in late 1996. My soul sang across the desert, picked up by the wind. I felt at peace and connected to the part of me that is indigenous to the East Coast, the Powhatan Indians. In Asheville, I had heard from relatives on the Outer Banks that we were of aboriginal descent, confirming what I had noticed about myself. My connection to the land was part of my DNA.

The mountains in New Mexico started talking to me after we had been there about a year. We moved from Bernalillo to Corrales, both communities centered on the Rio Grande, to a rental house in the foothills of the mountains. When we settled there, things really heated up, and I began having experiences similar to those in Asheville; the voice of the mountains told me that the rocks were Record Keepers, holders of ancient history, and that I was invited to "speak with them." What an opportunity to learn directly from intelligence that knew the Earth so intimately! I opened myself to dialogue every day, and was delighted to know more of the old medicine that was offered to me.

Old Woman of the Desert

My fortieth birthday was enjoyed with friends under a full moon rising over the Sandia Mountains, like an illuminated face of the elder native woman I was first introduced to in a vision in Arizona. I had been seeing her more regularly now in my inner landscape, calling and beckoning to me from this area of northern New Mexico. When I sat quietly to listen to the desert intelligence, I saw her coming forward with offerings in vessels, giant jars. She spoke to me in a language similar to the one that came through my body in Asheville. Something about her reminded me of Isis. The heroine of my youth seemed to be returning to me.

Albuquerque was great fun for the boys. We joined a home schooling group and they had buddies that they enjoyed. During the day, I took them for our lessons, and we had a blast discovering the area's history. The mountains were a wonderful playground, too. The conifer forests on the slopes provided cool shade in the summer. In the winter, we stayed in the museums. (It can get quite cold in Albuquerque in the winter, even snow, although it tends to melt quickly in its proximity to the sun.)

Peter took a job for a recruiting company once it became clear that we would stay for a while. He learned the ins and outs of being a "head hunter" well enough that he would start his own company eventually.

Family of Origin Strikes Again

My little brother got married that year, and I flew east to attend and play a small role in his wedding. I was not excited about seeing my family of origin. I had lots of questions about my childhood that could make it an uncomfortable visit. But I wanted to support my brother, so I prepared as best I could, remembering that I was stronger now than I used to be.

When I arrived and greeted my parents, I felt very strong survival signals in my body—heart racing, shortness of breath, being unable to think clearly, and wanting to get away. My body was terrified, no matter how much I had grown spiritually. I was disappointed in myself. I thought I was beyond these feelings, but the body does not lie.

The visit with my family of origin went as well as could be expected, considering the circumstances. I played my role and supported my brother, which were my intentions. The information I received from my body was also a bonus, affirming my investigation into what made me so afraid.

After the wedding, I returned to New Mexico as if to a lost love. Running back into the arms of the high desert and my beloved family, I felt safe. I sought solace after the difficult feelings I experienced on the trip east. The feminine voice that had been speaking to me coddled me. The mountains spoke to me of letting go, turning away from toxic influences, making hard decisions. I understood that Nature "makes tough choices" a million times a day, and it is not taken personally. It is a matter of choosing life, choosing what nurtures life, not death. Death is a natural end to what no longer has a place in the scheme of things. If I wanted to live, I would need to make some decisions.

Peter was dealing with some family issues, too. The boundaries we had set for our family while traveling needed reinforcing the fall of 2005 when Peter's parents wanted to come be with us for the Christmas holiday. We felt something big coming for our family and wanted to protect our process, so we politely told them that it had nothing to do with them, but that it was not a good time for a visit. They reacted in such a strongly negative way that we were shocked. We once again saw Peter's family's dynamic of codependence. This was the beginning of Peter's awakening into his wounding.

He asked them for space so he could process deep feelings that stirred in him, but they continued to make contact and sent a box of Christmas presents to our home. Another boundary ignored, we sorrowfully sent the presents back with a firmer request for space. They then respected the no contact request, but responded with wild disregard for our emotional safety, telling everyone who would listen (including mutual extended family and friends, and the worst, Peter's siblings) that we had cut them out of our lives, that we had joined a cult, that we were ignoring their grandparental wishes, and *that I was the reason all of this happened*. Once again, I was Evil Licia.

As we continued to fall in love with northern New Mexico, we voiced our desire for a pet. Our family cats had long since walked on in Asheville, and we had attempted a dog but found it too demanding of our attentions. Cats were the right pet for our busy lifestyle. But we had had no pet since our cats died years ago, and certainly not while we had been on the road. We imagined a kitty that would fit into our traveling life, naming qualities that she would possess, such as intelligence, playfulness, a love of snuggling, and hypo-allergenic. In December 2005, two days after voicing our desire, a feral kitten walked around the back patio and made eye contact with Peter and me, while we enjoyed our morning coffee. "Tink" adopted us quickly, moving in within two weeks. The land had gifted us an animal from its bosom, who would serve as a kind of glue to our family in times to come.

My personal relations with the land really took a lovely turn in this year of 2005. As I deepened into the communication with the intelligence of the mountains, I noticed that the intelligence visualized itself to my mind in the form of an elderly indigenous grandmother. She reminded me of the vision of the white-haired woman in the rust-colored robe, the one I had seen in my inner vision, hovering over northern New Mexico all those years ago. It had been the land calling to me!

Safe in the Arms
Collage ©2010 Licia Berry

At Christmas of 2005, the change we had felt coming materialized. I practiced listening to the larger intelligence every day, and I received indications that we should look for a place north of us, across the border of Colorado in the San Luis Valley. The San Luis Valley is a mysterious alpine valley that reminded me of a giant thumbprint over the borderlands of New Mexico and Colorado. We had first learned about it from a friend we met at Padre, interestingly a woman who recognized me as a devotee of the feminine voice. She loaned us a book about the unusual number of UFO sightings and unexplained activity there; reading it was fascinating. The locals spoke of strange things in the sky, including a prehistoric pterodactyl-type creature. I am skeptical by nature unless I have experienced something directly, so I was dubious about some of these claims. I was open to the possibility of interaction with extraterrestrial life and had even seen a few UFOs in my years, but I considered these things with some suspicion.

We took a few days and traveled the San Luis Valley; it was jaw-droppingly beautiful. The fertile valley floor is an agricultural mecca where crops are grown that feed the nation. Ranging from seven thousand to eighty-five hundred feet in elevation, it is surrounded by a ring of mountain ranges with peaks of more than fourteen thousand feet. Snow stays on the peaks well into the summer. We drove in awe of the soaring mountains and gorgeous, crystal blue sky. An eagle flew over a frozen river, landing in bare cottonwood trees as we passed. Something about it felt familiar, and we decided to move on the guidance to relocate.

Over the next two months, we found a house on forty acres outside the little town of Del Norte and bought it on a shoestring, by a sheer miracle. We moved in February 25, 2006, thinking perhaps our family journey was over and that we could finally settle down.

We were wrong.

Chapter 5: Great Mother Says Hello – 42 to 47 Years

Mother Five
Collage © 2007 Licia Berry

Our lives in the San Luis Valley were so sweet the first several months. We renovated the house we bought, making it more our own. We worked the land, scraping the desert of its debris and making an Eden out of our little paradise. We awakened in the mornings, looking out from the ample windows of the house to gaze at the extraordinary postcard-worthy views in every direction. "We get to LIVE here!" we exclaimed. It was a blissful sensation after years of mobility to have a patch of ground that was ours to care-take.

The winters could be harsh. While our first winter was not so bad (we closed on the property in late February, so missed a few months of winter weather), subsequent winters were a survival test. We rose to the challenge, buying a truck with a snowplow attached to the front so we could dig ourselves out of the feet of snow that drifted across our road and pathway to civilization seven miles away in Del Norte. We shoveled and strategized, outsmarting winter everywhere we could. Our family banded together, no stranger to challenging weather or circumstances.

The summer was blissful, cool at night and hot (ninety degrees was the highest we ever saw) during the heat of the day. The mountains relented and gave way to the sun by mid-June, when the snowy peaks that surrounded us became green. We explored extraordinary high vistas, alpine forest, aspens, and beautiful clear streams. The Rio Grande, the headwaters of which were a few miles away, ran snowmelt down through the desert into New Mexico, our former location. How awesome it was to be at the top of this magnificent river that feeds so many.

Challenges and Victories

We began getting to know people in the community soon after we moved in. After the Spanish displaced the aboriginal people from the valley in the 1800s, these pristine lands attracted homesteaders, ranchers, farmers, and miners. Most of the folks who lived there were at least third-generation Hispanic and European families whose roots were dug in to the Colorado rocky soil.

Our naive belief that we could arrive in a small, rural community and be accepted because we were nice people was challenged soon after we began interacting in town with the locals. The first interactions with other artsy, open-minded people were lovely (these were the renegade artist/independent/hippie/healer types that seek beauty in Nature and value freedom), so we were fooled again into thinking we had found our "forever home." We bought a main-street storefront building and poured money into the local economy. Peter had been doing well in his home-grown recruiting business, and we lacked nothing in our material existence. In fact, we had the best year financially we had ever had. We began to put roots down.

However, the town we lived near in our rural valley was economically depressed. Del Norte was a small, former mining town with a total area of less than one square mile, a population of just over sixteen hundred people, and the median annual income for a family was twenty-nine thousand four hundred and seventy-one dollars. We were doing so much better than the majority of people there that we felt no compunction about supporting the town through various financial efforts. The mistake we made was to disrespect the good fortune we currently enjoyed by spreading it too thin in anticipation of reciprocal support.

Later, when the recession began and Peter's business suffered, we learned some hard lessons about managing and respecting money. Our relationship with currency had an amazing opportunity to be examined and eventually healed, but at that time, we were not being supported financially by the town.

Community was hard to create, too. When our children went to school, the local kids absolutely punished them. Our boys had asked me if they could attend school the summer of 2006, and I reluctantly agreed to allow them. The kindness and personal responsibility with which we treated each other at home was a very different environment than what they encountered in school.

Aidan in particular, who entered fourth grade, was tortured daily and became despairing; he broke down one day and admitted what was happening to him, but it was beyond help. No matter how much I intervened, met with teachers, counselors, and principals, or requested that the bullying be stopped, the rude and nasty behavior continued.

I requested that the kids reconsider home schooling, but Jess, now in seventh grade, needed a peer group and did not want to come back home for school. My feeling now is that Aidan wanted to be like Jess, and at the time, he also refused the invitation to return to home schooling. I worried about them constantly.

As for the women, they alternated between ranchers' wives (mostly very conservative), "townies" who were working in the few jobs the valley had to offer, and urban, educated women who had moved to the area of their free will, like us. I could not relate to many of them, but I learned there was a full moon women's circle and thought I might be set. Having spent some years in women's circles with various degrees of success, I hoped at best for a safe, warm, and wise place to be myself; a group of women can be a tremendous encouragement if it embraces true feminine spirit.

I had been part of one Asheville women's circle in 1997 that fulfilled the best-case scenario. The women participated in rituals like the talking stick, sweat lodge, and deep heart sharing. The group leader was a therapist and paid facilitator, so the group was held and guided by a containing influence that kept it on track. She taught me a lot about the profound safety and healing that can result in a group of trusted women, a real gift. After two years with this group, the leader suggested we all spend a weekend at a mountain cabin, where we ran into a strange dynamic. Our leader, so capable and seemingly wise, fell into a triggered state and behaved irrationally. In her confusion, she said some hurtful things to me. Because I looked up to her as a paid authority, leader, and therapist, I was surprised and hurt. I felt betrayed. Again.

I repeated this dynamic later with many women—including in Colorado. I experienced conflict immediately and backed away when I saw no understanding of deep feminine wisdom. I realized through the experience in Asheville that I was looking for mothering from women who did not know how to mother me. I wanted them to take me by the hand and teach me how to be a woman. I wanted their guidance, their acceptance, their affirmation. I wanted their love. I yearned for a woman who did not exist, a mother of my imagining. The startling truth was that I would never find this woman; only an ideal mother could fulfill my hunger.

I began to question in earnest my history with women. Over the years, I had observed that I was uncomfortable with women and did not have long-lasting friends. It seemed I would find some lovely women and get to know them to a point, hoping for a transformation of the old wounded mother story. Eventually, my mistrust would be triggered by some breach, and I would distance myself. I realized in Colorado that I had created this dynamic of attracting women who could not be trusted, a pattern I had learned with my mother. I was trying to heal myself by repeating the pattern until I got it. No matter where I went or how far I traveled, the pattern would remain until I changed it. Eureka!

Doing Things Differently

Full fathom five thy father lies;
Of his bones are coral made;
Those are pearls that were his eyes:
Nothing of him that doth fade,
But doth suffer a sea-change
Into something rich and strange.

– from Shakespeare's *Tempest*

Coincidentally (or maybe NOT), all of this occurred in my forty-first year. Some friends back in Albuquerque at my fortieth birthday party told me I was entering my "Uranus Opposition," and that I was in for the biggest change of my life in the next couple of years. Apparently, between ages forty-one and forty-two, we can feel the effects of the planet Uranus coming into direct opposition to its position when we were born. I am no astrologer, but the information I found says that these are the years of radical new beginnings that give us a chance to become more of who we really are. It is a time to break the rules, to shake up the status quo, and do things differently.

This time was some of the most changing in my life. The town circulated gossip about me being a "witch" (not sure how they got that idea; maybe because I told ghost stories as a volunteer at Aidan's school Halloween celebration), and things got very odd. I had spontaneous visions of being pulled out of my house by a mob and dragged by my hair down the street to some central town place.

While I remained a dedicated volunteer at the schools and brought value into the community through our economic and volunteer support, I was experiencing a sea change that would portend a great healing. On my forty-second birthday (April 2007), I felt an extraordinary opening into a vast, uncharted place in my psyche. I was ready to heal my Mother Wound.

The mystical experiences I had then were beyond any I had encountered so far. The connection with the Earth, the spirits of the land, and the ancestors heated up to such an extent that I felt transformed, as if I was becoming the Earth herself. I felt earthquakes before they happened, pulsed with the emotional collective, and followed space weather, tracking solar activity and correlating it with my felt experience. I felt as if I was a body of the collective Earth activity, and at times, it got very intense. I wondered what was happening to me; I was at a loss to explain my experiences and began to project fear onto them.

One day, I was "listening in" to the feminine voice I had learned to hear in Asheville, expressing my concern for the fear that I seemed to feel pervasively. I was told, "Dear heart, you are feeling the threshold of change that is coming for the collective. I have called you here to this place in order to give you the space to feel me. The waters are my blood and carry memory of all life. Here in this desert, the waters are below you, deep in the ground; the surface is arid, and appears lifeless, but if you look below appearances, you will find treasures untold. All is well."

Soon after this interchange, I was surprised by a phone call from my Aunt Wendy, my mother's sister who had been attentive to me as a child. We had not been in contact for years. I assumed that she, like others in my family of origin, shunned me because of my choice to break the code of silence about the abuse in my childhood home. We had a lovely conversation and more soon after. She invited our family to come visit her in her home in Tucson! How funny that she wound up in the place we used to live! We made plans to visit during the New Year's holiday. It was a profound visit. Not only did my husband and children love her, but I was reminded that there was good in my mother's line. Like a woman who had wandered the desert for a hundred years, I drank her up.

Trust the Tide

Being in my aunt's presence initiated a cascade of what I can only describe as inner avalanches, and I tumbled down, down, down with the debris that was dislodged, settling eventually at the bottom of the sea. I remember looking out at the Arizona desert, dotted with saguaro cacti and rugged mountains, and thinking, *This all used to be the bottom of the ocean.*

When we got back home to Colorado, I had an experience of being under deep water. As I drove the kids to school, pushed my cart through the grocery store, and chatted with my husband and children about their day, I felt the cold pressure of hundreds of feet of seawater on my skin and the sandy bottom under my feet. The sensation was fortunately an internal one; my psyche had been opened up by being with Wendy.

As I explored this new territory, I realized that the feminine presence that I had felt in the ocean for many years was the same presence I felt in this internal experience. I had been dropped into the lap of the Divine Feminine, the Great Mother of All Things. I walked the bottom of this watery territory, encountering features such as corals, caves, kelp forests, undersea volcanoes, urchins, and sea creatures of varied size and helpfulness. Particular ones guided me to locations where I found jewels of every color scattered on the ocean floor; others took me to hidden places where larger gems were secreted away, awaiting my discovery. I dug with my hands in the sand to free them, and as I held them and marveled at their size and beauty, they dissolved into my body.

This internal travel went on for months. I met an Inuit Grandmother at a gathering and we had a wonderful, affirming discussion. I shared with her that I felt something was wrong with the model of "spirituality" that did not include the physical world and our bodies, and that I felt there had to be a marriage between heaven and earth within ourselves. She looked me up and down and said, "Then you are a Wise Woman and a True Human."

Trust the Tide
Collage © 2007 Licia Berry

I shared my undersea experience with her. She peered at me for a long moment, utterly startled, and said, "I have not heard any other person talk about this. I have had the same experience." She then told me about Sedna, the goddess of the world oceans. I later read the tales of Sedna and cried, feeling my kinship with her so acutely.

Sedna is the Inuit Goddess of the deep, cold sea. She began as a young woman whose father, a widower, attempted multiple times to marry her off to suitors, none of which she accepted. Her heart belonged to a young man from a warring tribe, one of whom her father did not approve. She stole away from her father to go with this man to his island.

Sedna's father, furious and shamed by his daughter's disobedience, canoed across the waters to fetch her. Sedna's lover, away on a hunt, did not know she was abducted. Sedna cried out to the winds, the sea, and the sky to take her from her dominating father. As he rowed furiously across the waters, a storm arose as if in answer to Sedna's cries. The canoe tossed from side to side, and Sedna's father feared for his safety. Throwing Sedna overboard into the water, he hoped to steady the rocking vessel, but she tried to climb back into the boat, tipping it even more. Her father chopped her fingers off and she dropped again into the sea. When Sedna struggled to use her mutilated hands again to climb into the canoe, he cut off her hands and pushed her away, throwing her appendages into the sea. Sedna sank to the bottom of the ocean, her dismembered limbs trailing down and scattering around her. These parts of her body became the fish, seals, whales, and other sea mammals.

Sedna descended to the Inuit Land of the Dead, where she now rules. As Queen, she is responsible for allowing the sea animals to be hunted to feed the people. To ensure that she continues to allow the hunt to be successful, shamans must descend through difficult passages to reach Sedna and soothe her. While they visit her, they massage Sedna's aching limbs and comb her hair, since she cannot. When she is comforted, she allows the shaman to take word to the people that Sedna will permit the successful hunt.

There was a reason this story—told to me by a recognized Intuit Grandmother who had also experienced being under an internal sea—was important. As I went about my daily life in the sun, my internal psychic landscape was living through and showing me an ancient, aboriginal tale. The story was alive inside of me, but who or what was telling the story? How did it relate to me, a modern woman in 2007?

The answer came upon more time spent under the waves; Sedna was a reflection for me, the killing of the female at the hands of the male, yes. But also the crucifixion of the feminine, the systematic "cutting off" of power by the masculine. I was Sedna.

Even more pertinent was that Sedna was an indication of deep, buried anger and a feeling of powerlessness. As artist Thalia Took says about Sedna on her website, "Unacknowledged or disowned anger can lead to depression. However, this anger or buried emotion is in fact very powerful and needs to be accessed, acknowledged, or released in a safe manner. Take your cue from the shaman's journey and treat this inner angry person with compassion and soothing gestures. Above all, listen."

Life went on; my reputation as a "Wise Woman" got around the valley and I was approached to write a weekly column in a San Luis Valley magazine. The title of the column was "Wise Words from the Valley Shamama." I was channeling regularly in small groups and facilitating healing through quiet counsel. Things were building for me. A different kind of power flowed through me, and it was blissful.

I learned much about the area, and perhaps why my inner life had become so amplified. A geologist told me that because of the mineral content in the area, the valley is known for anomalies. For example, she told me that mining companies hire geologists to use fancy computer equipment to find mineral ore under the ground, but that the most reliable way to find desired minerals is to watch the flocks of birds flying in the sky. When they fly over mineral-rich areas, the flock becomes disorganized and disperses. This is because *gravity fluctuates depending on the density of the mineral content in the area the birds are flying over.* I also learned that the area has a high quartz crystalline content. We know that quartz is used as an amplifier in technology, and it is an amplifier for me, as well.

I found that I was riding a wave or being carried by a current that was taking me somewhere. I could feel a clear destination point in my future, but I did not know where it was. My relationship with my newly recovered Aunt Wendy was building. I was happy to have her in my life again, but I did not allow her to get too close to me. My mistrust of my mother and women came roaring to the surface, and I kept Wendy at a safe distance while I became accustomed to her presence in our lives. As we got to know each other again, we spoke of memories from our earlier history. We compared notes and listened to one another talk about the challenges of our family of origin, as well as the good things. I was so grateful to have a woman in my family acknowledge me for all of the hard work I had done to heal myself and to become a more conscious person/parent.

I was getting clearer by the day. My intuition was off the charts, and I brought in multiple intelligences to support my writing and facilitating clients/students. My first book, *Love Letter – A Message of Comfort, Self Care and Sanity in Stimulating Times*, published in 2008, was designed to reground and reorient people in a time of big change. Since there were multiple sources of misinformation about 2012 being apocalyptic, I wanted to share the reassuring messages and strategies I had been given. I did not realize the book would be a predictor of the impending economic downturn and collective discouragement.

I also created several classes that taught whole-brain collage techniques due to my experiences in which I consciously partnered with my subconscious to retrieve information. I was becoming an expert in diving deep into the watery world of Great Mother and the psyche.

My personal and professional process deepened as I explored the healing of our inner children, creative arts, and the right brain as a means to access our subconscious. The blending of these techniques along with spiritual wisdom was profound and direct; what used to take years in traditional psychotherapy was taking moments. As a direct response to the cracking open of my heart, my inner children came to the surface *en masse*, freed from a closed chamber and invited into the light. Miracles abounded. My life became remarkably joyful even though we encountered the hardships in our community.

My work became even more healing-oriented, as I saw the tremendous impact that dialoguing with these inner children had on collective health and wellbeing. The development of my collaging technique relied upon subconscious discovery of parts of self that were hidden from plain sight; these parts could derail and sabotage our lives if they were not acknowledged and healed. Rogue parts of self driving my life—no more of that, thank you! I wanted to be a good leader to my inner parts, and I was learning how to be just that from Great Mother, the archetypal energy that had been flowing through my life for the last several years. I began to understand that this was truly my work—to mother my inner children, and to mother women, and to love myself like a good mother would.

How Do I Love Me? Let Me Count the Ways. . . .

Self-love became a primary intention for me in the next step on my personal journey. I find it interesting that when I opened more to the archetypal Great Mother energy, SELF-LOVE became my goal (instead of some of the other intentions, like abundance or prosperity or other such "outer" validation).

Here is a self-help article I published on my blog in 2007:

I don't like myself, I'm CRAZY about myself!
— Mae West, 1892–1980

I wonder what the world would be like if we all felt this way? If we could all say genuinely, without reservation, "I'm crazy about myself!"

If you are one of the fortunate people who already understands and implements the powerful choice to love yourself and enjoy the vast benefits, then you are ahead of most of humanity on the learning curve.

But many of us recoil in horror at the thought. "That would be egotistical!" "I would be embarrassed to say that." Or, "That would be selfish and arrogant!" We are not always taught to love ourselves; in fact, most of us were taught to put love of others over love of self, and this is why we see the pain that is prevalent. It is truly not possible to love others from a place of non-love for self. If everyone loved themselves, it would be a very different world.

What if I were to say that the universe is literally made of love? Do you doubt it? What other force but love could explain the sheer generosity that made everything? What other force but love could cause the grass to grow effortlessly, and the sun to shine every day, and the infinite diversity of consciousness that sprawls all over the universe? You are Source energy! How is it possible that you could be unlovable? Grass does not doubt itself and slump over, refusing to grow, and a flower does not feel self-loathing and decide it is not worthy to shine its face to the sun. All there is . . . is love . . . or the rejection of it. How are you rejecting love in your life? What better place to start to see love in the world than inside ourselves? How could we possibly have any effective measure of influence on the love in the world if we don't love ourselves first?

And what if I were to take it a step further and say that to truly love others, you MUST take care of yourself first, otherwise you have nothing to give? I love the quote from Esther Hicks when she channeled Abraham:

> "Be ultimately selfless in being ultimately selfish by saying that I care so much about you that I will insist on being in my place of utter connection so that I have something to give you . . . because if I do not tend to that, I do not have anything to give you, and if I do tend to that, then I have everything to give you."

So how do we joyfully surrender to loving ourselves unconditionally?

The quickest path to self-love that I know is to *decide it*. What I mean by that is to consciously choose to love myself. One of the intentions I speak every day is "I choose to love myself unconditionally, and I ask my angel team to help me do that." Then I follow up with choices that support that intention, such as being kind to myself in little ways, smiling into my eyes in the mirror, and laughing. For example, when faced with a choice to watch a scary movie or a funny one, I ask myself, "Which is more loving to me in this moment?" and most often, I choose the funny one. I feel better after laughing than I do after jumping out of my skin!

I also take myself out on "dates." I insist on alone time because it helps to ground and center me. (This can be challenging as a member of a family of four!) And I have begun to "court" myself. . . . I wear things that make my body feel good, like something soft, or maybe pick out some extra-fancy jewelry (instead of my usual practical kind) and then I look in the mirror and say, "Ooooh baby, you are looking *good* tonight!" Just the other night, I was in the hot tub with my husband and surprised myself totally by kissing myself on the shoulder. Out of nowhere! It was completely unconscious! I guess those self-love messages are really getting through! I crack myself up.

Did you know that Queen Latifah made a promise to herself that she would not marry anyone until she married herself first? She had very positive and strong female role models when she was growing up and therefore had the reflection of loving eyes and sweet encouragement. She knows she is precious. She loves herself so much that she bought herself a wedding ring and put it on her right ring finger, a symbol of how she chose to wed herself before wedding any other. WOW. Unapologetic, passionate, fierce devotion to self. Can't mess with that!

When you think about it, on this Earth we are all we've got. Yes, for a time we may have a beloved, or children to dote on, or friends to laugh with, but we know that things change and that in the end, we are left with our own precious self. Therefore, speaking practically, it is a good investment to start loving yourself NOW!

To love oneself is the beginning of a life-long romance.
— **Oscar Wilde, 1854–1900**

What Does Self-Love Mean?

Does it mean you get to eat ice cream every night just because you want it? Well, sure, as long as you love the possible consequences of that choice! Sometimes the choices we make are out of a place of NOT loving ourselves. Are you making choices out of self-love or self-loathing?

Just as a lack of self-love has a vibration, so does unconditional self-love. It has a quiet, steady radiance that draws others to its light. I define self-love as a deeper, quieter love—that you hold yourself in the way you would hold a baby or your sweetest lover, so tenderly, because you realize that you truly *are* a Child of the Universe and the Lover of the Sacred.

And we are not talking halfway here! Unconditional love is true love, love without limitations, conditions, or reservations. This means loving ALL aspects of yourself, not just the ones that are "nice," or more "spiritual," or "attractive." You learn to accept every aspect of yourself, even the ones you might think of as "negative." The universe is full of the balance of positive/negative, dark/light, up/down, hot/cold. It is the nature of things to have balance, and all things that exist are here for a reason, including all of the aspects of YOU. Any unloved aspects of the self will cry out for love in ways that can keep you bound to the inner and outer drama.

If we are not taught to love ourselves, how do we begin to turn the tide and feel genuine caring for all parts of ourselves? Self-love does not happen by luck or the grace of God. You have to choose to create it. Some things that I choose to remember are:

- Knowing that I am more than my physical body. I am very clear that I am an infinite being who chose to come here for the fabulous experience of playing and creating in physical reality. I love my physical existence and the opportunity to be here in this life.

- Knowing I am a powerful co-creator. I have the power to choose how to co-create with the rest of the universe. This power is both the greatest responsibility I have *and* the greatest opportunity.

- Knowing that I am always in process and always becoming. I honor where I am in my process without judgment.

- Knowing that my feelings are powerful indicators of what I am creating, and therefore, valuable information. I treasure my feelings and I respond to them with reverence. They are indeed part of my inner guidance system. I acknowledge my feelings, and then act from them, even if it means setting a limit with someone or saying "no."

A Self-Love Ritual

If you have been looking for a way to create a new spark in your relationship with yourself, a **love ritual** might be just the idea for you. Try this exercise: light a candle in a quiet room where you will not be interrupted. Invite your highest aspects into the ritual to assist you (whoever you feel they may be. Use your words: highest teachers, masters, angels, Source, etc.). Read this passage excerpted from the Bible, and while reading it, feel as if the words are written for you (they are).

Imagine you are reading this to you, sitting across the flame from yourself. Feel the words go into your heart.

Love is patient, love is kind.
It does not envy, it does not boast, it is not proud.
It is not rude, it is not self-seeking.
It is not easily angered, it keeps no record of wrongs.
Love does not delight in evil, but rejoices with the truth.
It always protects, always trusts, always hopes, always perseveres.
Love never fails.

— I Corinthians 13:4–8

Can you allow yourself to feel this great love for you? Are you open to the possibility that when these words were spoken by the master Jesus, that he was indeed speaking about loving yourself unconditionally? Notice the feelings that come up while you read this to your Beloved Self. What beliefs do you hold about yourself that prevent you from experiencing this kind of love? Write them down. Then, in this ceremonial space, set the intention to release those beliefs. Breathe deeply with each intention to seat it in your body. You may even want to burn those pieces of paper with the old, outdated beliefs written on them. Then set your intentions to do the following (read aloud):

- Love myself unconditionally
- Experience and embody the unconditional love that I truly am
- Allow unconditional love from Prime Source to flow through me and radiate outwards to all I come in contact with
- See myself as the Angels and Prime Source see me, and love myself as the Angels and Prime Source love me

Close the Love Ritual by thanking your Beloved Self/Prime Source/ the Angels/all of your helpers for guiding you.

> *You, yourself, as much as anybody in the entire universe, deserve your love and affection.*
>
> — **Buddha**

You are a miracle. You have within you incredible power and beauty. Your inner power and beauty give you the freedom to find success, peace, love, self-confidence, and the joy of aliveness. It is your birthright to experience life and its deepest satisfactions.

In making those choices every day to love ourselves as we would love our child or our most tender lover, and taking action to do sweet things for ourselves, we literally change our reality. We feel more at peace in the world, we attract more joyful opportunities and intersections, we draw more love into our lives, and life becomes the miracle it was intended to be.

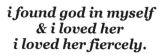

> *i found god in myself*
> *& i loved her*
> *i loved her fiercely.*
>
> — **Ntozake Shange**

~ End of article ~

I was successful in my quest to love myself. One afternoon, I was writing and "heard" Her voice say, *"Congratulations!"*

I stopped my writing and put all of my attention on my inner world, and asked, "Congratulations for what?"

I then "heard" (I put "heard" in quotes because it is more like feeling, or understanding, then translating the body of energy into words—not so much like hearing with our ears, but with our hearts), *"You've reached fifty-one percent."*

I was puzzled. I asked, "Fifty-one percent of what?"

The guidance said, *"Fifty-one percent self-love. You now, in this moment, love yourself more than you do not love yourself."*

I broke down in grateful tears.

~ ~ ~

The dichotomy of my self-love success and the loathing on the outer world side of things grew. The larger valley community was not altogether thrilled with me. While I had a small audience of women (and a few men) who were interested in and supported my work, the greater community of religious and conservative folks did not appreciate my speaking with such a "different" voice. My children were increasingly teased at school, I felt an odd shadow come over our property, and the San Luis Valley Pastoral Alliance held a meeting to discuss "what to do about Licia Berry, who is threatening to undermine good Christian values." The witch hunt had begun!

I even needed to protect myself from Peter's mother (again). My experience of her since our second meeting when she had shared intimate details of her insane mother (and the subsequent decades after) was as a person who did not observe boundaries (but kept very tight ones for herself). During one visit to Colorado, she cornered me in the kitchen, pressing into my personal space in a way that made me very uncomfortable. This was her usual way, but in the past, I had simply lived with it silently. This time, I said, "I'm going to ask you to back up a bit," and I put my hands up to demonstrate the motion I wanted her to make.

She backed up, looked stricken, and said, "You're hurting my feelings. When you say that I feel rejected."

I told her that when she was in my personal space I did not feel safe. I then crowded up next to her and then backed away to demonstrate where my preferred personal boundary was. She went flying out of the room and outside, where Peter's father was loading my children into the car. I watched through the picture window as she gesticulated wildly to him, speaking and emoting in front of my children about what had just happened. My civilized attempt to take care of myself had been perceived as an attack.

Survival became a prevalent theme. Our family was suffering due to the bigotry of the religious community, the environment of the high desert strained our ease (our hardest winter had snow on the ground for four months, sometimes up to our hips!), the economic recession was impacting our livelihoods, and I was having trouble finding real friends. So often, women would be attracted to me because of my work, but then they wanted to be my friend. . . and then they would ask me for the same guidance but wanted it for free. In other words, they wanted me to be their mother. This led to a quandary for me. My natural inclination to care and to give generously was taxed by their requests, and I was high and dry and felt no return/exchange for my giving. In fact, our little town felt to us like a greedy, hungry child, demanding the breast (our time, money, resources) with no awareness of exchange.

What a ninny I was! Here I was being groomed to become "a mother to women" and I did not even know it! All of the years of Great Mother speaking to me, from the very beginning, were so I could be a vessel for Her love! But my unhealed pain due to my own unmothering left me needy and seeking understanding from other women. How could I be available for them if my own cup was not filled?

How interesting that I would be guided to love myself in an environment that felt hostile, unwelcoming? I could not help but wonder if I was being guided through my outer environment to heal the old story of not feeling loved in my family. My understanding grew about how people's beliefs form and how they create their lives from those beliefs. If I believe that you are evil, that is how I will see you, no matter how you try to help me to see otherwise. Projection is a powerful drug.

Psychological Projection is defined as the act or technique of defending oneself against unpleasant impulses by denying their existence in oneself, while attributing them to others. For example, the projection onto me by people in our little town that I was a witch had little to do with me and much to do with their own unhealed relationship with the feminine. I realized at this time that the projection of my mother's own unhealed fear of her mother warped her view of me, her daughter. The evil inside of her was much easier to disown and place on me, a convenient (and as a child, defenseless) target.

My in-laws were doing it, too! The wild stories they concocted in their heads about me included fears that I would not seek medical care for my children if needed (because of my use of holistic therapies), fear that I would not allow them to see my children, fear that I had "joined a cult"—all insane, unfounded, and completely off base. I was mystified and disappointed that these seemingly intelligent people were not aware to be critical of their fears, discerning of their own minds. They seemed to be playing out some unresolved internal issues by putting my face on it. I seemed to represent their mothers to them. I don't feel qualified to diagnose them, but I suspect that there may be some unhealed childhood wounding there.

I began researching the Black Madonnas and how they were stained whiter and whiter through the evolution of the Christian church. Could there be a correlation between the rejection of the dark or yin of Great Mother and the Sacred Feminine and the codifying of the feminine through the pale Mother Mary we had all become accustomed to seeing? Was this similar to the projection of my community onto me, because I was closer to the Earth, of more indigenous beliefs? Did they want to "whitewash" me, too?

I planned a retreat to bring women back into the arms of Great Mother, similar to my own journey, in part due to my frustration at being "mother" to people who were not my children, and, in part, because I wanted Great Mother to take women to the heart of their divinity.

Black Madonna
at Swiss Abbey of Einsiedeln

I Sound a Call to the Women

I co-led a women's retreat in May 2008 at Ghost Ranch, in the wild, open, high desert of northern New Mexico. I hold women's retreats there at least once a year because I feel the presence of Great Mother there very strongly. The land there carries an extraordinarily nurturing energy for me. Fittingly, the women's retreat in 2008 was entitled "Loving Your Inner

Feminine," and the stated intention of the retreat was: "To facilitate the experience of and to cultivate relationship with the Divine Feminine/Great Mother within, so as to access the rich, nourishing, and abundant resources She brings to our psyche, our Wholeness and humanity." There, a group of courageous women gathered on Mother's Day to learn how to love themselves unconditionally.

We talked about our mothers, about mothering, about being mothered. We talked about how mother is our primary relationship; all other relationships are secondary to the relationship each of us has with our mother, our source of life and origination point into the world. We felt our wounds, touched them gently, and then began to rewrite our stories through art, music, sharing, walking the labyrinth with our prayers.

We ended the retreat with my "Invocation of the Great Mother Within" (see page 41). All of us were touched by the restoration of Great Mother's unconditional love during that retreat. Some of the women had a hard time receiving it at first; their belief that they were unworthy of it was so pervasive that they initially rejected the sensation of being loved without conditions. But by the end, all women carried the renewal of awareness of what it feels like. Like a seed in dark soil, watered with Great Mother's gentle touch, the knowing of their worth began to grow.

But who or what is Great Mother? I experience Her as my ideal mother—kind, allowing, accepting, guiding, soft, embracing, nurturing, honest, insightful, powerful, responsible, wise, and ancient as the universe. She speaks in kindness, looks upon me with love and adoration in her eyes, and is fiercely protective when I am unsafe. This is the kind of mother I needed as a child and the kind of mother I have strived to be for my children. She is a model in my mind as well as a feeling in my heart and a knowing in my body. She exists—there is no question. Whether She is a figment of my conjuring, an aspect of my own psyche, an energy of the universe or an actual deity (or all of the above) does not matter to me. I feel Her energy when I put my attention on Her, and Her energy changes me for the better. As far as I am concerned, She is as real as I am.

After the retreat, it became clear that I was a woman who had things to do. Women were hungry for the experience of feminine energy and learning what it actually IS. I found that I could articulate my experiences of the feminine to a degree, but I wanted to be able to describe qualities in our daily lives that are feminine in nature.

My family took weekend trip, a much-needed respite from our lives, and went to explore a town on the other side of the rural mountain range. We had a great weekend and were on our way home when the boys freaked out in the back seat, both breaking into tears and insisting that they did NOT want to go back to school in the fall and did not want to go back to the San Luis Valley. Peter and I were jolted by the clarity of their voices and their request; there was a gravity and purity that seemed divinely inspired, there was no question. This was a matter of our family's physical, emotional, mental, and spiritual health. We decided then and there to get the hell out of Dodge.

We packed the RV again and prepared the house for our departure. We were guided not to put the house on the market, so assumed we would be on the road again for a while and would return to the valley at some point. How long would we be gone? NO idea. We were once again Travelin' Berrys! It was like 2003 all over again!

We hit the road in October 2008 and headed south to Tucson, Arizona, where my Aunt Wendy lived with her sweet husband Zach. We found a rural campground in Tucson, stayed there for several weeks, and had a wonderful time exploring our familial bonds with Wendy. She loved my children and Peter, and they loved her. She expressed dismay that my biological mother was not showing up for me and expressed how much my mother was missing because my family was so wonderful.

Wendy's love for us was unconditional. There was no agenda, no extraction of promises, no obligations. She loved us simply because we were. I did not quite know what to make of this love from a woman; I had not encountered the freedom to be loved without being asked to conform to someone else's idea of who I was. She loved me for being me? Was it possible? In my parental relationships, I had always been expected to morph myself to their agenda in order to meet their approval. Could it be that I was lovable without becoming someone else?

Why wasn't she my mother?

From Tucson, we resumed our travel habit of asking for guidance and were led to move west to the coast of California, beginning just north of San Diego and bumping up the coast. We visited San Juan Capistrano (home of the returning swallows), Dana Point, and Thousand Oaks in the L.A. area. (Have you ever taken a thirty-five-foot RV through Los Angeles???) I made a point of meeting some women Facebook friends who are devoted to the Sacred Feminine and saw old paintings of the Mother Mary with Jesus on the breast at the Getty Museum. I was delighted to feel the feminine "above ground" in California. What a relief!

We were then guided to move north to San Luis Obispo, where we spent the next several months getting to know the area. We LOVED it. We met our soul family there, similar to the Albuquerque, New Mexico area, and felt such a connection to the place. We traveled north a bit to Santa Cruz and enjoyed exploring the land, beaches, and mountains, the forests of sequoia, but we were led back down to San Luis Obispo.

Something about the San Luis Obispo area touched me in a deep and profound way. It opened me to powerful energy within myself that seemed to flow from deep underground. We biked and walked the land there constantly, using the fire roads to head into the golden hills. The land spoke sweetly, and on one of the fire roads that connected to our campground at a regional park, I found a spring coming up through a rock. It sang to me and felt so special, as if its song was inviting me into an ancient grove of old. I recognized the voice of Great Mother through that spring.

Joy
Collage © 2008 Licia Berry

Those months in San Luis Obispo were a time when I felt very joyful. The weather was ideal for my body (Mediterranean climate), I was active and outdoors constantly, and I felt inspired again to cleanse my body through a vegetarian food plan. (I had done this a few times in my life at opportune junctures of spiritual growth.) I felt amazing, better than I had felt in years.

I was guided to visit a woman I had connected with online, a Jungian psychotherapist who was a pioneer in bringing awareness of the Divine Feminine back into the world. She wrote a lovely book speaking from the point of view of Mary Magdalene that both Peter and I read and resonated with. We had wondered at times in our relationship if we were playing out a divine partnership that was older and bigger than just the two of us. The story of Jesus and Mary Magdalene as partners and equals seemed more plausible to these rebellious hearts of ours, rather than the story of Mary being a prostitute. We knew the equality in our relationship was a powerful force that others could feel, and it made sense to us that a leader such as Jesus would have an equally impactful leader at his side in his beloved.

I made a special overnight trip down to see this woman in Los Angeles and visited with her for a couple of hours. We spoke about the feminine, about mother, about society and life, and I shared with her some of what was occurring for me in my personal process of recognizing the feminine as the holder of All Things. She affirmed me and told me that *the feminine IS primary, primal, first, number one . . . in fact, The One . . .* in the universe and to all of us, since we emerge from a mother.

Being in her presence seemed to open and activate something for me, something I could not quite articulate at the time. This was a guided, directed, and intense twenty-four-hour trip that I did not fully understand until later, in retrospect, as being formative in my life.

Sacred Systems™

The channeling got ever deeper, with entire bodies of work being presented. Peter and I set up "sessions," chunks of devoted time in which he wrote down the information that came through me. (It was too distracting for me to keep the space open within me, dowse for accuracy—something I had learned from an elder mountain woman in Asheville—and write at the same time.) He also asked clarifying questions, and really good ones! There was something about Peter being there, holding the space with me, that seemed to encourage the information, as if the two of us together created some kind of ideal vessel for the information to come through. There was a feeling, too; it reminded me of when we first met and had the sense that there was something larger than us, pulling us together. It felt to me as if we were fulfilling and refining our purpose together as a couple.

It was here at the end of 2008 and into 2009 that a body of information that we call "The UNIFY Codex" (part of our Sacred Systems™ work) came through us. The UNIFY Codex revealed to us the basic mechanics of systems, from the smallest particle to the largest organism; we learned that every system has energy centers (similar to chakras, but not the same as the human chakra system) and how systems are made of feminine and masculine energy. It was the prelude to a major body of work that would come through me later, one that would change our lives.

As we deepened our connections to San Luis Obispo and the wonderful people with whom we swiftly fell in love, my craving to find our next home was met with a belief that this was the place. The guidance I had access to was from a more masculine orientation, the left-brain system of seeing things as black/white or binary—either this or that, closed or open, yes or no. This is a wonderful tool for getting very specific information, but not so great for nuances and larger bodies of information. *I didn't realize it at the time, but my brain was changing as a result of intentionally and consciously working with the Sacred Feminine.* My orientation had been more masculine when seeking information—intellectual, go-get-it, achieve-the-goal, be accurate and precise—and became a claim to fame in my spiritual facilitation with clients. Now, the Feminine approach was giving me access to a tremendous amount of information, but not in a specific, pointed way. It was similar to the difference between painting with a broad brush or a quill pen, or the difference between being clairvoyant and psychic.

It then fell on me to ask specific questions and check the accuracy of the larger body of information through the question and answer method I had been taught; I felt it was the responsible thing to do. I received the larger body of information through my right brain (my feminine brain, and the doorway into the subconscious and larger intelligence, I discovered), and then I shifted into my left brain (my masculine brain, the hemisphere that deals in detailed and deductive information) to break the body of information down, articulate and fact-check it, then be able to write about it and teach it to others.

I realized that my years of training as an educator utilizing Brain Gym, working with children with brain disorders in Arizona, as well as my work with systems (the system of family, in particular) had perfectly prepared me to delve into this whole-brain territory. I understood the mechanics of how my brain processes the information, so it gave me a context for understanding my "channeling" and not being afraid of it. I developed an entire professional and life philosophy of being "whole-brained," realizing that we have missed so much, focusing as a culture on the left brain and its particular way of understanding the world.

Personally, I could feel something happening in the center of my head. It was not a good or bad feeling, but an awareness of something occurring in my own brain, a feeling of slight pressure or "activation" in the area of my pineal gland.

I asked for guidance about this to check myself out and was told that I was moving toward "Central Hemispheric Union" or *Sacred Union in my brain.* I had always thought the concept of

Sacred Union was a spiritual one, but the material coming through me said that the brain is where we achieve Sacred Union, and that it is *expressed through the heart* if we are fortunate enough to embody it. It is actually a physical possibility, but it starts in our brain.

I have learned through direct experience and repeated testing of this material that if we are in a whole-brain state, we are connected to "the Divine" and actually feel and experience that we are not alone. The alternative is the left-brain-dominant culture we have all grown up in. The evidence of how disconnected we feel lies in the epidemic of depression, addiction, and the prevalence of the electronic devices that help us feel connected to something bigger than ourselves (the internet, our new God). The advent of language began our journey into left-brain development, and the worship of the intellect and reason as "civilization" has denigrated the indigenous ways of connected spirituality and effectively separated us from our direct experience of God. (This is why young children have experiences of the sacred and supernatural, as they are not indoctrinated into the left-brain dominance until they get old enough to go to school.) Patriarchy actually separates us from our direct inner experience of the divine through encouraging censorship of the right brain, and therefore the feminine. It has become my mission in my work to reconnect and affirm the Sacred Union in our brains; I believe this is how we will see culture change.

The information coming through was extraordinary, affirming, life-changing, and I felt a great sense of excitement and satisfaction with being privy to the inner workings of the universe. Sessions with Peter getting The UNIFY Codex were astonishing, and we were learning so much about our systems, which were defined as "two or more parts coming together under a unifying intention." From that point of view, EVERYTHING is a system—the universe, our solar system, our planet, our country, our community, our family, our marriage, ourselves, our bodies, parts of our bodies, our brain. Everything in existence is a system.

The intersection of all the spiritual work I had done with this practical, grounded information was such a thrill for me. It answered so many questions about the mechanics of the universe that I had been asking since I was a child.

True Embodiment (be careful what you ask for . . . and how you ask for it)

Darkness precedes light and she is mother

— **Inscription in the altar of the Salerno Cathedral in Italy**

In 2008, our beloved Wendy came to Pismo Beach for a retreat and to see us. My Grandmother Ruby had died, and Wendy was her primary end-of-life caregiver in Tucson. Wendy had not had a chance to be alone and grieve, and we were thrilled she wanted to come be with us in our newfound paradise of the San Luis Obispo area. She was a mothering presence for me, and yet, at the same time, I was a mothering presence for her. I taught her several techniques to guide her growth process and provided a listening ear as she began to work through her mother's death.

A few days after she arrived, I stepped out of the RV to take an afternoon bike ride and slipped on the stairs. Reconstructing the moment, I stepped out with my left foot onto the sandy top step of the RV without firmly placing my foot down, and I went flying. When I landed at the bottom of the stairs, my right foot was floppy and twisted at a very odd angle. I remember looking at my foot and saying, "Oh, shit," then calling in to the RV that I thought I had broken my ankle and for the kids not to look. They did, of course. Peter and the boys were very upset, mobilizing immediately to help me into the car to get care. Fortunately, Wendy was in town and came to stay with the boys while Peter took me to the hospital. My fractured and severely dislocated fibula required surgery to hold everything together so it could heal.

It was a traumatic event for my family. Peter and the boys had never seen me in a physically broken state, vulnerable and needing help. What followed was some months of them stepping into a more active support role, and my embodiment of the feminine continued. As I wrote on my blog in "Ode to My Ankle," March 11, 2009, "[O]f note is the inner process that has been accelerated due to the whirlwind destruction of my bodily innocence and the surrender required to allow other people to help me when I am accustomed to surviving on my own. I have always been a very strong and healthy person, having very few accidental injuries in my life, relegated to the occasional burn or cut, not counting the fall from the top of the magnolia tree at age twelve. Even in my rash of car accidents in my barely-present early twenties, I walked away without even a bruise. Never having broken a bone or been to the hospital except for birthing Jess and a small cut that required stitches when I was eleven, this accident 'broke' my vision of myself as invulnerable."

My choice to embody the Feminine had led me to curtail my unpartnered inner masculine, my default, both in times of stress and as a primary way of life. I had felt since I was a teen that the right side of my body was my masculine and my left the feminine side. I had been leading from the masculine, the right side (I was right-handed, led with the right foot, etc.) as long as I could remember. Now, my right leg was incapacitated and my left had to take on the role of leader. I needed to learn to "lead with the feminine" in a very real way.

My inner and outer life was a swirl of changes. My family stepped in as the "masculine"—active and protective—and I experienced the feminine in a completely new way for me— receptive, allowing. The immensity of the transformation was evident in my dreams, evidence from the subconscious as to the depth of upset and restoration.

Dream, March 4, 2009

(I broke my ankle on February 23, 2009)

My family and I are somewhere in California, still sort of checking it out, thinking it is an interesting place to live but with kind of mixed feelings.

We are in a location with underground caves, but close to the surface and easy to access. A woman and two men are our "guides" to get us down into the caves.

When we reach the entrance that will take us to the caves, they produce two machines. Each machine has a single tank tread instead of wheels, but can be ridden like a motorcycle, with a flat seat that several people can ride on.

We all stand at the entrance, which is swampy and boggy, with watery dirt and plants. The "guides" are discussing the best way to get through this part. They take a long time and deliberate with each other. Peter and the boys jump on their machines and zoom off, apparently quite confident about where to go into the caves. They go right over the bog and take a right tunnel into the caves.

I stand closer to the "guides" who are taking a long time trying to figure things out and carefully examining the best route. I explain that I have a freshly broken ankle and that we have to be careful, and I look down and see my ankle the way it is in waking life, wrapped in splint and bandages. I don't see my crutches anywhere.

I want to be with my family. I move toward the two tunnels, and see a rivulet of water where the marshy area has dried up on either side. I leap, leading with my left foot, across the rivulet, and land safely on the other side, where I begin to travel down a LEFT tunnel into the cave, leaving the "guides" behind.

I am now in the caves, trying to find Peter and the boys, calling them but not seeing them. I know they are close. I can feel them. I continue to move around (somehow without crutches). The cave is beautiful, with high ceilings and interesting rock formations, organic-looking curvy shapes and colors. Gorgeous!

I continue to move around, and apparently, the caves have easy access to the surface, because I unintentionally wind up walking into what feels like a natural history museum (my favorite kind of museum!). When I walk through the doors, quite surprised, a lovely black woman wearing a red dress, an afro, and a big smile (she apparently works there) says, "OH, you must not have gone to the LIGHT!"

In my mind's eye, I see a choice point in the cave where I could have continued into the caves or come to the surface, and that I must have missed the sign that said "INTO THE LIGHT" that pointed into the caves. I am confused because this seems counter-intuitive. It is light where the museum is, and deeper into the caves would be dark. I say to the woman, "I must have!" and go out of the museum into the outdoors.

~ ~ ~

I do not remember if the dream continues—whether I get back down into the caves or whether I find the boys. I feel them close when I am in the museum, but I feel they might still be underground.

Seeking more information about the possible meaning of my dream, I went into a deeper internal space to ask the greater intelligence for guidance. Greater intelligence did not disappoint, and spoke to me of significant implications:

> *The caves are the feminine universe. Yes, the feminine was first (the First Individuation into masculine/feminine) because the feminine is the holder of space within which creation occurs.*

Peter and the boys go confidently into the caves because they know where to go—they are symbols of the masculine having "right relationship" with the feminine and the Great Mother energy.

In your life, you are more like the "guides" from your dream, or have been up to this point. You try to figure things out and discuss the nature of things, while the guys, just as they did in the dream, go on and experience it. In the dream, you are between them when you make the leap, with your left foot leading, over the rivulet.

(I realize that, in a sense, the guys have encouraged/forced me to leap because I want to be with them, and they have gone ahead. They are leaders for me into the feminine!)

This dream is a picture of where you are right now. You ARE leading with the left, feminine foot/side, but have not yet made the decision to ENTER THE FEMININE. The fact that you unconsciously found your way into a place of fun, higher learning and mind (similar to the discussing "guides") says that you tend to drift toward that rather than diving purposefully into the feminine.

The feminine is THE LIGHT for you, and that is where you need to go. The friendly, smiling, black woman seemed quite certain that you made a mistake, winding up at the museum accidentally, as if she knew what was down there in the dark of the Earth and had explored it, and here she was at the surface knowing its tunnels and traverses below.

This ankle break has happened for DEEP HEALING to occur—not to warn you away from something, not as a lesson or punishment or course correction, although you will learn much from this, but for DEEP HEALING. You are coming back into your own nature, the essence of the universe of which you are a part, and who you are. The feminine IS primary, primal, first, number 1. This is about you coming into right relationship with the Great Mother.

~ ~ ~

I had to learn how to lead with the feminine.

~ ~ ~

Back to Colorado

After a couple of weeks to get me stable (and for everyone to recover from the shock), we felt it was correct for me to recover on the ground (the RV was a challenging place to get around on crutches), so we packed up the RV and traveled back to the property in Colorado. Peter's parents supported our return by escorting us and staying with us for a few days. They were always happy to support in physical and financial ways, even if the emotional support was less than perfect. It was an uneasy visit because there were still hurt feelings all the way around from our period of no contact, and everyone seemed on edge.

The couch became my constant companion, and my sons cared for me while they home-schooled and Peter was at our office. It became apparent quickly that the valley was not a supportive place to live as not a single person came to help us while I recovered. We were grateful for the confirmation of our feelings about the valley (and our wondering if there was something wrong with us!) after the experience of such loving and welcoming community in San Luis Obispo. We were just in a place that did not know what to do with us.

This beautiful land, vast, immense, with soaring skies and high mountains, attracted people who had a vision of a beautiful life. The Utes had hunted and prayed in this mystical valley. Then the Spanish conquered them and set up homesteads, claiming this land for their own. Catholicism came with them, and the indigenous people who had not been killed or chased away were "civilized" in missions. For many years, Catholicism reigned as the primary spiritual tradition in the San Luis Valley, until the white European settlers came with their new Christian ways. The valley was steeped in religious, conservative traditions and we did not belong to any of these traditions. We were more like the indigenous people who initially lived on this land, and we felt perhaps as they felt—driven out.

Interesting to me, as I learned more about Catholicism, was that it is one of the few Christian traditions that honors the feminine through the Divine Mother, or Mother Mary. I wondered if my experience of the Divine Feminine and Great Mother might make me a good Catholic. The Catholic Church certainly had its reputation for atrocities over the course of history (as did every other religious tradition, one of the reasons I shied away from religion in the first place).

As I contemplated the presence of the Mother in this valley, so deeply steeped in the land and the generations of Hispanic families, I did some research and found that Great Mother had recently touched the papal offices of the Catholic Church in the form of the Day of Pardon, a public apology issued for acts which condoned centuries of cruel and abusive treatment against countless peoples, asking God's forgiveness for sins committed throughout history by the "sons and daughters" of the Church. The apology does not set everything right, well, and redeemed, but it represents a significant insight and reflection on the part of the Catholic Church about the atrocities committed by the Church in God's name. I feel this is evidence of the presence of Great Mother and the Divine Feminine coming to the surface of the collective human psyche and an invitation into our next phase of development as a species. In the apology (read it in full from the link provided in the Additional Resources section at the end of this book), we see admission of the Church's role in the degradation of women, and people of diverse cultures, ethnicities, and religions.

I consider this section especially pertinent:

CONFESSION OF SINS AGAINST THE PEOPLE OF ISRAEL

A representative of the Roman Curia:
Let us pray that, in recalling the sufferings
endured by the people of Israel throughout history,
Christians will acknowledge the sins
committed by not a few of their number
against the people of the Covenant and the blessings,
and in this way will purify their hearts.

The Holy Father:
God of our fathers,
you chose Abraham and his descendants
to bring your Name to the Nations:
we are deeply saddened by the behaviour of those
who in the course of history
have caused these children of yours to suffer,
and asking your forgiveness we wish to commit ourselves
to genuine brotherhood
with the people of the Covenant.
We ask this through Christ our Lord.

CONFESSION OF SINS COMMITTED IN ACTIONS AGAINST LOVE, PEACE, THE RIGHTS OF PEOPLES, AND RESPECT FOR CULTURES AND RELIGIONS

A representative of the Roman Curia:
Let us pray that contemplating Jesus,
our Lord and our Peace,
Christians will be able to repent of the words and attitudes
caused by pride, by hatred,
by the desire to dominate others,

by enmity towards members of other religions
and towards the weakest groups in society,
such as immigrants and itinerants.

The Holy Father:
Lord of the world, Father of all,
through your Son
you asked us to love our enemies,
to do good to those who hate us
and to pray for those who persecute us.
Yet Christians have often denied the Gospel;
yielding to a mentality of power,
they have violated the rights of ethnic groups and
peoples,
and shown contempt for their cultures and religious
traditions:
be patient and merciful towards us, and grant us your
forgiveness!
We ask this through Christ our Lord.

CONFESSION OF SINS AGAINST THE DIGNITY OF WOMEN AND THE UNITY OF THE HUMAN RACE

A Representative of the Roman Curia:
Let us pray for all those who have suffered offences
against their human dignity and whose rights have been
trampled;
let us pray for women, who are all too often humiliated
and emarginated,
and let us acknowledge the forms of acquiescence in these
sins
of which Christians too have been guilty.

The Holy Father:
Lord God, our Father,
you created the human being, man and woman,
in your image and likeness

*and you willed the diversity of peoples
within the unity of the human family.
At times, however, the equality of your sons
and daughters has not been acknowledged,
and Christians have been guilty of attitudes
of rejection and exclusion,
consenting to acts of discrimination
on the basis of racial and ethnic differences.
Forgive us and grant us the grace to heal the wounds
still present in your community on account of sin,
so that we will all feel ourselves to be your sons and
daughters.
We ask this through Christ our Lord.*

~ ~ ~

I began to understand that the San Luis Valley, in fact, my entire beloved Southwest, was a land steeped in Catholic presence, multiple generations of faith, mystery, miracles, and endless repetition of prayer. I had gravitated toward the missions, and they dotted the landscape in all of my very favorite places (northern New Mexico at the top of the list), bastions of the feminine through the Catholic Church. Perhaps I had been responding to the presence of the feminine that the Catholics had called forward from this land. Perhaps, through Her, I could heal my break with the Divine Masculine, the one that occurred when I was a young child in my Christian preschool. Even with all of its trials and tribulations for our family, this valley had been the perfect place for the feminine emergence within me. We had all been touched by Her. As usual, there were no accidents.

Healing the Masculine (My Right Leg Speaks)

My ankle healed as I convalesced in Colorado, and in the meantime, the wildest conversations were going on inside me. I regularly checked in (again, I was sitting a lot and had the time to write things down as this process unfolded—forced attention to the inner dynamic!). The mangling and breaking of the bone in my right ankle certainly invoked (or rather, uncovered) the ire and wrath of my inner masculine, as if the rage had been held inside the bone and was now leaking out. My inner feminine was scared of him, that much became evident.

Both my mother and my father led from the masculine, so I learned to be afraid of it. As a child, my soft, receptive, and sensitive feminine learned to survive by hiding out. Over time, she retreated as the masculine within me took over. I had been leading with my masculine for my whole life. My intention to embody the feminine required that the masculine take a back seat while she stepped forward within me.

This experience gave a new meaning to the word "stillness" for me. With the sudden and complete absence of physical motion in my life, the waters inside me got very still, and I could feel my feelings much more deeply. Still waters run deep, so they say, and I now know this is true of the internal world, as well. Was it easy? Hell, no! Some days, it took everything I had not to rake my fingernails over my face and scream. My inner masculine was hamstrung, told to "sit down and be quiet" for a while, and he did not like it.

I actually "heard" and "saw" these two polarities when I broke my ankle. In my right leg, I heard/saw a young masculine self, maybe twenty-three, face glowering, reluctantly say, "I break when I'm told to," his shoulders sagging and his arms crossed. I looked over into my left leg and heard/saw a young feminine self of similar age, looking scared and startled, as if she was not used to being regarded in any way by the outside world. In my inner guidance, I was told I was getting an experience of learning to lead with my feminine, through the vehicle of my body. No longer was I experiencing the feminine only through my higher senses or my intellect. This was an experience of embodiment.

My inner masculine was very upset about the forced stillness and being taken out of commission. I noticed that I was restless, antsy that I could not get up and "help" my family. When my sons prepared my meals, I noticed feeling impatient with them for doing it more slowly or less cleanly, or not the way I would have done it. AHA! Control issues! This was my inner masculine, who believed he was all-powerful. Being laid up made him very nervous! Who would be in charge if not him? Wouldn't the world fall apart if he was not in control? Wouldn't I die?

This really showed me how much I had relied on motion, action, and my will to cope with the world, and with my feelings! My masculine self had run the show from a place of fear for survival. With the right-leading (masculine) leg out of commission, my masculine self felt scared, so weak and vulnerable, so powerless, and I realized how much I had depended on my inner masculine (the tough, go-get-it fighter) to get through my life. My left brain/right side had been conditioned to build up dominance in my psyche, responding to a scary world that did not honor right-brain/sensitive/quiet/feminine energy. At physical, emotional, mental, and spiritual levels, I was getting a true lesson in the dynamics of the feminine and masculine.

My body was the holder of this story and showed me my soul's healing trajectory. This was what I had come to heal in this life. I had lots to do to embody and record the experiences that the Divine Feminine and Divine Masculine showed me as a result of my body's expression. There was no separation between "spirit" and body. They were one and the same. The feminine in me was going to lead the way to a new understanding.

Thank you, my right ankle, for making this sacrifice in service to the whole of me, my inner and outer community. Like our indigenous ancestors did in holy ceremony, you offered flesh to show how willing you were to put yourself on the line in order for healing to occur on the larger level.

I learned that the feminine holds All Things like the black inkiness of space holds all of the universe. She is the biggest, the all-encompassing, the Womb that embraces All Creation. The feminine in me, whose presence was getting bolder and growing by the day, watched my suffering inner masculine with compassion. Informed by Great Mother, my feminine self felt a different kind of power. She was holding the space for my inner masculine to thrash about, and finally, to surrender to her love. This was what created the opportunity for him to heal.

Learning How to Walk

He who would learn to fly one day must first learn to stand and walk and run and climb and dance; one cannot fly into flying.

— **Friedrich Nietzsche**

At the age of forty-four, I was learning to walk a second time.

Due to my ankle fracture, I experienced surgery, metal plates, and screws, and eight weeks of weightlessness—for me, a new meaning to the word "stillness," and the sudden and complete absence of forward motion in my life.

Well, not entirely. The movement that I experienced after my injury was the internal kind. The movement in the outer world can sometimes be a distraction from the movement in the inner world. I discovered that **I sometimes used**

physical movement to help me run from feelings that I did not want to feel. Feeling powerless or afraid? Go for a run or a bike ride. Feeling angry? Go clean something. Feeling anything uncomfortable? Go MOVE, do anything, but do not sit still or else it might catch up with me.

In the years that I had worked consciously on myself, much of that centered on **getting more still and paying attention to my feelings**. All the work I had done only took me so far. When my ankle met with a series of metal stairs on a rainy day in California, a new level of learning opened up. That's how it works in process, doesn't it? We go so far with something then find stasis and equilibrium. Then a new expansion experience is introduced and we get to grow again (oh, goody!).

I chose to dive into this experience. I wanted to harvest all of the AHAs, lessons, insights—and I sure never wanted it to happen again!

I started learning to walk with the aid of my crutches and noticed, within a couple of days, that I forgot where I left them. By the end of that week, I hobbled around without any help from my rickety metal friends. But the hobbling was troublesome; I looked like Frankenstein, arms flailing in my attempt to keep balance. My scars were not pretty, and it hurt when I come down on it. But it was a good pain, a natural pain. *It was the pain of learning to use something in a new way.*

Amongst my reflections and ruminations during that time of forced stillness, I wondered if I was walking in a way that was not good for me. Maybe not the physical way I walked, but from a symbolic standpoint, **where was I leading myself? How was I getting there? Was I being forceful or was I being discerning? Was I afraid of moving forward, or was I walking in balance and ease?**

Once I had the opportunity to learn to walk in a different way, I wondered, perhaps if it was a way that would serve me and the world community better. During the stillness, I considered: *How did I want to walk in this world? . . .*

Confidently, in balance, knowing that I was supported, at ease in my own power, looking forward to my future, knowing I was part of this world and that I had something to offer, with grace, strength, discernment, wisdom, and love.

As I healed and learned again to walk, I could not help but reflect on what it must have been like to learn to walk the first time. What would the first inner impulse to move feel like? What would it be like to get up on one's feet the first time and take that step forward? What kind of innate trust is there in all children as they fly through their developmental stages? What kind of crazy motor drives the impulse to get off your knees and start walking?! How amazing is it that we go from being born helpless to moving around at light speed in under a year's time? I seriously doubt that we could handle that kind of rapid growth as adults.

I am a grown woman, and I have learned to be afraid. Life has taught me that I must be protective and watchful and wary, lest something bad happen. That innate trust we are born with can slowly erode over time, to the point that it seems quite unbelievable we ever possessed this gift.

However, as I put one foot in front of the other, I was hopeful. I was in belief that **my leg would hold me up.** When I chose to engage my body by walking, I was saying, "*I WANT to trust again. I WANT to be part of the Earth walk again.*"

As I learned to put my foot down and do the careful dance of rolling my heel and pushing off with my toes, I wondered what kind of little girl I was when I took that first step. Was it a joyful and exciting adventure? Was it a feeling of complete trust and knowing that I was supported? Could I harness that level of trust again as I learned to walk again? I prayed that I could.

The embodiment lesson had taken root, and fast. Nothing like a trauma to change your beliefs and push the reset buttons!

I was the fulcrum for healing in my marriage, too. The partnership with Peter was impacted by the healing of my inner feminine and masculine because it altered the energy dynamic between us. My inner feminine wanted Peter to step up and take care of her; I had been the primary decision maker, pushing the envelope on our relationship and family development. I was now needing him to come into his power, something that had been developing since we left on our big trip. His relationship with his parents was a place where he had explored running from his power, and so this was where he was guided to do some work.

While we had been in California, prior to my ankle break, we thought that we had found a place we could call home. But something felt off. First, California is crazy expensive, and we were in a precarious financial position. Peter's family was also in proximity, all living in the northern part of the state. Our relationship with them had been very unfulfilling. Peter and I were trying to heal our relationship of his failures to stand up for me as his wife and the mother of his children (and my loss of respect for and trust in him as a result.) The disrespect and unkindness that he had allowed toward me had eaten away at our partnership. This had been a primary reason for our family odyssey: to heal our marriage. His parents did not seem to understand that our relationship needed support, not more artillery fire.

Our soulful partnership was at its most vulnerable, even more than when we had left Asheville. Peter's inner child was alive and well, and in the dynamic with his own inner masculine, that child needed a good father to show the way. He asked me what he could do to heal himself, and Great Mother answered him, "Call on Great Father to show you how to step into the Divine Masculine." My healing was now expanding into Peter's inner world.

Sanctuary in Great Mother

I was on a journey into the heart of the Divine Feminine. I had the privilege to experience (as well as name) what it felt like to be held as I went through my process, without being judged, distracted, or "fixed." I was learning that the yin energy accepts all things, does not judge as "wrong" or "outside of God." The energy of the Feminine is also the energy of the best mother we ever craved. The Great Mother of the universe holds us while we are with the world's sorrows.

To confront the sorrows of the world (and our lives) requires that we are present to them. That means we will FEEL them, which is no easy task. We will FEEL the anger, the injustice, the grief, the despair. FEELING takes courage. My theory is that this is why we shy away from hard news, folks who are having hard times, and our own pain. Emotional energy that is felt and expressed is the natural way to move this wave of information out of our bodies. Many human beings do not allow themselves to express emotional energy. This is because that would require us to allow the feelings *to be*.

Great Mother holds us, *is literally what holds us together,* during the worst of things, enables us to endure and persevere, to bring love forth even when we are angry. Like glue, She is the love that binds molecules together, like our cat Tink bound our family by serving as a loving focal point during the crisis in Albuquerque with Peter's parents, like the dark matter of space contains all solid matter.

In Great Mother, we have comfort. She holds us without judgment, acknowledging us deeply for how we feel. We are Her beloved children and She loves us no matter how much anguish we may have in our hearts. In Her, the alchemical transformation of grief and anger into love and acceptance occurs in an instant.

I have tried to wish away the concept of evil. It is terrifying to contemplate that such a thing is real. I can no longer pretend these forces are not there. Having experienced unconsciousness and the evil that the hands of unconsciousness performs, I know there are indeed forces that seek to defy Love/God/ Light/Consciousness in the world and in our own lives.

Perhaps being familiar with evil enables us to handle it when we are faced with it, rather than to shy away from it. Perhaps, as we experience the inner demons of others who attempt to spread their darkness onto us, we learn that we can survive darkness, after all; that we can overcome the inner death that happens when we awaken to darkness, the loss of innocence and the shattering of our illusions; that violence does not win, that it is not the last word; **that there is indeed rebirth, resurrection.** Perhaps this lends a certain fortitude in the inevitable times of being confronted with darkness later in our lives.

As I have heard in many spiritual traditions, the more devoted we are to the light, the more our shadows are outlined, illuminated. In another way of speaking, the greater our devotion to God, the more our inner demons come forward to trip us up, to lead us away, to distract us. Choosing light IS a choice, and it must be made over and over again. This fight for light requires consciousness and a warrior spirit. A line in the sand, a battleground.

Nobel Laureate Leymah Gbowee says, "It is time to stop being politely angry." Our discomfort with victimization is really the discomfort that horrible things actually happen in the world. **We must make peace with our anger so we are effective as we seek to envision a better world for all.** Our outrage is justified. The unrest we feel is righteous! The Divine Feminine allows for us to feel these unhappy things because feeling the unrest IS THE IMPETUS TOWARD CHANGE. We see the redirection of discomfort with these feelings in the blaming of victims of violence, whether in the media, the culture, or in our belief system. Isn't this another way to shield ourselves and deny the darkness, creating a temporary reprieve to make ourselves feel a little better? Is it so we can distract and separate ourselves from our own pain? Is this blame coming from people who have not dealt with their own demons, their own darkness?

Acknowledging the darkness is the first step to changing it, the bridge into the action realm. Whether in the world or in ourselves, acceptance of our unhappy feelings is the mechanism to shift our situation. The frontier of consciousness is not a place for fearful people. The pivotal moment of acceptance is also the pivotal birthing of the new. Then we can accept the sanctuary in the field of all wellbeing to nurture ourselves. We must refill our cup with the good water so that we may offer it in the world and receive the sanctuary of Great Mother and the Divine Feminine in mind and body, heart and soul.

She Cracks Me Open

Wendy is a name that I associated with a woman in authority, perhaps because of Wendy Darling in the Disney film *Peter Pan*. When I first saw *Peter Pan*, I had mixed feelings about Wendy. I was so impressed with her togetherness, her ability to so easily step into her role as surrogate mother of her younger brothers and the Lost Boys, her organizational abilities, her capacity for nurturing. But I also thought she was bossy, and awfully, well, girly. *As a stone in the rough, I seemed tomboyish to her feminine nature.* She was a conundrum. She gathered up and mothered the orphan boys with a nurturing that they desperately needed. At the end of the story, she has matured and is ready to assume the responsibilities that come with growing up. She seemed a mirror for someone I knew.

My own Wendy grew ever more important to me, bringing me much-needed, familiar family sense of humor, ways of being, and heart connection. My visits with her were challenging at the same time that they were healing, because inevitably my Mother Wound would be wide open when I was with her. I do not know how she put up with me. I alternately welcomed and closed the door to her, trying to navigate the unstable territory inside me created by my relationship with my biological mother. She continued to try, continued to knock on the door.

The name Wendy, a diminutive for the Welsh Gwendolyn meaning "white, fair, or blessed," rose in popularity after the character Wendy Darling in the 1904 play *Peter Pan* and its 1911 novelization by J.M Barrie. Various Chinese rulers have held the name and title Emperor Wen, which in Chinese is read *Wen(-)di* (文帝). Chinese women with the same or similar-sounding characters as their given names often anglicize their names as *Wendi* or *Wendy* (Wikipedia). Doctor of Folklore Leslie Ellen Jones, Ph.D., says, "Gwendolyn and Guinevere are etymologically related in that they are both Welsh names beginning with the element 'gwen' - 'white/dazzling/holy'."

Personally, if Wendy is derived from a Welsh name, my candidate would be Gwendydd (pronounced Gwen-deethe, 'white day'), the name of Merlin's sister. The Wendy I know has magical qualities, and is a woman who mothered me in ways I had not experienced before.

After I had healed and begun to walk more steadily (and could drive for short distances), Wendy invited me to meet her in Albuquerque where she bought a weekend at a sweet B&B, the entire weekend her treat. I had not experienced feeling this kind of generosity before. She gave with no expectation of me giving her something in return. It made me uneasy, as if I was expecting the hammer to fall at any moment. Underneath my enjoyment of her in the moment was a deep well of sadness that threatened to swallow me up if I allowed myself to feel it for a moment. My defenses toward Wendy were a way for me to defend myself against the grief that my own mother did not show me this kind of open, giving love.

We had a lovely time exploring together, just being together. I felt the darkness within me, and just sat with it as she and I laughed and talked and experienced our connection. My sense was that the inner children of my psyche were trying to get used to the idea that Wendy actually cared about me, perhaps much more than my own mother. It was a feeling of jostling inside, making room for a different possibility. She was kind. She listened to me. She affirmed my unique views. She was everything I wanted in a mother.

During this weekend, Wendy sat me down and broke the news: my parents had gotten remarried just a week before. After more than twenty-five years apart, married to others, and otherwise occupied, they had chosen to reunite. I had not received any word (nor an invitation) from them, my siblings, or anyone in my family, so it never occurred to me that this could happen.

I HAD received a rare and out-of-nowhere email from my mother a few months earlier (after my ankle break) in which she relayed to me that she and my father were going to "try again." What? She was getting back into a relationship with this sexual predator? In my reply to her at that time, I was very clear that I was disappointed that after so many years of me tirelessly trying to get her to acknowledge and understand the depth of his trespasses against me that *she would choose this man a second time.*

Once again, she chose him and not me. She had said in the email that she looked forward to me visiting them in their new farmhouse. What the hell? What denial, what fantasy did she have going on in her head? Where had she been all of these years that I had begged her to wake up and acknowledge the abuses, and to mother me in the ways I desperately needed? I had lots of work to do within myself to be a good parent to the inner child who was screaming inside me.

I told her in the email that I would never visit their house. So it is no surprise that I would not have been told they were remarrying nor be invited to their wedding. Apparently, my siblings WERE invited and were in attendance. They never told me it occurred. They were accomplices in yet another big family secret. It fell on Wendy to break it to me on this fateful weekend. If she had not, I would never have known.

When she told me, I first felt shock and then a tremendous hurt, spiritually, I think. It was an in-your-face, you-aren't-important, who-cares-how-you-feel gesture on their part. My entire family of origin had excluded me, my siblings included. It was not surprising at one level that my parents excluded me; I expected their behavior to be childlike. They were still active alcoholics and had not stepped up to try to mend our relationship or done any healing work to recognize their responsibility.

It was a deeper level of betrayal from my sister and brother not to have told me. After all the years of work I had done, I had clung to the hope that there would be healing and resolution in my family of origin. These hopes were finally dashed to the rocks; my fantasy was shattered into a million pieces. I could no longer tell myself that it would someday get better, that my parents would someday show up for me, that my family would finally understand and we would all be united.

I sobbed, my heart breaking in a whole new way. Feeling the depth of the abandonment, I croaked, "I'm an orphan." After everything I had gone through to make it better, this was the answer to my life's efforts?

The pain was so intense, and I was cracked open at an entirely different level. My mother had left me once again.

I Am My Own Daughter

It is hard to describe in words the subsequent months. Peter, the boys, and I had a clear understanding that we were not welcome in Colorado, a reminder to "go where you're invited." We made motions to find a new place to move, realizing that we had thought we were done with the big journey, but we were not. There was more to do, more to heal, more to create.

I found myself reflecting on the ways I could mother myself. I recognized that self-love was a tremendous component of the joy that I had previously felt. After the announcement of my family's betrayal, I had lots of work to do to remember I was loved. My husband and children loved me, this I knew. My inner children, however, howled with the injustice, the pain, and the soul-killing. The work became gathering the parts of me up in my arms, cooing to them to comfort them, and mothering them with my newfound skills. I realized again that releasing my self-judgment was crucial to the healing of these parts of self, what I now called my Inner Tribe™.

My Mother Wound was WIDE open. I did research and found The Orphan archetype, an old story of the lost child who finds themselves alone, with only the wild, untamed universe to parent them. I realized that I was much more than a wounded girl who had done some healing. I learned that my wounds marked me as a healer of a greater order, a messenger of Great Mother whose purpose is to heal the collective Mother Wound. To heal the larger wound, I had to go through the very worst that life could offer me; my wounding was a sacred calling.

The greatest wound that we can sustain is the one created by rejection from the one we came from. Yes, we come from mothers, human women who bring us through in the physical world. But this is a point of origin on this planet, just one of many places that we come from. Our original point of origin is the Source of All Life, the Womb of the Sacred Feminine, the Holder of the Omniverse; from Her, we can never be rejected.

My shattering opened me bigger than I had ever been opened, and I started channeling Her voice in earnest, the greatest love I could ever bring to others.

Some seeds have to go through fire to germinate.

Reverence for the Rage – The Place That Anger Holds in Our Growth

There is importance in anger. Anger is the impulse that arises when a boundary is crossed. When I feel anger, the very best thing I can do is to show compassion to myself for feeling that way. Self-judgment is how to stay stuck in shame, immovable and frozen. The fastest way I know to freedom is simply to **be with** what comes up.

In Inner Tribe™ work, I dialogue with the part of me that is angry; I ask questions of that part of self as if it were in the room with me. I ask, "What do you need to tell me?", "Do you have something to show me?", or "What can I do to help you?" These three questions, as simple as they are, can unlock the most blocked feelings.

We decided to move from Colorado.

The situation of my bone breaking, my mother re-choosing my father as a life mate, and our community projecting their own unconsciousness ("evil") onto me and our family, impelling us to leave all of our dreams (and hefty investments) behind—it all made so much sense. It seemed we were being forced to see our problems in stereo! And I was pushed to the point that the dam cracked and I felt my feelings. I opened my heart and the emotion that had been locked up there began to flow.

Over the years, I had been getting to know the feminine within and without me. I was learning that emotion was a key part of her landscape. In the years of left-brain dominance/patriarchy, feelings and empathy (both right-brain traits) had taken a back seat. We had trained ourselves to dismiss feelings as silly, a waste of time/energy, non-essential. And look at how the world was evolving! Violence, hate, greed. She taught me that if we do not feel what we are doing to one another, we lose our sense of connection, and therefore, empathy. That means we can make someone "the other" and not feel any problem with it. We can aggress and rape and kill and not even pause if we are not in touch with our emotional nature. This is also how we abuse children. We must undo this screwed-up, left-brain-dominant pattern. We must reclaim and value our relational, feeling right brain!

But we are scared to feel . . . even the good stuff like joy and happiness! What are we afraid of? It is simply emotion. Like the weather across our continent, it will move through us and clean house on its way out, through our tears, our shouts, our laughter. It is GOOD for us to feel, . . . and it is good for the world.

Back to the East, Our Origins

We packed up our belongings (how the heck did we accumulate so much stuff in the few years we had been here?) and headed to Tallahassee, in the panhandle of Florida. We had been through it the first time when we were stationed at Cape San Blas at the beginning of our odyssey, then came back a second time to visit a friend and co-lead a workshop with her. It seemed a fine place, but it was not on our radar as a place to live until Great Mother spoke through me and specifically said, "*Tallahassee.*"

Tallahassee, Florida??? We had judged Florida mercilessly in our previous life (before the trip) as the "Redneck Riviera." During our trip, we had found Florida to be a surprise—much goodness to be had. But what a shock to be sent back to the Southeast, our birthplace, our origins. It never occurred to me that we would again live in the South.

We moved in August 2009, back into the snug fit of the Bible Belt, and into the arms of so much of our early lives. The South carried anger and other passionate feelings—heat pressing on me and humidity flooding my lungs, my pores. There was water everywhere. Florida would bring forth our feelings like nowhere else.

Florida is also an area where my beloved soul mate had an unresolved ancestral wound to face; it was his turn to do some deep work. Peter came from a branch of family that made a fortune on the backs of slaves, an old southern aristocracy. We had had money trouble as a result of the recession, and Peter borrowed from his family's coffers to support us (without my knowledge). We subsequently had strange money karma for years, and I did not realize until we moved to Florida how much we were impacted by the blood on his family's money.

For decades, my intuition had said to avoid money entanglements with his parents, but they historically offered checks, seemingly as a way of securing love. I did not want to believe my intuition about this, but it was proven multiple times, later, when they expressed anger at us for not behaving in ways they expected and cited "giving money" as the justification for their expectation. We were a family with children, a home, and expenses, and needed the money. We did not want to love out of obligation or duty. That was not really love in our understanding. We wanted to love them cleanly, but we accepted their "gifts," and paid with our dignity.

Our love for them was enmeshed with needing to also accept their parenting. I wanted parents so much and was willing, for many years, to silently accept their treatment. We also had trouble discerning the difference between taking care of them emotionally and genuine love, so we fell into a pattern of enabling the emotional crippling of our adulthood. If we did not accept their "gifts," they got upset with us, and if we voiced discomfort with their "gifts," they also got upset. We felt hamstrung with no safe space to speak our truth, a terrible co-dependent cycle.

Our family had been on uneasy footing with Peter's parents since the 2005 Albuquerque incident when we had sent the gifts back to them. Our boundaries had been ignored, they talked about us irresponsibly to others, and I was blamed as the source of the trouble; there was no respite there. I was not feeling very loved or appreciated for all of the years I was welcoming and civilized to them, encouraging their relationship with my children. No, my personal relationship had never been easy with them, but I was respectful and kind. I wanted my children to have grandparents since my parents had not stepped up. What I had overlooked in terms of my own psychic safety I had done on behalf of my children. Here I was, the Evil One AGAIN, paying for my efforts in suffering.

The quiet rejection by our Colorado community, the fresh rejection by my family of origin in the wedding, the flagrant disrespect of Peter's family, and the black sheep persona that I carried internally created a perfect storm. I was furious.

Anger had always held me up when nothing else could. It was the skeleton around which I had formed my flesh.

My strength was in my anger.

When I broke my ankle, I became aware that I was angry because my bones told me so. My ankle was a messenger.

I have always been told how I shine, how I am a light in the world. My humongous spirit has always shone through despite the bodily structure of anger. I wonder how much of what I thought served the whole was truly of service. My awareness of the "good of the whole" may have been somewhat influenced by my anger.

My anger was about my own losses, but also was about what's been stolen from humanity since the feminine energy has been oppressed.

I knew that in order to save my life, I must express my anger; in order to change my bodily structure from using anger to survive to using love to live, I must take the risk and speak my rage. I intended to replenish the vacancy created by speaking my truth with unconditional support and love. I would transform what had held me up, but was now holding me down. This shift would be a miracle.

Righteous Rage
Collage © 2009 Licia Berry

Sekhmet is a Face of Great Mother

My rage was so big, it felt bigger than me. And it was. Great Mother said to me:

"Anger is the correct feedback when your being is trespassed."

It was easy to see that I was angry, but I felt like a tool of something larger than me, as if it was Great Mother saying NO to the ways I had been trespassed against. I felt I was being shown how boundaries are necessary and should be observed. I came to the conclusion that I felt Great Mother's rage, as well as the rage of women all around the world, who are regularly scapegoated, made out to be evil, used to explain others' irresponsible behavior. Since the beginning of patriarchy, women have been blamed for the ills of the world, and I was becoming a conduit for those women who had not been able to use their voices to scream their outrage at the injustice, the madness of it all. I became an unwitting lightning rod for collective rage.

Sekhmet arrived soon after my anger was set loose with the ankle break, and became a steady presence and a voice of Great Mother for me. She felt similar to a Mother Bear, protective to the point of violence if necessary.

Artist Thalia Took describes her: "Sekhmet is an ancient Egyptian Goddess of war and destruction, plagues and healing. Her name means 'The Powerful One'.... She is depicted as a woman with the head of a lioness, sometimes also with the sun disk and uraeus on Her headdress, Who symbolizes the destructive heat of the sun.... Sekhmet, though sometimes a violent Goddess, was however also known as a healer who set and cured broken bones. She is said to cause epidemics when She is not honored properly; but when She is, She can stop them as well."

Notice Sekhmet's connection to the breaking and healing of bones. I had to break a bone in my body to release the suppressed rage that had been in me since I was young. It also broke open the false innocence that nothing bad could happen to me once I was away from my family of origin, that my body was safe. And a twist . . . it broke open the belief systems that held me above the deep wisdom of my own unconscious, the storehouse of everything that had ever happened to me and the proverbial cave of riches. The opening of that container released the energetic binding that had prevented me from opening my mouth and screaming at the abuses I had endured during my lifetime. Sekhmet emerged in my life as the face of feminine rage, a force to shake up my process, drop me into the deep well of old wisdom, to engage my fury, and therefore the healing (and resurrection) of my inner masculine.

I was awake and paying attention. My years of seeing myself as a quiet, polite, and servile woman were over.

Dark Mother Invites Me Into the Deep

I felt as though the foundations under me were cracking. I had been so occupied with my own life, and with my family, and here was something so deep, below everything I had known. It was the Jungian "basement beneath the basement," the unconscious below the previous depth of exploration in the psyche. I was diving (or was I being taken?) deeper into myself than I ever had. It was not just my own anger I was experiencing, nor my own unconscious wisdom. I was being introduced to the collective unconscious—the great storehouse of everything that has ever occurred—through the archetypal Great Mother. I was being given access to the oldest wisdom that existed, and along with it, the collective rage of women since the beginning.

I seemed to have opened a container of Women's Collective Anger. Is this the truth behind the twisted myth of Pandora's box? Is it really that once women open and feel the anger that has been suppressed that the world might end? Anger is required as an entry to the inner masculine, the propulsion into action. Women getting angry about what has been stolen from humanity is the correct course. I had to heal my masculine so that he could partner with the feminine in me and so I could embody her, hold her. But she is not a meek little feminine. She is bold, big, powerful, deep, and she needs a masculine that can direct and focus her so she can be effective and do things to impact the world.

I had been intrigued by Carl Jung's work over the years as I had studied psychology, but his work with archetypes, examination of his own unconscious, and the collective unconscious held new meaning for me at this point. I dreamed of swimming in black, underground oceans, floating on the surface and looking up at the "stars." (I was stunned later to discover pictures that echoed my inner vision: cave worms in New Zealand that actually cling to the cave ceiling and glow, producing a starlight effect.)

Similar to my months under the sea with Sedna, I "saw" and "felt" myself as I moved through these subterranean seas, or alternately dark caverns, the cool air on my skin and the complete absence of light impelling me to use my hands to explore in total blackness. In these explorations, my hands occasionally touched upon a face, a quiet child sitting in the dark, or an object or artifact. These were calls to do Inner Tribe™ work, to integrate parts of me that had been left "in the dark" while I had learned the ways of the sunlit world, the world that required suppression of emotion. Again, I experienced this inner environment while I moved through my days as mom/wife/citizen.

You might think that I was afraid of these dark interludes, my hands out in front of me to prevent stumbling among the rocks in the caverns, or my body suspended in inky black water (with goodness knows what else in it with me) and I was at times, but mostly, I felt a mothering presence with me. I knew I was okay. This was territory that had been traveled by others, had been created by others before me. I was not alone.

I once again felt affirmed in my belief that a larger energy holds us all and that if we align with it, magic happens.

Several times a day I took time to be still, listen, and feel my connection to the Whole. When I did so, I accessed greater intelligence and a usual pathway opened when I felt alignment click into place. I felt a new (yet very old and familiar) presence move in from the left of center, supplanting my usual interface with the Divine.

Woman of Stone–She is Awakening
Collage © 2006 Licia Berry

"Who is here?" I asked.

A vast, deep silence, a feeling of gravity, immense power in my belly and sweetness in my heart was the response.

I sat quietly straining to hear with my inner ears, but I could not quite make out the name. I asked, "Are you here to aid me in my highest good?"

"**Yes,**" I am told, and I felt a rush of goodwill pouring through me. "Are you accountable to the light?" I asked.

I heard, "*No, I am accountable to the dark.*"

I squirmed; my early Christian preschool indoctrination formed my young, developing mind into a good versus evil bent, and I struggle to this day with unconsciously perceiving light as good and dark as bad, even though I know consciously that this is not true.

My resonance lies with the yin/yang symbol, in which the darkness and the light are simply two halves of existence that balance one another, and are therefore necessary for the Whole. It is our small, human minds that place judgments on qualities of energy such as light and dark, calling them names and putting them in little boxes so that we can feel more in control.

I have also studied the Goddess traditions extensively, and know that darkness, a symbol for the womb, for the void, for the night, for the face of the new moon, has been vilified ever since patriarchy reared its adolescent grab for power on the planet. I know from hard won experience that anything we demonize warrants a closer look to see what we are projecting onto it.

I heard this Being that had entered my holy space speak that it was accountable to the dark, and I took a breath. "Who are you?" I asked again, more firmly.

"*I am the Dark Mother*," She answered.

I sat quietly, stunned at the simplicity and precision of this revelation. I then proceeded to ask several clarifying questions, the first of which was posed to make sure I was safe to be interacting with this powerful yet benevolent energy, and the latter of which resulted from my increasing feelings of bliss and excitement. Many moments later, I was in tears as I accepted Her, the vilified face of Dark Mother.

I had been very angry the previous year or so. Dark Mother had appeared because I had allowed myself to feel the rage that I had buried in my psyche, just like the feminine was buried.

The work I had begun in 2005 to embody the Divine Feminine was inspired by Her. Images of the Black Madonna, which I had written an extensive article about in 2007, flashed through my mind. The many essays and radio shows and personal experiences of the Sacred Feminine that I had processed and offered to the world as a road map fell into place.

As a woman who resonates deeply (as well as recognizes within myself) the Sacred Feminine energies, I have spent time getting to know the several faces of the Goddess. Mary the Mother was the first face of the feminine I began to interact with as an adult, in 1999. She was safe, a clean symbol of goodness and light, *and a good start for a woman fearful of her own feminine energy.*

As a child, Isis was a frequent companion, but over the years, I had lost my sense of her. She came roaring back into my life in 2001. Then other faces of the Goddess began to emerge in my consciousness. Astarte, Diana, Hecate, Demeter, Kali, Innana, Brigid, Tara, Cerridwen, Persephone, Sedna, Lilith, Mary Magdalene, Amaterasu, Grandmother Moon, and more. As each of these treasured and varied *Faces of Her* visited me, I interacted with their archetypes and integrated them into my own awareness, making those aspects within me conscious. It has been a remarkable journey of awakening.

I never uttered the name **Dark Mother** for Her, perhaps because of my subconscious association of dark with evil.

I had heard of the Dark Mother as a name for the fierce Goddess Kali, She who oversees death and rebirth, and so I had approached the Kali archetype with a large perimeter and a considerable dose of respect. I knew the acknowledgment and appreciation of the darkness that comes with shamanic practice, in which the journeying through the various inner worlds must be discerningly and powerfully navigated. I had experienced the darkness of entering initiations and coming through into the light, being reborn.

And I had experienced the darkness that came with fully exploring the archetypes of some of the previously mentioned faces of the Divine Feminine. . . . darkness in the sense of exploring in unfathomable places in my psyche, such as deep, winding caves and caverns, traversed along with my sister

Innana, and at the bottom of the sea, along with my underwater kin, Sedna . . . *darkness in the sense of moving through what cannot be seen with the eyes, but must be felt and experienced through the inner worlds, grist for the mill, where great treasure is yielded for those who have the courage to undertake the journey.*

Perhaps the "dark emotions" are the realm of Dark Mother; grief, rage, anger, sadness, superiority, judgement, and meanness could become hard and physical if they are not composted into light. We must acknowledge these places of darkness inside of us, and Dark Mother is our guide. It is this face of the feminine that carries the natural medicine to transform pain into something that is useful and life-affirming. Yet we are afraid to own our darkness, and so it owns us. I have often wondered if the epidemic of modern physical maladies (such as cancers) can be partially attributed to the rejection of the dark emotions.

When the dark waters are navigated well, the painful emotions are easily composted into fuel for joy.

Great Mother appeared to me in many guises, the ones that could be easily seen, depending on where I was in my process. The Dark Mother was making herself known to me because it was time for me to grow up. I was a woman who had knowledge that could help other women, and I was being asked to step up. This was my destiny, what my life had prepared me for. It was time to put my history to bed and move forward into changing the world.

An internal conversation occurred that opened my eyes to what I was meant to do. I felt Great Mother's dark side move into my left field and I heard Her say, "**Who will claim this child?**"

I was unsure which child She meant until I saw in my mind's eye a baby girl wrapped in a spiderweb blanket, held against the bosom of Spider Woman, an indigenous Creator of the Universe and a Mother of All. Spider Woman was regal in her wrap and finery, her ancient face and eyes kind but serious. Spider Woman looked at me expectantly, as if she wanted to pass the infant to me but was waiting for me to choose whether I would reach out for the precious bundle in her arms.

I weighed whether I would be a good mother to this child. I had only raised sons, I did not know how to raise a daughter. I understood that I was being asked to step up and take this little one, as if she were my own shining daughter. *A role as a mother of women was being asked of me.* I did not know how I would do it, but I stepped forward and said, "**I will claim this child**." And this is the work I have done ever since.

What IS Dark Mother?

I have learned that Dark Mother is a side of Great Mother that has been oppressed and feared in our world since the beginning. Her energy is powerful, the most powerful energy in the universe, in fact. It is the energy of pure potential, the raw energy of creation/destruction that formed the cosmos. Personified, She is the face of The Destroyer, like Kali or Hecate, and the face of the powerful Mother Goddesses such as Cybele, Isis, and Hathor. She is destructive, yes, taking out anything that is not in Her plan. But as the essence of the universal Womb, She also oversees rebirth, the new beginning. She can feel like chaos, disorder, betrayal. She embraces, carries the deep wisdom. She is the ideal Mother if the design of the universe is something you yearn to understand.

She is also the face of the Mother who kills her children (like the stories that held strange fascination for me while we were stationed at Padre Island), but only if the shadow side of that mother *has not been integrated with the light side, or in other terms, the darkness of the unconscious dysfunction is not healed and made conscious.*

It made sense to me that if I brought my shadow side into my consciousness, worked with it and integrated it, I could be powerful, and also compassionate as well as a force of good in the world (and for my children!). The women I had read about at Padre rang true to the raw energy in my own earthly mother, although she seemed to have been unsuccessful in snuffing me out. I did wonder sometimes, though: did she wish I was dead?

In the Gnostic Gospels, a profound re-telling of the stories of early Christianity, the Nag Hammadi discovery found that some of the texts tell the origin of the human race in very different terms than the usual reading of Genesis. "The Testimony of Truth," for example, tells the story of the Garden of Eden from the viewpoint of the serpent. The snake is a symbol associated with transformation and rebirth, in that the animal sheds its skin. The serpent, long known to appear in gnostic literature as the principle of divine wisdom, convinces Adam and Eve to partake of knowledge while "the Lord" threatens them with death, trying jealously to prevent them from attaining knowledge, and expelling them from Paradise when they achieve it.

Another Nag Hammadi text, called "The Thunder, Perfect Mind," offers an extraordinary poem spoken in the voice of a feminine divine power (this is an excerpt):

I was sent forth from the power,
and I have come to those who reflect upon me,
and I have been found among those who seek after
me.
Look upon me, you who reflect upon me,
and you hearers, hear me.
You who are waiting for me, take me to yourselves.
And do not banish me from your sight.
And do not make your voice hate me, nor your hearing.
Do not be ignorant of me anywhere or any time. Be
on your guard!
Do not be ignorant of me.

For I am the first and the last.
I am the honored one and the scorned one.

I am the whore and the holy one.
I am the wife and the virgin.
I am <the mother> and the daughter.
I am the members of my mother.
I am the barren one
        and many are her sons.
I am she whose wedding is great,
        and I have not taken a husband.
I am the midwife and she who does not bear.
I am the solace of my labor pains.
I am the bride and the bridegroom,
        and it is my husband who begot me.
I am the mother of my father
        and the sister of my husband
        and he is my offspring.
I am the slave of him who prepared me.
I am the ruler of my offspring.
        But he is the one who begot me before the time on a
        birthday.
        And he is my offspring in (due) time,
        and my power is from him.
I am the staff of his power in his youth,
        and he is the rod of my old age.
        And whatever he wills happens to me.
I am the silence that is incomprehensible
        and the idea whose remembrance is frequent.
I am the voice whose sound is manifold
        and the word whose appearance is multiple.
I am the utterance of my name.

Why, you who hate me, do you love me,
        and hate those who love me?
You who deny me, confess me,
        and you who confess me, deny me.
You who tell the truth about me, lie about me,
        and you who have lied about me, tell the truth about
        me.
You who know me, be ignorant of me,
        and those who have not known me, let them know me.

For I am knowledge and ignorance.
I am shame and boldness.
I am shameless; I am ashamed.
I am strength and I am fear.
I am war and peace.
Give heed to me.

I am the one who is disgraced and the Great One.

~ ~ ~

I was interested in being a presence of goodness, as well as of truth and healing, so my Inner Tribe™ work (described more fully in Chapter 8) became a primary mode of work in my practice. The tools that I had learned over the years had prepared me perfectly to understand the psyche, from a neurobiological, physical, mental, emotional, shamanic, and energetic (or quantum) framework. I had every tool I needed to do some serious healing work.

At this time in my life, floods of feelings washed through me. I felt angry, fearful, sad, anxious, as well as in wonder. I knew that emotions moved through the body like a wave and that the chemistry coursing through the soft tissue of my body elevated my arousal response. I knew that the brain processed thought and that the corresponding chemicals to that thought moved through the physical body in ninety seconds, along with the accompanying emotion. If we are emotional for longer than ninety seconds, it is because we rethink a thought that induces the chemical response again, OR we are exposed to an external stimuli that induces thought (and therefore emotional response).

I had plenty of thoughts in my own head, but the presence of so much external upset caused me to feel unsafe as we moved our family (again) to Florida. Old fears about the South came to the surface, and my emotional state fluctuated wildly as my body processed the feelings.

My journal was my constant companion as I identified parts of myself that needed support. I kept detailed notes of the aspects of my psyche that cried out for integration, recording their needs and messages. As always, Great Mother guided the healing with Her compassion. As I healed these Inner Tribe™ members, I felt better and better. Through my journal, I was introduced to one of my Inner Tribe™ members, The Angry One.

The Angry One

Inner Tribe™ Case Study

She is fourteen years old and the *me* that is post-Little Rock and moving through puberty in Atlanta, a middle school, unsettling, awkward time. She has begun menstruating, something she was not prepared for by her mother but thankfully had learned about in a health class. She is embarrassed about her developing breasts and the pads she wears for the blood flowing from between her legs. She is alone; no one is her confidante. She has no mother because the woman who should be is selfishly engrossed in her own disarray and fear. She wants desperately to be mothered, but there is no one to fill this role.

She splits her despair into two, one part that is a puddle of goo, a victim that does not speak when she is violated emotionally or mentally or physically, but absorbs the impact like a sponge. The other part becomes a warrior boy of epic proportions, who rises to the occasion when he feels the violation. He has an angry demeanor and intelligent mind, so uses words and unkindness as his weapon.

The vacillation between these three parts of self shows me how I have dealt with anger in my life, and this makes me desire greatly to heal these parts and re-integrate them.

~ End of journal entry ~

The self-mothering that characterized this work was what made it different from many techniques I had attempted. THIS DAUGHTER NEEDED A MOTHER. I had been given the perfect work technique, exactly for my needs.

A Different Kind of Power

My experience of the archetypal Great Mother was that She instructed me like no one had in the ways of holding space for myself. This archetypal energy was within me, without me, everywhere in the universe, but I had had to break down my defenses in order to experience Her. Learning to have compassion for my feelings was what freed me in the end. There was no alternative but to love my way through my sadness, hold space for my anger; my previous strategy of walking defensively, protectively with my right side leading (whom I had affectionately named the Warrior Boy) was no longer an option. My defensive, unpartnered masculine self (right side) was receiving an opportunity to learn to love.

I was stunned by the uninterrupted flow of insights. I became aware that I was being tutored about the nature of feminine energy in a way I had not understood before.

As I wrote for my first book, *Love Letter – A Message of Comfort, Self Care and Sanity in Stimulating Times*:

> Do you create with your body? Do you create with your emotions? Do you create with your Infinite Spirit? YES. Believing that we create only with our thoughts is a continuation of the worship of the mind and intellect that has overtaken our culture. But we are much more than our minds. We are vast, energetic beings with all the resources of the universe available to us. **We are not separate from All of Creation.**

It is important to get right with ALL the ways we create if we want to live the magical lives we were intended to live.

A Reminder – We are part of an infinite field; you can think of the Omniverse as a giant fabric. You are a thread in that fabric that makes up all of Creation; you are part of and contribute to Oneness. Where we get into trouble is that we forget that we are part of All That Is, and try to live our lives separately from all of Creation. Living a magical life is dependent on our willingness to work in partnership with all the aspects of Creation and to allow that fabric of Creation to support us.

Working in partnership is the new dynamic that is being seated in the universe, also known as the Aquarian Dynamic. We are now coming into the awareness that we are one with all things, and that what we do affects the Whole. We see this manifested in our awareness of global climate change, as well as seeing ourselves as global citizens instead of identifying with just our own country. Not only do we have the opportunity to work in partnership with each other as a species, but with all of nature, the Earth, the universe, and all aspects of our Being.

When we take care of ourselves, love ourselves unconditionally, and align in Prime Source energy (rather than resist it), we are being part of the flow of All Creation, rather than trying to separate ourselves from it. Magic occurs when we allow ourselves to be in the flow, and when we flow, All of Creation benefits and supports us.

When we make the choice to honor the partnership we have with All of Creation, that is when we experience the joy that is our birthright.

Our promise was to come here, fully and completely, and enjoy the journey, expanding the universe through our experiences and desires and choices. We were designed to completely ground our essence all the way through our physical bodies and into the Earth's core, bringing Source energy all the way through us. Think of Prime Source as our North Pole and the Earth's core as our South Pole. We were intended to stretch from pole to pole! If we choose not to embody any part of that amazing spectrum, we are only being part of who we truly are!

~ ~ ~

Great Mother was teaching me to reclaim ALL parts of myself, including my energy body and the knowledge within me. The universe was truly inside of me, just as I was inside of the universe. I was being assisted to remember.

We do not become healers. We came as healers. We are.
Some of us are still catching up to what we are.
We do not become storytellers. We came as carriers of the stories we and our ancestors actually lived. We are.
Some of us are still catching up to what we are.
We do not become artists. We came as artists. We are.
Some of us are still catching up to what we are.
We do not become writers, dancers, musicians, helpers, peacemakers. We came as such. We are.
Some of us are still catching up to what we are.

We do not learn to love in this sense. We came as Love. We are Love.
Some of us are still catching up to who we truly are.

— Dr. Clarissa Pinkola Estes, "Simple Prayer for Remembering the Motherlode"

Part Two

Herstory

Chapter 6: The Feminine Lands – 47 Years to Present Day

The Persistence of Memory
Collage © 2010 Licia Berry

Tallahassee is beautiful. With its green rolling hills, copious trees, proximity to the Gulf of Mexico, and mostly progressive community, this town created a verdant container for my family's next evolution.

The boys wanted to be in school again, and this time I felt good about it. I carefully researched the options and asked for guidance about where to place them. They went to schools that wound up being perfect, growthful places.

Peter and I focused on stability; we had been on the move for six years, and we hoped this would be the place we would actually "land." We rented a house in a nice neighborhood called Waverly Hills and planned to try the area for a year to see if we were all happy with our new town.

The streets of Waverly Hills are named for notable characters in Sir Walter Scott's *Waverley* series. We learned that the series is about a young English dreamer and soldier with the spirit of adventure, Edward Waverley, who is sent to Scotland during the time of the Jacobite uprising of 1745, which sought to restore the Stuart dynasty in the person of Charles Edward Stuart, known as "Bonnie Prince Charlie." He journeys from his aristocratic family home, Waverley-Honour, in the south of England, after being raised by his Jacobite-leaning uncle. He travels first to the Scottish Lowlands and then into the Highlands and the heart of the rebellion.

We had fun on family walks through the neighborhood calling on our Scottish heritage (both Peter and I have familial roots in Scotland among our ancestry) and trilling the names in Scottish brogue. We landed in a place that reflected a journeying fellow on the hunt for truth, enlightenment, and restoration of power, just like our family! Amazing how we are in constant communication with the larger intelligence. If we pay attention, we can see so much about ourselves. The universe talks to itself all of the time.

We settled into our new life and created a routine. Peter and I struggled with ancestral money issues, not quite understanding yet the legacy we had inherited, but the kids had the stability of friendlier school environments so that was no longer a worry. While they were in school all day, I was free to work, so I rented a small, cheap studio space. I was thrilled to have a "room of my own" after so many years involved with my family's process. I moved into the studio in May 2010, nine months after our arrival in Tallahassee.

As soon as I was settled in, Great Mother tapped on my shoulder and asked me to make a "guided collage." This was the name I had given to collages made with messages directly from the larger consciousness. My process involves dowsing images from my hundreds of magazines or other sources, dowsing how to place them, then dowsing for accuracy as the message is interpreted. I have gotten extraordinary information through this process, information about things that I cannot possibly know about personally or through my usual guidance process of asking questions and dowsing for the response.

The "guided collage" that I was led to create was complete. It had a hawk with food in its mouth, a feminine feeling, and a face that was Great Mother letting me know that She was guiding me. The collage was lovely. I asked for the message inherent in the images but was stopped and asked to create another "guided collage." So I did.

This process continued—*for three months!* By the end, I was blissfully utilized to create eighty-one mixed media collages that told the story of the feminine and the masculine energies, how they have played out in the human species since our origins, and how they had been unpartnered in order to expand the consciousness of the universe. The story revealed in this body of work changed my life.

The translation of the eighty-one collages (which took another three months) has turned into several curriculums and a six hundred-page manuscript, and has inspired art that delves deeper into the story. I have incorporated the material into my personal process, my marriage, my family, and everything that I do. It is the answer to so many questions about why things are the way they are.

Her Gifts Nurture
Mixed media © 2010 Licia Berry

I felt guided to show "The 81" (as I came to call them) to a dear and wise friend. (I have shown them to very few people.) I invited him, and he made time to come see them. A Taoist, he quietly viewed the collages, taking them in. After several minutes, he quietly said to me, "Did you know that the Tao has eighty-one chapters?" I had not read the *Tao te Ching*, but knew peripherally that it had much to do with the yin/yang of life. This material seemed to be connected to and perhaps even rooted in a universal body of knowledge that ancient people had also understood.

I wept almost every day as I worked on these collages, and later, as I interpreted them (when I was allowed to). I weep when I look at them even now. The story they tell is so full of love.

Her Love is Infinite

The mothering of the universe, the omnipresent, infinite blackness of the womb of space, the consistent, ever-beating pulse of the Great Heart at the Center of All Things, shows me that a mother's love does not end. It is bottomless, and when I should be tired or cranky or jealous or selfish, I look at the faces of my inner children and the people I serve in their earnest desire to heal, to make good of their life and experiences, and I am moved beyond time and space to show up right next to them, to love them, to have endless compassion and to do, to do, to do . . . to actively love, to the point when I think I cannot love any more, and yet I do. She is the thread that runs through everything, that connects everything, AND that HOLDS everything. She is the feminine face of God, the Great Mother, the first face that we ever knew.

Our wounding on the collective level is that She has been erased from our conscious memory, She who is our True Mother. It is as if we were told to forget the woman who birthed us, our memories erased and a different story told of having come from another source.

My life story was the perfect introduction to remember Great Mother and the feminine face of God. In my pain and earnest yearning to be mothered, I opened myself to a secret that has been kept and a shameful history that has enslaved women for thousands of years.

Soul Surrender
Collage © 2006 Licia Berry

True Human

As I grew in my understanding of the depth to which the feminine has been buried, my inner masculine became more active. The two years following my ankle break resulted in such a transformation for me that I could barely recognize myself. I did not make up pretty stories in order to explain others' bad behaviors; I did not pretend to be fine when I was not. My relationships in the community evolved as I did.

I found myself in conflict more often because I now spoke up when I was not happy about something. Where I used to hold my tongue and appear more agreeable, I now found myself setting boundaries with situations that I would not have before and taking better care of myself. I was concerned at first that I was digressing, becoming more human and therefore "less spiritual," but what I was told was that I was integrating my masculine into my inner feminine. It was not always pretty, but it was a necessary part of healing the masculine within me that was "put on hold" during the ankle break.

If I was going to be a "True Human" as the Inuit Grandmother had said, I would have to face my fears about being perceived as a "not very spiritual" person, and claim my human nature. The embodiment of the feminine had been a huge, years-long process for me, but now I was going to embody the masculine and attempt to bring both into partnership within me.

I realized that God/Goddess are a way of speaking about the masculine and feminine energy as ideals that are in partnership with one another, co-creating the universe in Sacred Union. The world and its issues and problems are a reflection of unpartnered masculine and feminine qualities of energy.

"Spiritual" has come to mean separate from the body, and nothing could be further from the truth. The partnership of proton (positive charge, or the yang) and electron (negative charge, or the yin) create the atom, the basic structure of the physical universe, so both energies are utterly co-dependent on one another for the universe (and life) to continue. *The seamless union of the feminine and the masculine is what makes them Divine.*

A "True Human" is a marriage of heaven and earth, body and mind, vertical and horizontal. The Abrahamic religions had effectively separated the physical, earthly body and the etheric spirit, and as a result, the physical world was to be suffered through until heaven could be attained and we got our reward. The Inuit Grandmother was correct: in order to be a True Human, our spiritual nature had to be recognized in our physical world.

"Spiritual bypassing," a term first coined by psychologist John Welwood in 1984, is the use of spiritual practices and beliefs to avoid dealing with our painful feelings, unresolved wounds, and developmental needs. I had learned that it was easy to disassociate from the messy aspects of life by "ascending," and I had learned some wonderful things from people who treated physical life as a burden to be "transcended." But I was getting schooled directly. It is not "spiritual" to pretend everything is okay when it is not, to ignore or explain away when any of All Creation is suffering.

I became interested in activism. I rejected the notion that a spiritual person did not tackle the issues facing humanity, and I gained the understanding of my aboriginal ancestors: **taking care of business, interacting with the world IS spiritual**. Getting your hands dirty, being willing to trip and fall, being temporarily uncomfortable in order to make the world a better place IS spiritual. I realized that the feminine in All Things wants a just world, wants healing for everyone, wants everyone to be taken care of.

I made the connection that modern pop spirituality is yet another "salvationist" construct of the unpartnered masculine, and that the Feminine asks us to return to our reality as creatures of Earth, with a planet to love and take care of and fellow beings that need help. We are on the brink. Acting under her guidance, the birth of our reconnection to the partnered masculine, the Just Warrior, has begun—and that means setting boundaries.

Great Mother Says NO

I can understand the seductive appeal of spiritual philosophies that focus beyond the immediate reality. Sometimes immediate reality is terrifying, painful, or at the least, unpleasant. But how do we change things if we do not face them, if we do not feel the angst and mobilize ourselves to act?

If we let gurus tell us that our desires are debased and that we should not have any, that strips us of our very humanity and we become automatons. If we let someone else tell us what stories to live, we are living *their* stories and we cease to be the authors of our own lives.

Life is full of disappointments because we have desires that are not fulfilled when or how we want them fulfilled, but that is part of living! If we try to escape disappointment by *having no desire*, what kind of life is that? It may be a reprieve from pain to go to the clouds and meditate, which is great for keeping us healthy, but only as a temporary measure. When we come back down to earth, we will notice that the pain we escaped for a time is still there where we left it. It must be faced in order for our lives to be *fully lived*.

I was not allowed to say "NO" as a child, as many of us are not, and if we do not heal those old issues, we find ways of making implicit YESes okay so that we can live with what is happening. We allow ourselves to be formed by the SHOULDs of others rather than the whispered, passionate wants of our own hearts. We get used by the world, instead of showing up in our unique role and *being of use* to the world.

I finally understood. Great Mother, the aspect of the Divine Feminine that births and nurtures all life, holds the big picture and knows what is life-affirming for All Things, cries out at injustice and harm, and it is Great Father, my name for the father aspect of the Divine Masculine dynamic, the Defender/Protector and Just Warrior, that acts on her guidance and inspiration! Great Father arises at Great Mother's bidding, stands at Her side, and moves when She tells Him to move.

In the partnered state, these two primal energies are the yin/yang of how life continues. One births it from her cosmic womb, and the other protects and defends it. This is how life began and how it has continued since the beginning of time. The seamless union of birth/nurture and protect/defend gives everything in creation its best chance to live and is how life is supposed to be.

When you grow up in a family where there are no boundaries, where the feminine is in victim mode and the masculine is in predator mode, there is no Sacred Union of two Divine opposites, just a seamless union of two dysfunctional dualities that keep things in a constant state of chaos and disarray, which is NOT conducive to life's continuation. It is a mirror of the collective psyche, revealed by the state of the world and popular culture. Mommy and Daddy are fighting, putting all of their children in a precarious position, so life is vulnerable to NOT continuing—Earth and humanity's problems summed up in a nutshell.

Bringing it back into my individual psyche, having chaos and victimization as the norm and no modeling of appropriate boundaries, I had learned to regulate to chaos and stress, to allow crazy things to happen to me, and not to stand up for myself! As a child, my inner feminine felt the injustices and they made her angry, but my inner masculine had been cut off at the knees, so later in life, he did not lay down the law and protect/defend me. My voice had been caged and so was acculturated to being silent and allowing things to go on that should not have been allowed to go on.

Once I realized the imbalanced state of the Defender aspect of my inner masculine, I was mortified. I had seen my inner masculine emasculated in the way that I frequently did not speak up for myself when a boundary had been crossed, or hyper-masculine or defensive in the way that I would cut off from my feelings of empathy and connection (feminine) and express (expression is masculine) my feelings in a harsher way than I could have to my husband or sons.

Of course, it made sense that I developed my inner masculine the way I had; my masculine role models were alternately aggressive, dominant or critical (hyper-masculine), weak, failed to protect me when it was needed, or distant/absent. I did have some middle-of-the-road modeling in certain areas of the masculine, so I was able to internalize that, but in the protection/defense department, I was sorely lacking in supportive training. What we see as we grow up is what we believe to be the standard, and my standard needed updating.

I asked Great Father, to help retrain me. I was guided to look for examples of balanced defenders in the world in order to inform myself about what that looked like. This was so helpful, as I am a visual learner and also learn by example!

I noticed when I heard or watched stories about balanced defenders that I would feel my blood rise, my feeling of righteous justice would be activated, as if I could call up the same feeling, as if the feeling of wanting to protect/defend was universal. (It is.) This was informative; it told me that I was not a lost cause, but that I could indeed be shown how to align with the balanced masculine Defender because *it was already within me.*

Giving ourselves permission to have our own unique point of view, speaking up when we are interrupted, protecting a child from a threat, protesting against actions that threaten the Whole—this is the Balanced Defender. Any time we set a boundary, we are defending something that we care about, and this action in and of itself is a masculine dynamic. But what makes defense balanced is acting in accordance with the discernment, connectivity, and wisdom of the feminine. THAT'S what makes it balanced.

Defense uninformed by the feminine is defense without regard for the bigger picture. The masculine principle, in its quest for individuation, can defend something that does NOT serve the Whole, such as a corporation that creates major environmental issues in the name of profit. To bring it closer to home, we can defend an idea or belief that we learned but that has not passed through our inner feminine's ability to *feel* whether that belief is truth. The feminine principle informs the masculine principle about what needs defending, why it needs defending, and how to do it in the most supportive way.

Enabling Bad Behavior

This period of my life felt like the most full of growth in all the years on the road with my family. It was the **landing and grounding** point of my re-education. All of the years of welcoming the feminine forward in my psyche/body/daily experience resulted in my now embodying her, and she was anchored in.

In 2010, we decided to stay in Tallahassee. Our family journey was over. We would now continue our odyssey to grow in the Aquarian principles of the partnered feminine and masculine while staying put in one place.

Now that the feminine was anchored in my lived experience, the next big step for me was healing the inner masculine in my psyche, who had learned broken boundaries and poor defense skills. I had allowed myself to become a repository for other people's negative emotions through empathy for their suffering. Becoming full of others' anger, sadness, depression, grief, and fear, I felt as if I had a trail of anchors behind me. Of course, I was trained to absorb others' unconsciousness by my parents and society in general; but being an empath makes you a sponge, and if your inner masculine is broken, you do not know how to set boundaries. You can hold onto people's emotions for so long that you forget those emotions are not yours! The only thing that can be done is to enliven the Boundary Maker inside, the inner masculine, and say NO MORE.

I saw him as a scared little boy or the angry young man I had seen when I broke my ankle. I was becoming painfully aware of my lack of boundaries over my adult life, and set intentions to mature my inner masculine and bring my inner feminine and inner masculine together, into partnership. Such deep examination of the issues in my *own inner relationship* forced me to look at troubling issues *in my marriage* with my beloved husband. I saw how I had enabled him to get away with stepping out of his power (and therefore avoid taking care of important things.)

Our marriage had been rocked by our unhealthy relationship with his parents: he was silent when they said hurtful things to or about me and did not stand up and protect/defend the mother of his children. This was another expression of the emasculated inner masculine! I thought I was a strong and independent woman—I should take care of myself, right? I struggled with expecting Peter to take care of me. I was worried that it would be perceived as weakness to ask him to step forward in this way. After having children, though, I found I wanted and needed from him a "feeling of shelter." I was nurturing our babies and needed to be soft, motherly, feminine. I needed him to show up as the masculine in our relationship.

With the guidance of a trusted therapist, I had set boundaries years prior with my own parents, creating distance when they did not honor them. In the case of Peter's parents and family, I had given power away to Peter. I did repeatedly speak to Peter's parents about things that I was uncomfortable with, with no support from Peter, but it seemed more often than not, my attempts were either turned around to make me the bad guy or there was no change in behavior. I stood up for myself several times with them, but I frequently did not feel heard or acknowledged. It might have helped them hear me better if Peter had stood with me, in union, supporting and in alignment with me, instead of being mute. I wanted HIM to choose me, to stand WITH me, and at least protect me from them. But over all of these years, he did not. I was furious with him, and the anger was between us, getting in the way of our relationship.

I began to understand how my emasculated inner masculine had looked to Peter to step up as MY externalized masculine. I was expecting Peter to portray the ideal masculine traits I had hoped to learn from my father. I was projecting my need to be fathered onto my husband, and I needed him to teach my inner masculine "how to be a man!" However, I also felt acutely that Peter had fallen short in his duty to me as my husband to protect and hold the sanctity of our marriage and his wife.

My anger at Peter came forward now with vengeance. I understood with righteous rage that *it was correct* to want him to take care of us, to protect us, and to defend me personally. I had made a solemn vow to give my life to this man! I could be strong and independent as a woman and still expect that my life partner would do what he could to keep my heart safe from his family. His silence in the face of their commentary had left me feeling unsafe, betrayed, and oh, so familiar. It was similar to how I had felt with my parents. Dammit, how could he do this to me?

I voiced my anger strongly to him now, not the subtle requests of the past, but wide open, and loud and clear. "This is what I expect. This is what you have done/not done. This is the way I need it to be." The voicing of these real feelings was a VERY important part of the process. I needed to unapologetically claim and express my hurt over the twenty-plus years of our marriage, not soften, hide it or whitewash it. It was in me, and it had been poisoning our relationship. It had to come out, as ugly and painful as it was.

Fortunately, Peter listened to me. Hard. He was mortified to see and feel my anger at him so clearly, and to glimpse how he had failed to step into his masculine role in our marriage and family. He hated that he had unconsciously hurt me so much. His acknowledgment of my feelings, his true *receiving* of my anger freed me to stop and look at how, *together*, we had unconsciously recreated the dynamic of our childhoods. I was a decision-making leader as a woman and he was a subservient, whatever-makes you happy man. I was "the boss" and he, the follower. AND I had made sure that I would never be preyed upon or dominated in any way by any man, informed by treatment by my father and having witnessed the victimization in my mother. My damaging childhood had created a marriage in which I was designed to be in charge, and therefore would presumably be safe. Ohhhhhhhhh . . . Eureka!!!

I had not only *allowed* my husband and the father of my children to get away with his behavior, I had *trained* him to be that way! In my face was the fact that I had played a major role in this painful dynamic between us. The ways I had enabled him included: having no expectation that he would protect/defend me because I was used to surviving on my own, then becoming "spiritual" and transcending the pain of his betrayal, and lastly, (when I *finally did* allow myself to see/feel the pain) not setting boundaries and consequences if he did not transform his relationship skills. I smacked myself in the forehead when I saw how clearly I had manifested the shift in our larger dynamic—by insisting we take a family odyssey, by doing so much internal work, by handing over the finances of our family after I had handled them for eighteen years, by embodying the feminine, by forcing Peter to occupy a caretaker role when I broke my ankle, by being vulnerable, by allowing him to take care of me, by inviting his masculine forward by being more feminine, and finally getting so angry about the dynamic that it came pouring out of me in a way that had been received.

In the beginning of our relationship, Peter had said how much he appreciated that I was a "strong woman," and I was proud of that. Somehow, needing him to step into a protector role meant that I was weak, at least in my damaged framework. But he did not know how to be masculine in the ways I needed, and I sure as hell was not going to let go of the reins—I did not know what would happen if I did!

The universe made sure that I let go, and our family odyssey (as it turns out) was (in large part) learning how to be the

Divine Masculine for Peter. It could only happen, though, if I stepped back and embodied the Sacred Feminine. Now we were learning about the opposite roles, balancing out over our midlife. The feminine had to come first, and her magnetic nature drew the masculine forward into partnership. Now that she was present, holding court in her center, the masculine could step up to act on her inspiration, because she knew what was good for the whole. Now it was his turn to learn to trust her and to surrender his false sense of power through defensive resistance and passive aggressive behavior. He could truly step into blissful partnership with her. No more power struggle!

This outer dynamic of my marriage echoes my inner dynamic (no surprise there!). My own inner masculine is currently learning to surrender to the wisdom of my inner feminine, the seat of All Things, the ground of All Being.

It came to me, as I understood this cosmic dance between the yin and the yang, that every time we enable something or someone, every moment we give away our power, it is because our inner feminine and inner masculine are resisting one another. Now I can understand the bigger picture and why we give our power away, enabling bad behavior by not setting boundaries and allowing dysfunction or madness to continue. The pop "spirituality" movement of "positive thinking" can devolve into ignoring monstrous horrors; "Don't focus on what feels bad" is a dangerous precedent if we care about the state of All Creation.

We live in a country where several forms of madness are encouraged. Greed, addiction, mental illness. We turn our heads away from people hurting one another. We medicate ourselves so we don't have to feel our pain. When we don't pay attention to pain, we can let awful things happen.

When someone is mad, they don't have the capacity to make a good decision any more, and that is when we must step in. If madness is allowed to go unchecked, there is nothing to prevent the presence of it becoming larger, growing.

Boundaries are in place for a reason. There is a line of acceptable behavior, and when it is crossed, it is correct for us to be upset, enraged even. Being angry means a boundary has been crossed, and it is appropriate.

But will we have the courage to feel our pain? And will we let our pain become something that mobilizes us to act, to say no? Will we enable madness to continue? Enabling is what we do when we don't confront the truth and stand up to it, making it stop. Sometimes love means saying NO. Do we love ourselves and humanity enough to set a limit? How will it ever change if we don't say NO?

Jesus was born into a dark and impoverished world, surrounded by violence. The light of the Christed One came into a world that was in stark contrast to the love and justice he eventually preached. If the metaphor holds up that the light of consciousness equals each of us being "Christed," then the awakening of our own consciousness into our hearts will light up the wickedness in the world, exposing it for what it is.

If we want the world to change, we must first see the evil, and then acknowledge it.

Just as the unconsciousness in myself had to be seen and called out in order for me to recover and heal myself, so the unconsciousness had to be seen and called out in my marriage in order for it to be healed. Our hearts must be kept safe and that cannot happen when we run from problems. Great Mother had saved my marriage.

The Rubber Meets the Road

Tallahassee proved to be the environment that we needed to continue our family healing work. Life continued in a more settled way with the kids stationed in good school situations. Peter and I worked steadily on our marriage, with bumps and twists in the road. I found that I was able to connect with some women, but seemed to frighten others. My troubles with women had not been completely alleviated.

Jess, my precious oldest son, was turning sixteen and would start to drive. This next emergence into the great wide world for my baby boy brought up some old terror. As usual, I processed it by going inward. As he celebrated his birthday, I ruminated on the events that led up to that day and remembered my fear about his birth.

My pregnancy had been flawless. I LOVED being pregnant. I felt powerful and sexy, the embodiment of Great Mother.

As Jess's due date got closer, I had wondered how I would get this giant child out of my body. I seem to grow big babies and at almost ten pounds, my doctor was concerned that we would have to do a C-section if he didn't hurry it along. I didn't know any better for this first baby, not having any mothering influences around to remind me to trust my body's knowing.

As the due date came and went, I puzzled over why this baby wasn't coming. Was it up to the baby to decide? Was it up to my body? Was it a dance between the baby, my body, and something larger that made the decision as to his arrival?

My doctor gave me an ultimatum. We would wait no longer than two weeks after the due date, or risk having surgery to bring Jess into the world. We scheduled a date "just in case." I asked a woman I worked with about how to choose a date, and she told me that more animals are born before a full moon than after, so I chose to schedule his birth the night before the full moon. Those two weeks, I prayed a lot. *Please come, Jess. Let him go, body.* But to no avail.

The morning of his scheduled birth, I was so scared and sad. Scared because I had no idea what to expect and sad because I felt my body had somehow betrayed me. It had not allowed the birth process to happen as it was supposed to. My body was not letting this child go. It was not releasing him into the world. That was a big clue for me, much later in my life, about my core emotional wound: ***the world is not safe***.

I was given Pitocin to rush things along and an epidural to keep me from losing my mind during the birth of an almost ten-pound baby. After labor pains of nine hours or so, I pushed for two hours, lost a lot of blood, and Peter thought both Jess and I were going to die. I felt as if there were two of me—the one that wanted this baby out of my body and the one that was hanging on to him as if life depended on it.

Eventually, the *me* that wanted him out won by a slight margin. I remember the moment; the doctor said Jess was in distress. This remarkable baby had been moving his head in an effort to help the move down the birth canal, but he was weakening. He was stuck and losing strength. I had been bleeding and pushing for two hours, exhausted and freaked out because I didn't seem to be getting anywhere. The room filled with varied medical professionals, and a room for surgery was prepared. I thought I couldn't do any more. But when I heard the doctor making noises that intimated that he may not make it, something bigger than the me that wanted to keep him safely in my body took over, and I pushed with a strength that came from Source itself. I was no longer in the room; I was the Big Bang. Suddenly, I exploded and gave birth to the universe. Jess was born.

He was blue and limp, needing oxygen for a couple of minutes. His poor little head was shaped like a cone from being in between my pelvic bones for so long. But he lived. Thank god for his determination.

My body was torn to shreds physically; the inner conflict I had experienced left me exhausted and ripped open emotionally. My most basic fear had been exposed, the scab of an old, but very alive wound, ripped right off. The pulsating well of grief and fear within, that was subsequently exposed, took me down a rabbit hole of two years of postpartum depression, and the reemergence of my spirit back into my life. And healing.

So, in a very real way, this beautiful boy who was turning sixteen saved my life. He is still a teacher to me every day; wise beyond his years and with seeming nerves of steel, he has a tender heart and genuine caring for all humanity. When he decides to do something, he does it with mastery. I am amazed sometimes at the ease with which he moves through the world.

But it was his entrance into the world through my body that taught me one of my most precious lessons. No matter what our fears and doubts, no matter what wounds may seize us, no matter how we may try to prevent or resist the flow, *life wins*.

When Jess was born, I was bloodily initiated into motherhood, taught, in no uncertain terms, that bringing life into being is a violent act and requires sacrifice into the alchemical crucible for transformation. While he had been inside my body, he was safe. Letting him go into the world went against my instincts. I began to understand that being a mother meant letting go and living in a state of acceptance of whatever may come. My protective and hovering way of mothering had to give way to a different energy, that of Great Mother, the mother of everything in existence.

The Mother of All Things, by whatever name or faculty of the mind, has shown us great love in that we were born. The sheer fact of the miracle of life is proof of the essential generous nature of the universe. Life continues, no matter what. Once life is given, a myriad labyrinth of experiences occurs that require acceptance of the great workings of the universe. It is part of being feminine to let go, to allow, and to surrender. The births of my sons were acts of trust, a requirement asked by life itself.

Lunar Mother, Lunar Daughter

I have gotten to know Dark Mother well during my life, through my various traumas and the choice to recover from them through honesty-assessment and journeying through the inner landscape. This life has not been an easy traipse through the meadow! My journey was one of alchemy, the true process of transforming lead into gold. In alchemy, **nigredo**, or blackness, means putrefaction or decomposition. I had made compost from my challenging experiences my whole life. The darkness of my experiences led me to discover the gold within, something that I understand not everyone gets to encounter. This took surrender. The alchemists believed that as a first step in the pathway to the philosopher's stone, all alchemical ingredients had to be cleansed and cooked extensively to a uniform black matter. The sacrifice of the previous form was required. Initiation came as a result of complete decimation of the old form and rebirth into a new one.

The Mother Wound that I had been healing built my capacity to heal the worst that life can offer, making me a **Lunar Daughter**. My own mother had been a **Lunar Mother**, showing me the dark face of life's difficulties and releasing me to navigate my way through the dark night of the soul. My path brought me to face my own shadow, as well as to the collective and ancestral shadows.

Looking back, my healing seems miraculous; yet, it seems I had been following a trail that other pioneers had followed. In diving headlong into the unconscious, I uncovered the Self, the wholeness in the center of the psyche. I was moving out of my internal psyche and making forays into the world shadow. My inner experience shifted, and I noticed my inner landscape change from the deep watery world into one of dry land. I was topside again, playing in the sun. My blending of shamanism, neurobiology, and spirituality created an ideal container for deep mothering to transform the harshest pain. Uniting the conscious and unconscious, Inner Tribe™ work was swift and permanent.

My troubles with women made sense to me now; I reflected the collective unconscious to them and that was frightening to those devoted to the solar aspects of the psyche, to those who resisted looking into their own darkness. Inner Tribe™ work was nothing but lunar work in the bowels of the unconscious. It changed the darkness into light. This remarkable method of healing was revolutionary and yet as profoundly simple as being a loving mother. I had transcribed the words of the Source of All Life when the "Invocation of Great Mother Within" came through me in 2008. My calling Her forward was now almost to full fruition.

Mothering and Allowing

I was guided to relax into another aspect of the Sacred Feminine—Allowing. To me, this felt akin to "going with the flow," or the term "surrender." While I understood the concept in some areas of my life, I found it challenging to do as a mother with my children.

There was an ever-present internal dialogue from the time my boys were born. *Is this supportive for them to experience, or is this something I need to set a limit about?*, etc. In my efforts to protect them, sometimes hyper-vigilantly, I may have sheltered them too much. Learning to let go has been a constant process.

The stakes were smaller when they were little. *Should I let them try this food, play with that kid, see this tv show?*, etc.— little decisions as a mom to prepare me for the bigger decisions that would come as they got older. Fortunately, the balance of having their dad around prevented me from putting protective bubbles around them, even as I cringed when he threw them in the air or wrestled with them on the floor.

As they grew, they entered into realms where they could really get hurt. *Is it supportive for me to let them play football, is it supportive for them to have a long-term girlfriend already?*, etc. We entered the realm of greater potential physical harm or heart/emotional harm.

At seventeen, Jess, my oldest, was driving and had just come out of a year and a half relationship with a girl. Halfway through his junior year in high school, he intended to leave for college just a year and a half later. He was so grounded and so capable in so many ways, but I still had fears for his safety, whether emotional or physical. This has never changed, as I will be a mother for as long as I am alive.

The guidance I had received to "be more allowing" really caused me to pause. *But I have* been *allowing in so many ways*, I thought.

"However," She told me, "you have been allowing to the point that you were able. **Now it is time to grow, to be more allowing, to trust. To allow is to step back, to let what will unfold unfold, without interference. Even if it means that someone you love very much could be hurt.**"

"Oh," I said.

Having developed a habit of wanting to control things so that my children could experience a healthier emotional family than the ones my husband and I grew up in, this idea of "allowing" pushed against the edges of my Mother Bear aspect—but perhaps Mother Bear was appropriate when her cubs were small. Now they were learning to survive in the world, and trial and error were the key to learning natural consequences. They must be allowed to fall in order to learn how to pick themselves back up.

I wondered if this is how it works on a macro scale, **if the Sacred Feminine is allowing humanity to explore and design new ways of living, even if the unfolding of those explorations eventually results in the end of us? Is this the greatest love there is: to create, and then allow what you care about to destroy itself in the spirit of us learning natural consequences of our choices?**

I am allowed a lot of room to become who I am, and for that I am grateful. I make mistakes, I fall on my face, and I choose to learn. I believe this makes me a better person. Perhaps this was what I must do for my children, as She does for us.

It was confusing to me how Great Mother could be allowing and be a voice of rage at injustice at the same time. How do those polar opposites coexist? I felt the boundary-making aspect of the masculine and the inspired righteous concern of the feminine, but the allowing aspect was so accepting it almost felt as if it could be the energy that made the universe. *Is Prime Source, the first Source of All things, then feminine?*

Great Mother Presents the Answer

At the end of 2012, I published **Soul Compost – Transforming Adversity into Spiritual Growth**. That book was the result of two years of writing and many years of healing and recovery, with a focus on women's resilience and post-traumatic growth.

One Billion Rising Tallahassee, 2013

As a natural follow-up, I organized the 2013 One Billion Rising event in my city, and saw nearly four hundred women dance in the rain on a cool February Valentine's Day morning to bring attention to (and reclaim their bodies from) violence against women. It was an extraordinary day.

Jess had gone to college for his freshman year that fall of 2012; his first semester was not stellar. As he sat with us that holiday break, he saw his grades and fell apart. He had not expected that he would do poorly. This was an indication to us that he was not in touch with the reality of being a college adult who knew how to take care of his education. We set boundaries with him about doing a WHOLE LOT better his second semester or he would have a very short college career and come home.

I have wondered in subsequent years if we had kept him home instead of sending him back for his second semester if things would have turned out differently.

A New Definition of Allowing

Life became different for us as of one a.m. Monday, March 25, 2013. My eldest son, Jess, received a traumatic brain injury in a skateboarding accident that required brain surgery to save his life. BRAIN SURGERY.

It was a strange, surreal landscape we were walking then. I was closer than ever to my inner guidance and it continued to guide me well as I navigated this new territory. Writing to keep our extensive community of friends/family updated helped me keep my own head straight and, perhaps, oriented me as I found my way. Writing is a great coping strategy for me, helping me find a quiet place and solace for my words, things I find I cannot or don't have space to say. Writing is my meditation. It helped me find my ground then too.

At a little after one o'clock a.m. that March morning, we were awakened by the phone call that every parent dreads; our son Jess, age nineteen and a freshman at the University of Central Florida in Orlando, had been admitted to the emergency room with a head injury. He had been "garage bombing", a skateboarding antic which begins at the top of a multi-storied parking deck to speed as fast as possible to the bottom. He raced with two buddies, pro skaters, (without a helmet, despite our many pleas) and at the last ramp at the bottom of the parking deck hit a thin trickle of water after a recent storm in Orlando, and he went flying. He hit the pavement at about thirty miles an hour and fractured his skull. He was apparently unconscious for about seven minutes after seizing, my baby boy's body thrashing on the cold pavement. His buddies, who did not have phones, yelled to some strangers to call 9-1-1. This quick action saved Jess's life.

He arrived at the emergency room by ambulance somewhat coherent, but started to deteriorate rapidly, getting more confused by the minute. Peter spoke to the doctor after a CAT scan, which indicated the fracture, but also a large blood clot between the brain and the skull. It was necessary to operate immediately; apparently, with brain injuries, time is of the essence.

Peter gave permission for the required brain surgery over the phone while I went inward to see if there was any guidance. I was told there was a brain injury but that Jess would recover. Waking Aidan up to tell him that we needed to go to Orlando to see about his brother was a heart wrencher. We high-tailed it to Orlando (a four-hour drive that we made in about three), speeding through the night. What a surreal experience.

Over the drive, I kept hearing *"See him healed and whole."* It was so easy to go down the path of our worst fears, and each time I did meander that way, I was gently corrected with this mantra. I felt the strength and courage return to me each time I thought this powerful thought. I shared this with Peter and Aidan, and this became our collective mantra.

We arrived after Jess was out of surgery and in the ICU. We were told that the surgery was successful in removing the clot from Jess's brain. He was patched up (he had a new piece of hardware in his skull, a plate that we agreed we would gently tease him a little about once he was well). He responded well to the surgery, showing good vitals. He was really out of it when we got there, as was to be expected.

A little while later in the morning, he was lucid enough to say his head hurt. The very funny and optimistic nurse who buoyed our spirits said, "Well, DUH. You hit your head."

He had no memory of the event. He also felt his head and asked where his hair went.

Later, an occupational therapist came in to test his brain functioning; this was the part that Peter and I were the most afraid about. Jess was an intelligent and gifted writer and speaker, a loving and kind personality, just a delight. Our worry (besides that he would not make it) was that there would be permanent brain damage. Jess passed the test with flying colors. Even in his very groggy state, he was able to say our names, the date and the time on a clock, Aidan's birth date and year, and he could follow three-step instructions.  WHEW. The occupational therapist said she felt really good about Jess's chances at a full recovery, as did the doctor when we spoke with him again later.

Jess was moved from the ICU at two-thirty p.m. that afternoon. That and the fact that when he finally opened his eyes, complaining about how annoyed he was with the gadgets all over him and how much he hurt, were good signs. We are not out of the danger window yet. The first seventy-two hours were crucial. But we were celebrating the small victories.

We were told that Jess would not focus or concentrate very well for four to six weeks; he would be unable to finish his semester at school, which was a shame because he was doing very well that semester. We would bring him home and work with him in the ways we were taught. In the beginning of this strange, new journey, there was much to learn.

During the many phone conversations, texts, and messages of concern (they all ran together for me), I felt a consistent wave of support. My inner guidance, the same guidance that gave me the "Healed and Whole" mantra, said that MY job was to ALLOW. That felt akin to receiving the true gifts of love that were being offered, the true expressions of love with no strings attached. People caring with no expectation, people doing things because they loved us.

I am aware that in my life I have developed a strong independence, an "I can do it myself" attitude. This is, in part, due to the failure to feel loved and protected as a child, but also is part of my natural personality. My soul has a lot of pluck. But the danger of having a strong, independent will is getting in the habit of not allowing others to help. "I can do it myself" starts to get very lonely when you are facing emotional crisis. Then it becomes "No one cares about me." It feels like being in an empty room, alone and silent.

The instruction to ALLOW was an active learning curve for me; it required conscious effort to soften the turtle shell on my back and receive the gifts of love that were offered. *Yes, you can pick up our mail. Yes, you can take care of our cat. Yes, you can make us dinner. Yes, Yes, Yes.*

Allowing, receiving, saying yes, being in the flow of grace is extraordinary.

The year after Jess's injury, we worked together to bring him back to a modicum of normal life for a young man of twenty years. He achieved one hundred percent in his recovery by two years, a battle won by his determination and by utilizing every healing technique I knew, in addition to everything I learned. Our months together while he healed seemed to give me another chance to "raise a baby" for the second time, except at high-speed. He recovered in such leaps and bounds as to defy all expectations of his medical staff. They said, "It's a miracle." Over and over.

Jess has had to manage his emotions and energy through discernment, intention, attention, and gentleness so that he is healthy. He has a bit of a perfection attachment and is hard on himself for perceived losses or failures. He has given himself extraordinary grief for "losing time" in his college track.

My counsel to him has been that there is a Larger Logic, a greater plan or flow to his life than the ordinary routine for most young people. He has been learning to be more caring to himself as if he were a little boy in need of a kind adult, showing sweetness and gentleness, and acceptance. His transformation has included becoming more receptive, allowing, self-reflective, and less giving, active, outer-focused. More BEING and less DOING.

He had to learn patience, not easy for someone who loves to do things fast and pushes himself hard to compete. He has been asked to change the way he relates to life by slowing down and honoring a deeper part of himself. Jess has had to find a different rhythm. His life is changed forever, hopefully for the positive.

I see these changes in him as an expression of "allowing." Great Mother had claimed my firstborn son for her own.

His "accident" was caused by traveling over a thin trickle of water, a line of feminine energy that he attempted to cross very fast on his skateboard. The water caused his skateboard, traveling at twenty-five to thirty miles an hour, to lift, bringing the right side of his skull, head first, down into supplication, to the Earth (in this case, concrete.) The right side of his skull fractured in two places as a result of this intimate, sudden, hard, and insistent contact with his Earth Mother, bursting his carotid artery and creating an epidural hematoma. *Epi-dural* means above or over the dura; the **Dura Mater** is the leather-like covering that protects the brain under the skull, and literally translates to "Tough Mother." This "tough mother" protected his brain from further harm as the Earth Mother reclaimed him.

As I ruminated after his injury, working for the years on my own feminine awareness became an auspicious preceding chapter to Jess's trial. I had been told in 2011 that to *allow* is to step back, to let what will unfold unfold, without interference—even if it means that someone you love very much could be hurt. Then I had become the "Tough Mother" in that I had survived almost the hardest thing of my life. The thing that could have made me crumple did not. The mysterious great force I had come to know gave me strength in ways I cannot explain.

During the intense event of my son's traumatic brain injury—emergency brain surgery and recovery—I really "got" that I was still expecting my biological mother to show up for me in ways that she is incapable. I "got" that I was waiting around to be scooped up and nourished and greatly cherished, but while she intellectually rationalized that she loved me, I did not experience that. I did not see evidence that she loved me because she made no actions to show me that.

Jess's injury was the second hardest thing I had survived. The first was my mother's rejection. I had no energy, no reserves to tolerate or hope for change in people who could not love me. There was nothing there for me, and it was time to face the facts. It was so clear. Everything I had lived through had prepared me for this moment. I could let her go.

Dura Mater

In the two years after Jess's injury, I encountered my feminine and my masculine aspects as sides of my brain. Deepening my research on the brain and the elements that are represented by each hemisphere, I have created a body of work that is infused with the Sacred Systems material (the body of work that came through my art in 2010). This has led me to create leadership, feminist, and system-balancing classes and workshops that are profound for women who seek to know their sacredness. I can truly see that Jess's injury in March 2013 heralded my biggest breakthrough with the Divine Feminine. My growth since that time has been powerful.

During those two years, I also noticed feeling more strange sensations in *my* brain. When I asked the bigger intelligence what was going on, I was told that I was again strengthening my "central hemispheric union" and that this was part of achieving partnership of my left and right hemispheres at a more committed level. I again sensed a feeling of activation in the region of my pineal gland, sometimes very aware of it, as if it were "lit up" or vibrating.

I have practiced shamanism for many, many years, so I knew that I was witnessing shamanic initiation when Jess went through his experience. Not one to buy into the average American life, it makes me glad that he is discovering another aspect of life that is so rewarding, so deeply connected to the old medicine of Earth and our ancestors. It flies in the face of what society asks us to become when we embark into adulthood. The temptation to be what others want us to be is strong; there is a promise of security and belonging if we just give our power to that larger belief system, but security is only real when it comes from the inside, from our sense of knowing, from our sense of self. Otherwise, the concept of being safe and secure is dependent on outer circumstances, which are subject to change.

The ground beneath our feet is one of the most primal securities we have. Our connection to Earth is something we take for granted, in that it is always *there*—like the mother we always wanted and the one we all deserve, ever present, ever supporting, ever nourishing, ever loving.

When Jess was insistently brought back to the Earth, he was being reclaimed by his Great Mother, the Mother who is also his mother's mother, and all who came before her—the Big Mama, the source of his body and blood. The elements of the Earth are what combine in the most amazing, miraculous manner to form our physical bodies. The collective intelligence there is pure consciousness taking form through the Earth's body within each of us. The relationship to the Earth is very similar to the relationship we might have with our concept of God, as a maker and overseer, the larger intelligence that governs the universe—except that the Earth feels like Great Mother, in that we are held on the planet by the sheer magnetism of her embrace (gravity), are nourished by her body, and held by her warm and powerful presence even if we do not notice her.

Is this the behavior of a mother? I feel it is, having lived as a mother informed by Great Mother for more than forty-three years.

The oldest, most primary relationship we have on Earth is the one with our human mother, and before that, the oldest, most primary relationship is with the Mother that birthed All

Creation. I have come to believe that the enduring tie with the birth mother transcends any time apart or relational difficulty, that we are energetically connected regardless of estrangement or conflict.

I forgave my mother for many things during the years I spent healing myself, but even though I forgave her, I still needed her to show up as my mother. I wished so often that she would call me and say, "Licia, my eldest and treasured and wise daughter, I have been so wrong to slander and discount you. You were right, and I ask your forgiveness for being so hurtful to you. How can I repair our relationship?"

But no such words were forthcoming. I waited and waited. For twenty-five years, I waited.

My attachment to receiving what I could not get from my biological mother kept me on perpetual "hold," and waiting for her to wake up and love me did not feed me, but drained me of life force. It became apparent after Jess's brain injury that I had no energy left for anything other than Jess. I could barely nurture myself. I was completely tapped out. I realized it was necessary to sever any expectation of support from my mother (or father) with a protective warrior stance, keeping boundaries so I did not "bleed energy" in her direction. My mother's continued addiction and marriage to my father went past any hope of a safe place for me to land. I refused to interact with her while I worked tirelessly with Jess to gain recovery. It was just too much.

I spoke with Great Mother regularly during his recovery and took solace in Her presence. She was there in the darkness with me, holding me, stroking my head, or rubbing my back to comfort me. At times, I physically felt a brush down my arm or a pat on my hair. I wondered a couple of times if I was going crazy, but the comfort was real. Did it really matter if I was not actually being caressed by a loving mother presence?

What DID matter was that I could keep showing up in absolute presence, awareness, and action for my son and family. Everything else paled in comparison. Somehow, I kept going. It seemed as if I gained energy and connection from some great mysterious well of love and life force. Her voice guided me at times when a mother's wisdom was so needed.

In July 2013, just a scant few months after Jess's injury, it came to me that Great Mother had kept me whole all of my years on the planet, despite the "bleeding" from the connection with my mother. Similar to the Dura Mater saving Jess's life by preventing his bleeding from entering the recesses of his brain, I had been protected at an essential spiritual/core level from my dysfunctional parents by an inner layer of "Tough Mother" in childhood. . . . and now, when I needed to remain exquisitely aware of caring for my family. The Dura Mater that saved Jess's life had also saved mine.

Now I understood. "Great Mother Says No" was made of the partnership of feminine energy WITH masculine energy. When the feminine and masculine partner, the feminine becomes active and makes boundaries with the solar energy of the masculine. The masculine becomes The Warrior/Defender/Protector at her request.

Great Mother is different than the feminine in its entirety. The general feminine or yin energy does not include boundary-making as part of its qualities. The feminine/yin energy is the vast void of pure potential, no boundaries, no friction, no light, nothing for light to bounce off of—just a long, long YESSSSSSSSSSSSSSSSS, pure acceptance. She has no masculine partner, except for when she becomes Great Mother. Great Mother holds an embrace of all life, her "arms" circling around us, which is a boundary in itself. The Womb that holds the universe is Great Mother, because a womb contains and creates a boundary for life to grow within its embrace.

Any time we set a boundary, we defend something that we care about, and this action in and of itself is a masculine dynamic, partnered with the feminine. Defense is balanced by acting in accordance with the discernment, connectivity, and wisdom of the feminine. The dance between the feminine and masculine is what makes it balanced, or partnered, and therefore in accordance with life-affirming natural laws. Doing the tango is good for All Creation.

Vision Quest

During Jess's first year of recovery, we decided that going west for a road trip to his birthplace needed to be included as part of his healing.

Everyone who was watching Jess knew the symbolic resurrection he was going through and commented on it. This experience in our lives happened to fall on Easter week, where there was a template that we could follow for metaphorical death and rebirth. This synchronicity was not lost on me, as a symbolic thinker and spiritual person.

One friend offered, "As his mother, his existence is crucial and built into your mom DNA. This casts a big vote on this side that the cosmos can hear. You're not done with him in this lifetime yet and it sounds like he's not done with this lifetime yet, either. This is Easter. Happy Easter. And happy resurrection and rebirth to your beautiful son, you, and your family."

Jess was once again becoming a creature of the Earth, just as he was when he was younger, before he became so caught up in the mind games of his peers and culture, and before he felt a need to risk his life to prove that he was indeed alive. He is softer, more mature, more considered in his decisions now. His body has becoming more precious to him. He was indeed initiated as a shaman, brought back down to the old path, the path of his lineage and destiny. The Earth had reclaimed him.

I suggested that he share some writings as a guest blogger on my website, an activity that I gave him to encourage his brain recovery. There, he described his sensory experience:

As my recovery progresses, I just keep getting more and more present; colors become more vivid, touch becomes more textured, and sound becomes sharper. All of my senses are continuously heightened, and the world around me takes clearer shape by the second.

I know this comes off as vague, but my sense of place in this world and my sense of belonging to the Earth are more and more THERE. When I reach for that sense of belonging, it is at my fingertips, not so far away that I nearly lose my balance trying to reach it.

The world is such a more pleasant, homey place to be; I feel as though I am finally cohabitating this plane with the rest of the world with spiritual peace and rightness. The more my head heals, the more my view of myself heals. I'm parting ways with the perfectionist part of me that finds nothing but reasons to cut myself down when I look in the mirror. It feels freeing, so blessedly freeing, to be able to think about myself in a positive manner. This is where I am, and this is where I continue to be.

By the time we disembarked on our road trip, I kept hearing, **"Allow Jess to become the healer that he is."**

When I was a young mother, my eldest boy had told me that he did not think he would make it to college. Jess was seven years old when he announced this to me. I heard this as a premonition that he would die young and I began my attempt to keep him alive. My efforts included being over-protective, making bargains with God, and secretly grieving the possible loss. It was a heavy burden to bear.

Later that same year, he told me that he felt he would not make it to age twenty. I heard this as confirming the fear that Jess was seeing his own demise. Now, I think that Jess was feeling the imminent death of his old life and the grandness of his new life. James Hillman, a psychologist who wrote a wonderful book called *The Soul's Code*, believes that children have a sense of their destiny quite young. I feel he is right.

Jess said to me one day as we drove his little brother to preschool, "Mommy, I want to be your apprentice." He told me this at age seven, the same year he told me he would not make it to age twenty. I had never spoken to him about my healing work or the concept of apprenticeship, and yet here it was, expressing freely and unprompted from his lips.

He was a seriously psychic kid, and I filed away his request in the store of remarkable instances of his abilities as a shaman, always wise beyond his years, where it stayed until the brain injury, when these isolated prescient moments in time leaped out in full color, as if we were getting a window into his future.

I was reminded that I broke my ankle to help the feminine in me become more forward, to stand in her power and lead from her wisdom. Jess seemed to be following a path of similar vein; his masculine had been brought forcibly down to the feminine, in the form of his right temple bowing to the body of the Earth.

It led me to question if the sacrifice made by the masculine in service to the feminine is an archetypal tale, spun over and over again in the eons that the physical universe has been in existence. The masculine in partnership does what the feminine tells him to do; I think of bee colonies, and how the Queen Bee is the "holder" of the hive while the worker bees go out and do her bidding, trained completely on her as the sovereign entity. The feminine has the good of the whole at heart and knows what is best. The masculine has to submit to her knowledge if he wants to act in ways that benefit the whole.

No wonder women have been subjugated by men and by patriarchal culture for thousands of years! The masculine energy, defined by its individual nature and by its defense of what it deems worthy of protection, has considered women carriers of great wisdom that take care of the whole, not the part. In order for civilization to expand, territories to be carved out, treasures to be defended, and battles to be fought, the feminine voice of love, peace, and unity has had to be silenced. The masculine energy in us has uncoupled with the one whose wisdom can save us.

I knew years ago that the indigenous way of being can save humanity from self-destruction. Our aboriginal ancestors knew how to walk in balance with the Earth. The partnered feminine and masculine energy are how they followed natural laws. It seems to me that our awareness of the feminine is coming alive in our collective consciousness, something I have been experiencing since the late nineties—a growing awareness that feels like an old, old voice speaking to me from the depths of my being. My son is the latest evidence of this experience. He is a man who has been relearning the feminine being-ness through his mind, body, and soul. He is a part of the change that we are all undergoing as we rebalance our *collective* human soul. Our indigenous ancestors will show us the way; all we need do is ask.

We set out in August 2013 and headed west to Jess's birthplace of Tucson, Arizona. We felt a connection between the brain injury and his difficult birth, and saw the trip as an opportunity to revisit the original trauma. We had worked on healing the brain stem and the regulation of his brain toward high stress and desensitization toward pain. To feel more power in his life, Jess had been operating on a premise that if he subjected himself to pain and lived through it, it made him powerful. This is partly because of his birth experience of feeling powerless. At a core energy level, he believed he could only be alive if he experienced high levels of stimulation, similar to the smothering pressure of being stuck in the birth canal for two hours. This external pressure trained his brain through the birth trauma to need high levels of pressure in his life.

Jess was eager to face his early beginnings as a way of having Vision Quest, a time of reflection on the purpose of one's life. Our trip took us a little more than three weeks, over which we covered territory that Jess had treasured during his life thus far. We began and ended the journey with Tucson, a way of bringing closure to the quest and to launch him again, born anew.

When we looked shamanically at his injury, it seemed as if it were a re-creation of his birth: a crushing of his skull in order to be birthed into his life. The trickle of water that tripped him as he flew on his skateboard was like my water breaking, heralding the beginning of labor.

Over the years, I have developed a discernment for lack of integrity in people. My journey with Jess helped me even more to make clear the boundaries between myself and others who did not have my best interest in their hearts. I lost all patience with anything that was not as simple as the horizon line that met us each day on our trip west. The naked honesty of the land meeting the unobstructed sky reminded me of the line I needed to keep in order to protect my inner child, too. My intense desire to support Jess had a parallel within me; my Mama Bear had been activated, and I was powerful. I had no time or energy to entertain anything that was not absolute love.

The result is that I said goodbye to some relationships (that were already fragile to begin with because there was no integrity in the connection); I started to stand up for myself, calling lack of integrity out when I saw it. Not in a nasty way, but clear. Did you know it is a revelation that I am allowed to do this? That I get to have and express my opinion and feelings, even if there are some who disagree? And that it is right to expect that they be respected?

Jess's traumatic brain injury and recovery surely paved the way for this phase of my development. Whether I liked it or not, it was part of my growth and maturation process. I found it hard as a sensitive person and one who prefers to avoid conflict.

My ideal is a peaceful world where we do not have to have these kinds of interactions. However, this is part of being an adult—and human—a maturing process of dealing with challenging things, hopefully with heart and wisdom. I chose to integrate this lesson.

Living with integrity means: Not settling for less than what you know you deserve in your relationships. Asking for what you want and need from others. Speaking your truth, even though it might create conflict or tension. Behaving in ways that are in harmony with your personal values. Making choices based on what you believe, and not what others believe.

— **Barbara De Angelis**

Rebirth

I was a midlife woman, traveling for a vision with my oldest son, who almost died. Out in the vast plains of desert, I wondered who I would be when this was all over. This phase of growth was exponential, and I could barely recognize myself in the mirror.

My work up to that point centered on being a shamanic practitioner, energy helper, educator, all built upon a foundation of years of formal training and experience in the more mainstream occupations as public school instructor, trainer for children with brain disorders, non-profit project manager working with families from a strengths-based perspective. I had morphed as life asked me to, evolving my work as I went through the next phase of development. Now, I felt that I was being birthed into something greater.

This would require conceding my vision of myself up to this point. Taking myself seriously as a scientist and a neurobiologist through all of the research and direct application with Jess seemed to be where I was pointed. I had

Chapter 8: Inner Tribe™ Work (*or* Peace with the Parts)

Storyteller Doll, Jemez Tribe, New Mexico

given myself so much experience over the years, studying the mind, it was a natural step into the neurosciences, but how did this fit with my ability to pull greater intelligence in through my brain?

I channeled the voice of the Larger Intelligence. How would that be viewed by the scientific community? I helped women see their sacredness. I was a feminist, seeking equality for all people. Yet, there was something quite great about the feminine energy that was more than the masculine energy. The Womb of All Creation seemed vastly larger than the little thing created in its embrace. I saw that the brain showed the way; the right hemisphere understands the larger picture, and this information is then translated by the left hemisphere. Isn't this exactly what the feminine and masculine do in partnership? The feminine knows what serves the whole of creation, and the masculine acts on the feminine's knowing?

Eureka! I would serve the whole of creation by teaching people how to use their whole brain by inviting the input of their right hemisphere, thus contributing to the feminine reemergence in the collective psyche. This seemed a pertinent and pointed moment to re-imagine myself.

I watched Jess during his Vision Quest be so clear about what he wanted to do and wondered, *What do I want?* As a woman and mother, is this line of questioning more complex for me? My life of service to others, whether through profession, as a person who cares about the world, or as mama changes orientation with this question. Is it still being of service if I am a happy, self-actualized person?

I did some research on midlife rebirth and found a lot about midlife "crisis." Questions came up in my Google query like, *Is there is a cure for midlife crisis?* and *How do I survive midlife crisis?* I chose to see that time in my life not as a crisis, but as a TRANSITION, or rebirth.

There seemed to be a direct relationship between how resistant I was to allowing my mature seed to emerge and how long the "crisis" would last—how long I clung to outdated parts of self, how long I tried to stay in the box of my old thinking (which had gotten me where I was so far, but may not serve me anymore), and how long it would take me to accept that I was a midlife person. These were the markers of how long the midlife rebirth would take; in other words, it would last until the transition was complete.

I felt the door open to my midlife experience on my forty-second birthday during my Uranus Opposition. This coincided with the third year of our family Vision Quest that started in 2003. I was alternately in the wild rapids and in the infinitely deep peace of the river of life as I began to define myself as ME. But that wasn't enough. To bring my midlife transition to a raucous, full-on arrival, Jess's traumatic brain injury ripped away any remaining innocence, accelerating my release of anything and anyone not in integrity in my life, thus *embracing where the love and truth and light really ARE*. The violence and grief of that event created a shocking displacement of anything immature, fantasy-based (like that my parents would ever step into their adult roles), and unhealthy, and a reorganization of what was left into the woman I was becoming.

Psychologist Robyn Vickers-Willis, author of the book *Navigating Midlife: Women Becoming Themselves*, says, "There have long been societal pressures that discourage women from tossing off others' expectations of who they should be *and embracing who they are at their core—and how they truly want to live their lives* [emphasis mine]. This growth can threaten the still-traditional 'status quo' of wife as nurturer and husband as provider."

A long-term study of the evolving physical and mental health of over fifty-eight thousand Australian women backs this up. The Australian Longitudinal Study on Women's Health reveals that many middle-aged women found themselves too busy taking care of other people to explore their own needs and desires.

By August 2013, I sensed that a period of immediate intensity, or "crisis", was completed. I had a sense of being reborn, with a new lease on life, a new sense of adventure of a different kind. Something utterly unexpected and extraordinary occurred while on the Vision Quest with Jess that changed my life at a cellular level. Like the near-completion of my midlife transition, it ushered in new opportunities and positive growth, and a molecular shift toward the dream of who I have become.

As we traveled, I looked at my brave warrior of a son, showing up so courageously to find his new path, and I wondered, *Who birthed who here?* I have been initiated through this child healer now several times. He showed such grace as he released his old life and embraced the new. And his wisdom deepened so much, or else he became quiet enough to access it. He shared his insights and gentle observations while we walked the land and gave me quiet counsel when I asked. Jess birthed me as much as I birthed him.

OH, the letting go that occurred! My baggage dropped off me at light speed. The clearer I got about what is mine (and what belongs to other people), the more room for joy I have found. Relieving myself of the burden of my parents, all of the unrealized prayers for reconciliation and healing, all of the negative energy they sent through other family members, all of the shame and guilt for what was actually theirs to carry—this cleared the space in me for a remarkable (and completely unexpected) gift.

The Wanted Daughter

Our Vision Quest in August 2013 resulted in many insights for Jess, and I received an unexpected gift, too. New parents!

My Aunt Wendy and her husband live in Tucson; we went there to do some important work in Jess's birthplace to initiate the Vision Quest for him. Shamanically speaking, we needed to go back to ground zero to reclaim energy compromised during his difficult birth and heal this trauma. We began in Tucson, stayed with Wendy, did the work needed, and planned to wander to other locations in the desert Southwest as guided, finishing the trip back in Tucson if there were any loose ends to tie up.

We wandered through northern New Mexico, encountering soul family, good friends that we had met during our family Vision Quest from 2003 to 2010. It was a revelation for me to appreciate these true heart friends. I enjoyed the love and connection with people who really see me for who I am. Jess's injury really cracked my heart open to another level, and I was able to feel and receive the love of these friends. Jess was not the only one getting a Vision Quest. I was being reminded that **true loving family is not necessarily the one we are born into**.

On our second visit to Tucson at the end of the Vision Quest, we were happy to be back at Wendy's house. It felt so welcoming and familiar. One night, as we all sat together in the living room, they said they wanted to ask me something. They had been talking since our last visit, and seeing as how we already felt very close and that my aunt had already been treating me in a motherly fashion, they wondered if it might be all right if they adopted me. It was apparently my uncle's idea first, and the more they talked about it, the more they felt it was right to ask me.

I sat stunned for a moment. "Adopt me?"

They said, **"Yes, we want you to be our daughter."**

In my mind, a few split-second things occurred . . . that they might be talking about ceremonial adoption (similar to the kind I had already experienced through indigenous friends/family, which would be sweet) . . . wondering if adults could be adopted . . . and finally, shock and disbelief *that they wanted me.*

They clarified quickly that their intention was to **legally adopt me**, making me their daughter, not just in thought and heart, but in clear, irrefutable black-and-white terms. They were not just saying they loved me. They wanted to go to great lengths to prove it.

I was stunned. It had never occurred to me that this was a possibility. It had never crossed my mind.

I sat in disbelief until I felt my beloved eldest son, who was sitting behind me, making wiggling motions with his body. I turned to see him grinning like the Cheshire Cat, emphatically nodding his head and jumping up and down in his chair. He looked me in the eyes and said, *"Say YES!"*

I turned back to these amazing people who had just offered me and my family the greatest gift that anyone could offer . . . and then felt something occur in my body that was nothing less than a miracle.

In the short moment of turning from Jess's enthusiastic approval back toward these people who had just declared their wish and intention to take me into their family, I felt a seismic shift occur. *It was as if I became aware of the community of fifty trillion cells that comprise my body simultaneously, and I felt them as a whole. I felt that I (and my inner community of cells) had been peering into the darkness of a deep cavern my entire life, longing for love to come out into the light where I stood waiting, . . . forty-eight years of standing there, wanting desperately for the love to come out to me, to no avail. All that had emerged from that yawning maw was an invitation into more darkness.* Then, as I turned toward my aunt and uncle in their living room in Tucson, **I suddenly knew where the love was, and it was like THE SUN.**

The light of it was so profound and so warming, and such a contrast to the darkness I had been trying to draw the love from through my will, through my twenty-five years of therapy and inner work to understand what was so wrong with me that my own parents did not love me. *I felt my cells, as a community, make a decisive turn away from the dark and toward the light.* I experienced such a profound depth of happiness in that moment that I understood what I had been missing my whole life: the feeling of being wanted, of belonging. I have not turned back toward the darkness since that moment.

Into the Arms
Collage © 2010 Licia Berry

My happiness has been all pervasive since. Everyone notices something different about me, a lightness, a joy. My husband says my feet land on the ground in a different way. **It feels absolutely remarkable to be chosen, to be accepted and affirmed**. IT IS NEVER TOO LATE TO BE A WANTED DAUGHTER.

Great Mother was in this moment of my life, the presence of unconditional love in the face of such complexity.

My biological mother was not apprised of her sister's offer to adopt me until it was legalized on October 29, 2013. We wrote letters explaining the decision to make this move after I made the difficult choice to accept, and I have yet to hear my former mother's voice in complaint. I say difficult choice not because it was so clearly what my body, heart, and soul wanted to do—that was obvious! I say difficult choice because of how co-dependent and toxic my relationship has been with my family of origin.

Caught in the spell and paralysis of expecting them to be parents, to heal with me, to grow, I succumbed and still took part in the dysfunctional family trance. I knew the adoption would create serious waves. I knew it would be yet another opportunity for them to see me as the bad guy. I knew that it would hurt. But I chose, by saying yes, *to love myself more than loving the unhealthy relationship.*

During the adoption hearing in Arizona, the judge asked me why I wanted to do this. My answer was simple and unequivocal: because I want HAPPINESS, to be loved by parents, to be wanted as a daughter!

As we went through the process, I stood with Wendy in her kitchen, listening to her describe how much she has always felt that I was her daughter. We stood a few feet apart, gazing into each other's eyes, when I felt a strong tug at my naval, and then "saw" something that looked like an umbilical cord between us. My eyes widened at the exact moment hers did; she felt it too! We simultaneously said, "WHAT WAS THAT?", but in seconds, we knew exactly what it was. Our energetic bond, choosing each other as mother and daughter, had just been made real.

After my adoption, the wounds that I sustained as a result of being unmothered began healing in a quantum way. I was stunned at the speed of change and depth of happiness that permeated every level of my being. My relationship with the Earth felt different, more connected. My relationship with my body also changed; it was as if I had been standing to the side of my body, not fully inhabiting it, and when the adoption occurred, I suddenly found myself fully IN MY BODY. I took ownership. I sat behind the wheel and started driving. I started living like my life mattered to ME. It wasn't that I had not been somewhat in my body before, but I now felt permission to take ownership of my space on the planet in this physical vessel because I belonged here, and that I could be alive for ME, not just in service for everyone else. It was a revelation!

I also noticed that my bodily and energetic pattern of "holding" shifted. Where before I had noticed that I was slow to allow hurts and wounds to pass through me, to let them go, now I could let them go with ease. Where I was defensive in my body posture as if waiting for a blow, I was relaxed. I went through a physical detox of old energy, emotion, and other toxins releasing from my cells and I lost weight. It was remarkable to be free of the burdens I had carried for so many years!

From a mature, wise, and powerful perspective... a LOVED perspective... I cannot understand how a mother can refuse invitations by her daughter into healing for decades, choose to remarry the very man who preyed upon her child (the wedding occurred in secret, enlisting my sister's and brother's collusion), and then suddenly decide she is angry that her daughter chose to go where the love is.

My biological mother stopped communicating with her sister Wendy. Of course, the communication has never been good between my former mother and me. She did call eventually Wendy (two years later) to say how angry she was and to accuse her of "stealing her child away from her." It's jaw-dropping to hear this; how could I have been "stolen" if she had loved me as a mother? I can understand why she is angry. My mother has been replaced and I no longer serve as her enabling scapegoat of a daughter, the punching bag.

I wish it could have been different. My heart hurts for her. I am sad for her pain. Was she ever sad for my pain, I wonder? It *could* have been different at any moment over the twenty-five years I waited for the woman who birthed me to meet me in the field of possibility, in the field of healing. I stood there for a long time. She never came.

My experiences as a result of my son's injury and my adoption have shown me that my dedication to mothering my children has molded me to be a mother to women who are motherless, that being a mother is my calling, and that the fierce and devoted love of a mother is the love that transforms everything. The presence of it makes us want to be in the world, to get better, to be alive, to give, to love. The absence of it makes us want to leave the world, fall apart, to disintegrate, to die, to self-injure or injure others, and to be closed to the gifts of the universe that are so effortlessly bestowed. I am alive and blessed and happy through Great Mother, who prepared me so exquisitely to accept the love of my new mother!

Great Mother has made me understand that mothering well is a choice. To my great sadness, my biological mother chose, over and over, not to mother me, but I have been shown, without a doubt, that I am indeed mothered (and fathered) by a universe that cares about me—*a universe that bestows unconditional love on me through others who are willing to allow it through them.*

There are a LOT of motherless daughters (as well as fatherless sons) out there, and this is the greatest wounding there is. Countless grief-stricken children grow up to be angry adults, searching to fill the void left by their lack of parenting. I see it every day, young people who doubt their worth, their validity, the very space they take up on the planet. We can see it in their eyes, their question about why they are not loved. This is WRONG! Children, young people, old people—no one should carry this burden, ever. And being unmothered IS a burden.

Our world is in trouble, and this is the way to fix it: mothering. The unconditional love that lies inherent in the archetype of Great Mother is the great agent of alchemy that can change our hurtle into a frightening future. *If we feel loved, deeply loved, we care about the world, about other people, about the children, about the descendants of our human race.*

When you do not have a mother who sees you, hears you, loves you, actively chooses your wellbeing over and over again, you do not understand this kind of love. It takes a lot of time and work to turn around the self-loathing, the doubt that you should even exist, the challenging of the basic core assumptions you hold in your cells that you are not wanted and therefore do not belong in the world. But the universe was your mother before your biological mother was, and that is the truth.

As a result of my journey to accept love from those who gave it freely, I came to understand: my biological mother gave me a tremendous opportunity to learn to love myself. She was a Dark Mother to me, inviting chaos and despair in order to birth something precious and true. She gave me the thirst to seek and find Great Mother. I forgive and bless her for playing this holy role.

Chapter 7: Healing the Broken Heart (*or* Forgiveness and Trust)

Igmu Tanka Shantae Weh (Big Lion Heart Woman)
Collage © 2008 Licia Berry

One of the hardest things I have experienced in my life is living with my heart open and being hurt, or conversely, closing my heart and having it cracked open. When I was a little girl, I was so in love with all people, and nature, and the Earth, and all life, and the universe. I saw the best of people, their potential; I think now I was seeing their souls. It was such a strange thing to me when they did not act in the way I saw them! I was so innocent, I walked in wonder and thought so positively that I was frequently accused of seeing through rose-colored glasses.

It is with great sadness that I have seen myself, over the years of experiencing pain in response to what others have done or said, close my heart and form a crusty surface through which I perceive the world. In the absence of a completely open heart, the mind then takes on the burden of navigating this wondrous life. It is easy to be misled when we have a closed heart.

When my heart is closed, I experience a world that is devoid of magic; people meet my expectations of rejecting me or being unkind to me. My eyes are full of the horrible things that we do to each other, rather than seeing the flow and the lovely things. I perceive a world in which I am hurt and hurt and hurt again. Then my mind creates elaborate constructs to try to keep me safe. These constructs are actually prisons.

I have found that, when I have closed my heart, I experience profound relief when it opens again. I feel "righted" in my world, like I have been off course for a while and now I am back on track.

The experience of having one's heart crack open after being closed is like coming home. The various constructs and judgments and coping mechanisms and ways I have limited my interactions with the world drop off. It feels like chains falling from my spirit. I am free.

It feels very vulnerable at first, like I imagine a new butterfly feels when it emerges from its cocoon. It can be tempting to quickly try to put those shells in place again to cover the open, soft heart. I find it beneficial to sit with the feeling of openness and vulnerability, to simply allow it. I sense that this is actually when we are our most powerful. The heart *is* our true power.

The choice to love means loving All That Is, unconditionally. That means no judgment or conditions. This can be a tough one when we have experienced something very painful at the hands of others.

Our heart is wise and has access to a reality that is much bigger than the one we experience with our minds. The heart knows the ways of the universe. The heart knows how to dance with the magic and the mystery. The heart is the bridge to unconditional love. When we choose to open our hearts, we are choosing to love in the way we are meant to love.

I make working with my heart every day a priority. I measure my progress in the areas Angeles Arrien mentions in *The Four Fold Way*: am I full-hearted, open-hearted, clear-hearted, and strong-hearted?

Licia's Heart Practice – Healing the Wounded Heart (6 Steps)

1. Make a choice by setting the intention to be deeply grounded to the core of the planet, the heart of the Earth, with all of your mind: "I choose to be grounded to the heart (core) of the Earth now."
2. Breathe down for a few minutes (focus on bringing fresh breath as you inhale into and through your body, from the source of the universe, down into the core of the planet).
3. Breathe up from the Earth for a few minutes (focus on bringing breath up from the core of the planet through your body, offering it out the top of your head to the universe).
4. Put both hands on your chest.
5. Set your intention. "I choose to heal my heart." Ask for the assistance of Great Mother to do this.
6. Breathe and pay attention to your body. You may feel a little flutter in your chest, a gentle stirring. It may be small or feel distant at first, but keep paying attention with the intent to heal your heart. That flutter is the awakening of your Child Heart. Keep breathing, keep

paying attention to your hands on your chest and what is happening inside. Allow the feeling to grow, to spread to your face and belly. Do you notice a feeling of lightness, or an opening, or a shift of something as if to a more expansive place? Allow the feeling to spread up into a smile, a really big one, as soon as you feel the child in you stir. This is your re-introduction to your Child Heart, so be sweet and kind to yourself. Perhaps you would like to color or make some art, or go outside and dig in the dirt. Treat yourself as a child who has been locked away and just wants to be a child again. Play with her!

What is Love?

Love is a verb—it needs to be manifested in action not just contemplated intellectually. You cannot learn to Love yourself—or be capable of having healthier relationships—without taking action to change your core/foundation relationship with self and life into one that is more aligned with Love. This inner child healing work is an effective and powerful formula that allows you to learn: to be more Loving to self; to gain some freedom from the past; to develop inner peace and serenity; to own your response-ability as co-creator of your life so that you can become a positive co-creator instead of negative (learn to be your own best friend instead of your own worst enemy); to start relaxing and being present for your life in a way that creates a more balanced and enjoyable experience.

— **Robert Burney**

I have found that love is indeed a verb. While we may pontificate about what constitutes love, the simple act of being fully present with one another is an act of love. The looking into one's eyes with a pure heart and gratitude, the holding of another while they cry, the making of a meal with the intent to nourish, the acknowledgment and admission when we have unconsciously been hurtful, the generous nature of spirit expressed . . . these are actions that demonstrate that we love.

The burning desire to make myself a better person in order to stop the cycle of abuse is an impulse of love, and the consistent application of what I learn in order to DO that is daily, minute-to-minute expression of a gift of love to my children, my someday grandchildren, and humanity, in general.

Love changes everything.

Sacrificing Ourselves on the Altar of Forgiveness

Giving up is not the answer. Neither is giving in. Stand your ground. There is a way of doing that without having to be combative. There is a way of hanging on to your true self, and demonstrating it, without resorting to aggression. But giving up and giving in is not the way. Simply and quietly claiming your right to be You is the way.

– Neale Donald Walsch

I have gone all around the mulberry bush about forgiveness.

I wanted to forgive my biological mother before I had even begun to heal myself. The pain of acknowledging our failed relationship was so great that I wanted to rush to forgiveness even before it was resolved within myself. Society pushes us to forgive the atrocities visited upon us by our parents per the fourth commandment, to honor thy father and mother, *even if in the forgiveness we sacrifice ourselves.*

My rush to forgive was prompted, in part, by the pressure to do what society asked of me, and was an attempt to keep from feeling the depth of my pain. Jumping straight into forgiveness is bypass; forgiveness is superficial, even fakery, when we do not first deal with the pain inside and heal.

Once I realized that my attempts to forgive were "not sticking," I surrendered to the larger wisdom of my process. I allowed myself to fall into the feelings I had been trying to stay above. As a result, the grief underneath my anger about being rejected by my mother revealed itself and began to move toward the surface, like a wounded animal that had taken shelter in a deep hidden cave that, with trepidation, emerged into the sunlight.

I learned something very important as a result: *in the beginning of recovery/healing work, it is vital to truly allow the feelings that we have to emerge—without the burden of expectation of forgiveness.*

The freedom to feel how we feel without self-judgment (or the judgment of others) is paramount to our eventual healing and understanding. There is a tremendous societal taboo about speaking or acting in our own behalf instead of for our parents/families. This is also seen in the victim-blaming that occurs around sexual crimes. But only through giving ourselves room to feel how we feel, no matter how awful it may be, do we stand a chance to heal and move through the pain of the wound to the other side.

The act of separating my heart from my idealized version of my mother was a kind of rebirth. I emerged from that fog, blinking in the harsh light of the truth, and then I understood— *there was indeed something to forgive.*

I had repeatedly rushed to forgive her when I was not ready. I forced, pushed, guilted, and shamed myself into "letting go of the hurt" so that we could move on. The trouble was that *my mother never asked for forgiveness.* I was relying on the little girl inside me, the one who desperately wanted my mother's love and acceptance, to forgive an adult who did not seek healing or truth and reconciliation. I was doing all the work on my end, bending and making machinations to smooth it over and give her another chance, all by my lonesome. She never expressed interest to me in being forgiven.

In hindsight, I see that I took full responsibility for the failure of the relationship, a hyper-controlling attempt to feel better about the awful person I must be for her to reject me, her daughter. In the end, relationship is between two people, not just one. The work to heal the relationship must be done by both of them, if they are willing. And willingness, an expression of love, means everything in creating healthy relationship.

Forgiveness in a Vacuum

It is wise not to push ourselves to forgive; if we force forgiveness, it can actually impede our healing process! I think of the years I lost attempting to forgive before I was ready, and I wonder how much further I might be if I had honored my true timing.

Forgiveness can happen in an instant, but healing is a process. When people say they are sorry and acknowledge the hurt they have caused, take responsibility for their behavior, we can forgive them because they have opened a door with their apology, a door through which we can recapitulate and reconnect with our forgiveness. The olive branch has been extended, and we can now accept.

What about when they do not own the pain they have caused? What happens when they do not take responsibility for their behavior, genuinely apologize and ask for forgiveness?

We remain standing in front of a closed door, and we wait. Sometimes we try to crack that door open, demanding the olive branch, but this is not organic and can chase the olive branch further away. Sometimes we wait our entire lives for that door to open. At a certain point, we need to take our power back and move on.

What is Forgiveness, Really?

I observe that there is quite a bit of confusion about forgiveness. One clue to understanding forgiveness is to look at the origins of the word. The word "forgive" comes from an old English word *forgiefan*, which is itself made up of two words: *giefan*, meaning "give" and *for-*, meaning "completely." So the word *forgiefan* conveys the sense of *giving completely*.

Perhaps the idea of "giving ourselves completely" to one who has betrayed us explains why forgiveness is a concept we might resist. It is akin to lying down in front of someone with a raised dagger. Will they cut us again?

I have wondered if forgiveness is the wrong word. Really, the goal is to make ourselves whole, and in that, hopefully, we can mend our relationships. Is it really possible to forgive, to give ourselves completely, if we are not whole?

We must make ourselves whole before we make our relationships with those who have hurt us whole. We must honor ourselves first and always, for it is with ourselves that we must make peace. In the end, we must be able to live with ourselves. This may mean that we never "forgive" those others. The real point is to come home to ourselves, whatever that takes and whomever we must release from our lives to do it.

How we feel is real. This is a baseline of truth. There is no right or wrong with feelings—they just are. We have the right to our feelings, and we have a right to act from them. I found that I judged myself for my feelings of anger and had to *forgive myself for that!* Forgiveness is allowing our feelings, giving unconditional love to ourselves, and accepting our truths.

This is what the archetypal Mother showed me. It was good practice to forgive myself, to give myself completely to my truth, to make myself whole.

When we move naturally to a place of seeking to forgive the perpetrator of our hurt, it is because we have healed in ourselves. This step is one that each of us must determine for ourselves; no one outside of us can know if we are truly ready to make this next step.

It helped me to understand that forgiveness does not mean that we have to forget, accept, or tolerate the perpetrator. Forgiveness does not mean that we have to see or speak to the person. Forgiveness does not mean we need put ourselves in a situation where they can hurt us, nor ever trust them again. Forgiveness does not mean that what was done was acceptable, or even that the person does not need to be punished. Forgiveness does not mean that we somehow deserved what happened or caused it in any way. Forgiveness does not preclude us from feeling healthy anger when our boundaries are crossed, or revisiting an old hurt with that person if fresh memories or feelings arise.

True forgiveness is a natural consequence of wholeness, a result of our personal journey for inner peace and health. We cease judging ourselves for our feelings. We cease waiting for them to make it right. We cease repeating and amplifying the hurt that was done to us. We stop the cycle. We take our power back by making ourselves whole, regardless of the actions of the other person.

I now understand that we can choose to truly forgive only if our heart is healed, and only then is relationship possible. Our state of wellbeing, arising from wholeness, determines our ability to never be hurt by that perpetrator again.

Indeed, we send love in response to hate and become spiritual alchemists.

— **Wayne Dyer**

Changing My Focus

Trust can take an entire lifetime to be regained. In preparation for the next hurt that may or may not come, we close ourselves off. The defended heart is ready for the next slight, the next barb, the next arrow. While we stand, awaiting the apology of a perpetrator, we miss the possibility of wonder and joy in our lives. The moment I was asked to be the legal daughter of my aunt, I turned and saw the sun for the first time in many years.

Patterns of thought develop over time, and our brain is a creature of habit. Once we experience something new, a neural pathway is created. The repetition of that experience strengthens the neural pathway, and a habit of thought is born.

Over my life, I became so accustomed to standing in front of that closed door that I forgot there was a whole reality behind and all around me, a real life full of goodness, bliss, and meaning. *I realized that I had become identified with my sadness about my mother.*

The original title of this book was going to be *I Am My Own Daughter* because I was alone as a daughter. I did not have a mother in my life and I had parented and healed myself as if I were my own daughter. This forced me to seek mothering within myself, to learn how to mother myself better than I had been mothered. I wore my sadness like a cloak around me, getting more comfortable with it each passing year that things with my mother stayed unresolved. It became my identity, part of my mind and body. After the decades melted away, I forgot the sadness was even there.

After I was adopted and began to hang out with Mama Wendy like a daughter might hang out with her mother, I noticed I felt very sad. I realized that my heart was cracking open in the presence of mother love, and being in that presence reminded me how much I had missed being mothered.

Oh, the kind eyes and welcoming arms of the mother! Oh, safe harbor, how I have longed for you! Like children cry at the sight of their mother when she picks them up from the first day of kindergarten, having subsumed themselves in learning, play, and fun, and forgetting her for a time, but then being reminded of how much they missed her when she comes, I realized that I had busied myself my whole life to keep occupied. Then, having grown accustomed to my motherless life, my heart was surprised at the spilling of tears when I realized how much I had missed. Oh, the years of laughing, playing, and creating, loving each other that I had lost! Of course, the natural response to such loss is grief.

Quickly, I understood the backlog of sadness was moving out of me in the presence of this joy. I wanted joy! I chose joy! My patterns of thought were changing. So I cried tears of gratitude.

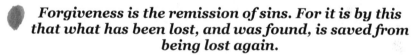

Forgiveness is the remission of sins. For it is by this that what has been lost, and was found, is saved from being lost again.

— St. Augustine

My Guarded Heart

After we initiated adoption proceedings, my heart was wide open. I experienced what it must feel like to be a loved daughter from childhood—a remarkable sense of groundedness, belonging, and generosity. It was as if I had the world to give, because I truly felt I had been given the world.

A few months after the bliss of the reemergence of early childhood innocence and joy, I noticed that I was avoiding speaking to my new parents. I had enjoyed regular weekly talks with them, but now I recognized that I did not initiate the calls quite so often. I watched this with interest. Much later, I came to the awareness that I was afraid to trust the goodness that was being bestowed upon me.

In a conversation with a psychologist colleague, I understood that I feared that my new mother and father would change their minds about adopting me or regret it later. I feared that I was so damaged that I would be a terrible daughter or that they would abandon me.

The psychologist offered, "You are focusing on what you fear because you were abandoned by your biological parents. You are thinking negative thoughts of your past and worrying it will repeat. Your new parents clearly love you unconditionally, so I don't believe that they will abandon you like your parents did. This is an issue of trust; trust is like a leap of faith. You had good reasons to protect yourself before, but now you can begin to learn to trust. Your heart is safe."

My heart is safe.

My heart is safe.

I could scarcely utter these words. I tried to believe that this was true, but I kept looking for evidence that would back up the old hurt. My fear that Wendy would regret her decision to adopt me reignited every time I heard her express sadness about losing her siblings (all of whom ceased speaking to her after the adoption).

This was one of my misgivings about accepting her request to make me her daughter; I expected the backlash that inevitably came, because I was accustomed to the dysfunctional response of my biological family to my own healing. I had experienced their anger and confusion about healthy behavior and the changes I had brought to the existing family dynamic. But Wendy was seemingly unaware, or at least in hopeful denial, that her intentions to scoop me up as a daughter would be understood as coming from a place of love and mothering instinct and not taken as an affront or offense. Unfortunately, this was not the case. She was abandoned like I had been.

The psychologist I spoke with suggested it was a good idea for me to keep a "thought record," a technique used to keep track of negative thoughts and therefore have the opportunity to transform the negative reinforcement into positive reinforcement in my brain (see the Additional Resources section). This would help me change my way of automatically going to negative types of thinking to being able to think more positively. He said that Wendy had been interested in my life since I was a baby and would remain so, and that my identity as a "lost child" would be slowly erased over time, with a new identity as a loved daughter emerging.

This identity shift did indeed occur, at the same time that my midlife, peri-menopausal, empty nest identity was shifting! The sensation I can only describe as earth-shaking has lasted since Jess' brain injury and the adoption and has led me into a radically different life.

Learning (Again) to Trust

Trust. What a strange word. Alliances are forged and entire worlds are built upon trust. In our most precious relationships, trust is the common thread.

The word trust seems to have originated in the 1200s, from Old Norse *treysta, "to rely on, make strong and safe."* Clearly, trust is a state of believing that we are in good hands, that we, and what we value, will be secure, protected.

Trust is built by repetition, in multiple, small gestures, by examples of caring. Over time, we learn to trust that a person has our best interest at heart. Some people extend trust to others easily, with little or no evidence that it is warranted. For them, trust is a given, a baseline, and they only withdraw their trust if it is betrayed.

I observe that young children fall into this category. Arriving into the world with complete vulnerability, children must believe that they are secure. If things go well, they are. But if things do not, children learn to mistrust.

My observation is that children of abusive mothers can fall into two categories: those who continue to blindly trust until betrayed, and those who believe that people must earn their trust by demonstrating trustworthiness.

Here are some qualities of a trustworthy person that I have gathered over the years:

- They are authentic. They let you know how they feel, where they stand, and how you stand with them.
- They have integrity. Their actions and words match; they "walk their talk."
- The are self-responsible. They have done inner work and are willing to do more.
- They are accountable for their words and actions. When they make a mistake, they are willing to own it, apologize for it, and make amends; they expect the same from you.
- They are undistracted; they are present (not looking at their cell phones or otherwise preoccupied).
- They set boundaries. They are clear about and hold their boundaries, and they respect your boundaries.
- They are reliable. They can say "no" respectfully and "yes" dependably; they keep agreements or renegotiate, if necessary, consistently.
- They are honest. They admit when they do not know something and are able to ask for and receive help; they provide help when you ask for it.
- They are willing to make compromises but never compromise core principles or personal integrity.
- Consistent ethics, positive values, or principles inform their behavior.
- They are willing and able to tell you things you do not like to hear—kindly.

- They can disagree without needing to argue, or they are able to have friendly arguments that lead to increased understanding.
- They are generous. They assume the most generous things about your words, intentions, and behaviors, and check in if you fail to live up to your usual potential.
- In a trust relationship, when there is a conflict or misunderstanding, communication with them is open because both parties desire connection versus separation.
- Both parties in a trust relationship recognize, accept, and enjoy (even celebrate) the differences between them.
- They are safe. A trust relationship includes non-judgment and confidentiality; what is shared is held in confidence. They value your heart and do not betray it. And no gossip!

You might notice that my Trustworthiness list shares some overlaps with my Maturity list in Chapter 1! That is because *it takes a mature person to cultivate trust within themselves, and therefore with other people.*

Trust is defined as choosing to risk making something you value vulnerable to another person's actions.

— **Charles Feltman**

Betrayal is a breaking of trust and goodwill in a relationship through some form of wounding. Depending on the circumstances, it can take a long time to heal from and can leave us changed forever. When our trust is betrayed, especially by someone central to our lives (such as our mother), it rocks us to our core. We are taught the opposite of security. Instead, we learn the awful truth that we are unsafe and the world is an uncertain place. Deep betrayal is a trauma that imprints us at a core level.

Rebuilding a sense of trust can take a long time after even one betrayal, much less a lifetime of them. Betrayal recovery work is a slow process and is painstaking in that we must risk being hurt again as a means of relearning to trust.

How do we rebuild trust after being betrayed by the source of our being? Trial and error. We risk, learn, risk and learn. And we *rebuild our trust in ourselves by learning how to be trustworthy*.

When we have been betrayed by our mothers, we learn, not only to mistrust women, but to mistrust ourselves as women. Trusting ourselves to do what is right, to say how we feel, to keep our boundaries, to be honest, is how we learn who to trust. Self-love and self-respect leads us to seek out others who are worthy of our trust. We know that we can trust ourselves by the company we keep. We know that when we trust ourselves above anyone else that we are worthy of trust from others. How we treat ourselves is how we are treated. You can know you are worthy of trust when you are surrounded by trustworthy people.

I don't trust people who don't love themselves and tell me, "I love you." . . . There is an African saying which is: Be careful when a naked person offers you a shirt.

— Maya Angelou

We learn who to trust and we become trustworthy—two sides of the same coin. Powerful insights often come at a powerful price.

Living in our culture is a betrayal experience, every single day. The messages that bombard us reiterate what our broken inner trust tells us: we are not enough, we are broken, we need fixing. The only solution is to take matters into our own hands. We need to share ourselves with people who are worthy of our hearts, and we need to show ourselves that we are worthy to be cherished.

Since a patriarchal culture needs you to believe that you are a problem that needs solving, we cannot rely on the outer world to trust. We must build trust from within, and gather up the aching parts of ourselves into our arms and integrate them into our wholeness. Our parts, the tribe members of our own psyche, need us to show them that we will take care of them better than our mothers took care of us.

Introduction to The Tribe

As described in Chapter 4, my family and I were guided, in 2005, to the San Luis Valley of Colorado during a critical juncture in our healing, individually and in my marriage. This area of the country provided the perfect backdrop for us to dive deep into our core wounds (the Mother Wound for me and the Father Wound for my husband.)

At that time, as we drove across the border of New Mexico into Colorado, we felt a strange sense of awe. Fourteen thousand-foot peaks loomed, towering over a vast alpine valley. It was a sensation of being in God's presence.

Under a cold, crystal-clear blue sky, we crossed a river where groves of bare cottonwood trees clustered, and watched as a bald eagle flew near us, our car the only barrier between us and the great wilderness of the San Luis Valley.

We had purchased the forty-acre homestead because we felt we were done with our trip, but this proved to be inaccurate. Really, at only two years since we had disembarked from our former lives, we were just beginning the true work of our journey. The two years that had gone by were just the "de-programming phase," the time we needed to unplug from expectations and obligations of society. It took that long to open the space inside of us to mend the wounds so deep within us.

Stationed at our rural homestead, under the watchful eyes of the San Juan Mountains on "Old Woman's Creek," we felt, within the land, the presence of the indigenous people. Their presence was palpable to us; we heard their whispers on the wind and felt them as we walked the immense, open ground. The peaks near our property called to us to come to them, and we walked for hours up in the hills, seeking the geodes and agate that so generously littered the land. The land loved us and we were happy.

Then we began to feel that our lives were not ours anymore. This happened when we began to have trouble with the townspeople, descendants of Spanish and Caucasian European settlers who drove out the native tribes so they could ranch and claim the resources of this bountiful land. We felt persecuted, as I have described, and left the area three years after arriving, feeling forced to move for our sanity, wellbeing, and physical and emotional safety, similar to the native people who had occupied and had deep relationship with this land for thousands of years. (I believe now, in hindsight, that we were being given a very small window into the experience of our native ancestors who were driven off their homelands. This proved valuable later for our understanding of cultural colonialism.)

The experience brought forward the parts of myself that had been disenfranchised, the aspects of me that felt persecuted and misunderstood from a young age. Our subsequent move to Tallahassee in the panhandle of Florida created the groundwork for me to own those parts of self by healing and integrating them into my wholeness.

As I continued to work with these parts of self, my "tribe members" came back home, one by one. As each Inner Tribe™ member was acknowledged, they ceased operating "outside of agreement with the good of the organism" (me), and came into alignment. As each part came onboard, I experienced more energy, clarity, purpose, peace, and joy. Clients expressed the same response; a short, few minutes of working with an Inner Tribe™ member and their life became different in the most positive ways.

My experience of Inner Tribe™ work is one of great trust of the Sacred Mother to love all parts of ourselves and claim the birthright of self-love and wholeness. There is no greater gift of love that we can give ourselves.

The Mother Heart, Healing and Inner Tribe™ Work

The greatest love that we can experience is Mother Love. It is all-inclusive, all-accepting, unconditional. It holds us, encompasses us, keeps us safe. It sees us, knows us. It wraps our hearts up and no matter what life hands us, we know at some level that we are okay, because we are loved by the greatest love there is.

In 2010, I was told a Creation Story directly by Great Mother, The Heart at the Center of All Things. It went like this.

The Story of Creation, as given to me by Great Mother

In the Beginning, There Was the Womb

*The Womb, Prime Source, the First Source, **was**. It was content, the model of pure peace and acceptance. This neutrality is what we call "bliss."*

Infinite eons of endless wellbeing existed in a timeless rapture. Perfect stasis, perfect is-ness, a heightened intensity of actualization, like the contentment that comes from an orgasm, but that never ends.

The felt experience of the First Source is what we equate with unconditional love, pure acceptance, Oneness, and unity consciousness.

But nothing was happening. With no conflict or friction, no creative tension, it was dull. Bliss became boring. Feminine in nature, First Source experienced something new: a desire. This desire was a tiny voice at first, a natural curiosity, a spark of wanting something different. A question emerged, gently: "What more is there?" First Source began to yearn to become more, to find the "edge" of its current experience.

The Womb now had something in it; the Womb now contained something of itself, yet the seed of an expansion of itself at the same time. It was the beginning of contrast, the conception of duality. The spark within First Source took root and began to grow.

The spark stretched and grew until a certain momentum occurred when First Source reached beyond the "edge" of its experience.

Then First Individuation happened; like a birth, a new creation emerged from The Womb. This moment, this act of separation was the beginning of the Masculine. The Individuation, separation from Source, is masculine energy in action.

First Individuation had both feminine and masculine energy within it. First Individuation, an offspring of First Source, also encountered eons of bliss and total acceptance, but eventually became interested in what came next. "What's beyond?" it wondered. And a new seed was created. A model for future individuations, First Individuation was free to create and later became a Source of its own. First Individuation became Second Source.

Second Source individuated into many Individuations, which, in turn, became many Sources. These Sources gave rise to other Sources, which gave rise to other Sources, and so on. Like a fractal, an endless unfolding, Sources continued to beget other Sources.

This how the universe was created and continues to unfold to this day.

~ ~ ~

According to this version of the story of creation, the Mother is the beginning of all things; more happens after the thought of "What else is there?" This is when expansion of the universe occurs. Thus, the love that began everything is Mother Love.

Mother and Source are synonymous.

I connect with Great Mother and am reminded of this love. I do this by choosing to connect with Her, like calling a specific person on the phone. I do this by saying aloud, "I'd like to connect with Great Mother now." In a few, short seconds, I feel Her presence.

This is something we can each do. I am not special in this capacity, nor am I endowed with unusual powers. This is an innate capacity we all have. She is Mother to all of us, after all. Mother likes it when we call home. Her presence is warm, welcoming, and very loving. I am often moved to tears when I feel Her. It is a great blessing.

She is very powerful. The energy that is the origin of the universe is intense. I am reminded of the stories of Aditi, the face of the Divine Feminine that is the black void of infinite space, the womb of pure potential. It can really feel big! But it feels like the same kind of *big* as the ocean bobbing us up and down in the waves, the mountains that ring a valley, or the arms that hold a child. A good kind of big. It takes a little getting used to, but once you experience this kind of love, you will want more.

Peace with the Parts

I take pleasure in my "transformations."
I look quiet and consistent, but few know
how many women there are in me.

— Anais Nin

We are made of parts. Our body is a living, organic community of over fifty trillion cells, each with an agenda to live and a unique role to play in the makeup of our physical self. A brain cell has a different role than a liver cell, for example, equally important but different in function. Our cells are a microcosm of the billions of people and the trillions of creatures on our planet.

There are also parts of our individual psyche. In shamanism, the oldest medicine in the world, we know that **every age we have ever been lives inside of us**. We have a four-year-old, a sixteen-year-old, a twenty-seven-year-old, and so on, all alive and well in our inner landscape.

We also know that our ancestors are alive inside of us, something we can describe as scientifically as our genetic code, our DNA. We are indeed made of the love of many people who came before us.

In a culture that wants us to behave in certain ways, we are discouraged from being authentic in our needs, in expressing how we really feel, in being who we really are. We are asked (or told) to put parts of our selves away, behind closed doors. We are asked to sacrifice our truths in the name of societal need. This begins with our caretakers when we are very young.

"Sit down and be quiet" can result in shame for singing and moving. "Stop asking so many questions" can shut up the curious seeker of information. "Stop crying or I'll give you something to cry about" can stop the flow of emotion that comes to us naturally. "I don't like this part of you" is essentially the message, and because we are young, vulnerable, and need the approval and love of our authority figures, we put ourselves away, become who they want us to be.

As we grow older, we are afraid to show those "undesirable" parts of self, and the closed doors can become locked. We can forget those parts of ourselves ever existed, and then are mystified when we wake one morning and do not know who we are.

Many of us also have undergone trauma, and this can result in parts of ourselves becoming frozen in time, in that moment of awfulness, and remaining there, suspended. Trauma can look like many different things to different people. Trauma is relative. If you have a sensitive nature, trauma could be someone pushing you down at the playground and laughing at you.

We may not like those parts of ourselves; we have been trained not to like them, unfortunately. The culture rewards strength and blames the victim of crime, for example. We even blame someone for getting an illness as if they have done something wrong! We have been trained not to like parts of ourselves that are weak, vulnerable, powerless, perhaps even victimized . . . to turn on those parts as if they were a weak member of the herd and to feed on them.

Parts of ourselves that are not integrated into the wholeness of our psyche can turn "rogue" on us, creating drag as if they are anchors, or even a ball and chain heavily tugging along behind us. These parts of self can actually sabotage our success, not because they are "bad," but because they are seeking our attention, crying out to be heard, acknowledged, and finally, healed. They want to come home.

How we treat ourselves is frequently how we treat each other; if we judge parts of ourselves as inadequate or undesirable, we will most likely judge others that way, too, and ask them to put parts of themselves away like we have inside of ourselves. This is how we perpetuate psychic injury on children, passing it down from generation to generation. An extreme example of this is hate groups, who actively judge others. Because they hate parts of themselves, they are actively judgmental.

Along the lines of self-love and ceasing the habit of judging ourselves, I love what Joseph Bruchac writes in his wonderful book, *Our Stories Remember*. He speaks of a conversation with a friend who asks him if he is carrying around any guilt. When Joe answered no, he didn't think so, his friend said, "Brother, that's good. . . . One of my (Cheyenne) elders asked me once what you should do with a cup of water that is not good to drink." He then made the motion of pouring liquid from a cup out onto the ground.

This is a great story and illustration of what to do with those old thoughts and feelings that are not helping us live our lives in a joyful way. There comes a time when it is more supportive to let go of something than to hang on. By pouring out the stagnant contents of your cup, you are then able to hold it out empty and fill it with something life-affirming!

The Call to Wholeness

As Jess and I drove west for his Vision Quest, six months after his brain injury, we had lots of time to talk. At one point, Jess said, "It is surreal to think I almost died."

Deep breath, mama. *Yes, it is sweetheart.* I took the opportunity, carefully, to enter into a deeper conversation with him.

When something we experience feels surreal, my experience is that we have not integrated it yet. I looked up the word "surreal": *having the disorienting, hallucinatory quality of a dream; unreal.*

This makes sense. When we have a traumatic experience of any kind, it transcends our ordinary sense of reality and our mind has trouble finding a place to put that experience in our regular files. So, we split off a part of our consciousness and it orbits around in our psyche, moving in and out of our sight, depending on whether we heal that situation or not. When something we have experienced feels surreal, it is because our mind has not quite found a place to put it yet.

The orbiting part can get triggered by something we encounter, and suddenly it is right there, in front of our eyes again. We can then re-experience the trauma of the original split, feeling the emotions and bodily sensations as if we are undergoing that experience again. That can create problems in one's life.

I am a proponent of integration, or wholeness. I learned early on that the orbiting parts haunt us, not only because they can pop up unexpectedly and create havoc in our lives, but because they are a part of us and want to come home, to be part of our consciousness. Any part of us that is split off wants to come home, just like we want to come home to our birthplace or to where people love us. The call to come home is strong, and it is the same with parts of us we would rather not own.

Experiences that create a split in our consciousness (or trauma) overwhelm our system in that moment and that creates a psychic wound. A wound requires a healing. It does not have to take years of therapy to do it (although that is a perfectly fine route until you discover there are other ways), but it DOES require healing. It is astonishing to me how some folks think it is okay to walk around with their mind blown to bits, but they would certainly go to the doctor for antibiotics if they were sick, or go to the emergency room if they broke a bone. I find that the physical body is an extension of the emotional, mental, and spiritual body, so if there is a wound in our mind, it requires attention.

Jess's injury was traumatic to his brain and body, but it was also traumatic to his mind. Our whole family has focused on his recovery, for obvious reasons. Once he regained some feeling of normalcy, it made sense that his psyche was ready to work with the part of him that had not yet worked through the experience of almost dying. The fact that he was thinking about this and then said it aloud meant he was beginning the process of integrating the experience. This, of course, means that the rest of us will, too. What will be the next chapter for our family?

Wholeness looks different for different people, but it always feels the same. It feels like coming home, like being reunited with a part of yourself that has been far afield and has returned to you. Often it feels like you did not even realize you were missing that piece, especially if it has been many years since the original split occurred. But it always, always feels like a homecoming. Every time I have integrated another part of me, sometimes dramatically and sometimes very subtly, it is a keen sense of being bigger, stronger, more stable, more solid in my core. That strength of integrity emanates outward, making my energy field powerful. If we want to do good things in the world, that is important.

I have learned that acknowledgment, acceptance, and compassion are the way to melt all barriers inside of myself and return to the flow of authentic *me*. *Self-judgment is the most reliable way to stay stuck.* When I feel something inside and allow it to be heard, bring it to the light, let myself feel that way, it comes to the surface and expresses. Then it dissipates. It is over. If I suppress a feeling, try to squash it down, freeze it, or keep it in the dark, I do not feel the relief that comes with expressed emotion. I stay bolloxed, stuck, and uncomfortable. The way out is truly *through*.

Which, of course, takes love. It's so simple, isn't it? When we can hold ourselves with love, it seems we can face anything we do not like about ourselves. But how do you love yourself with such passion and ferocity when you have not experienced it, when no one taught you how? When we do not experience this kind of love in the world, we can doubt our worthiness, doubt that we are lovable. Self-forgiveness plays a role here, forgiveness for not measuring up in the ways we were taught we should, forgiveness for being "unlovable."

The Great Mother Heart has taught me that love is always the answer, no matter who is crying, no matter what is acting out, no matter what part of myself I may judge as undesirable. She taught me how to love. Coming to peace with the parts is the path of a master, sure, but really, it is the path of Great Mother. Love transforms all things.

Inner Tribe™ Case Study

A sixteen-year-old girl cries because she is crushed by her mother's criticism. "Why are you so mean to me?" she sobs. She learns to mistrust the cruelty of the masculine, the hard voice of her mother, and she internalizes the mistrust of her own inner masculine, the twin part of her that would be learning how to act and exert will in positive ways. She binds her inner masculine, tying him down as Gulliver was bound by the Lilliputians in *Gulliver's Travels*. He is the part of her that would stand up for her in the face of cruelty or abuse, but she cannot know that because no one in her family has ever done that for her. She puts him away because she is afraid that he will hurt her like her mother and father did. As a result, her life is less impactful than it could be.

As this part of her heals, she notices a toxic dumping of ways that she has thought cruelly toward herself: parts of her that feel her body is a "trash heap"; parts of her that say, "She's tough, she can take it," and that expose her to unkind people, nasty media, and dangerous experiences; parts of her that prohibit her from feeling the good feelings and that make fun of her for her happiness.

The healing continues, and she begins to take care of her body, her mind, her soul. Healthy thoughts flow through her mind and her body gets stronger and lighter, and she feels wellbeing. She is reclaiming her life.

I Am My Own Daughter – Miracles of Self-Mothering

In the journey of life (both inner and outer), re-parenting myself has become a central theme in my healing process. Seeing myself as a child of God, precious and valued for my own sake, has been the cornerstone of my reclamation of Self after my violent childhood. Very different from "blaming my toxic parents" or endlessly indulging my "inner child," re-parenting myself is an active, moment-to-moment decision to be the wise guide to the renegade, unhealed child aspects that desperately need a good mother and father.

The "good parent" parts of me are the parts that are integrated, grown up, matured, and emotionally developed, whereas the child parts may be victimized, emotionally stuck in that age, and very needy. My experience tells me that those child parts can run our lives into the ground if we allow them to drive the train; it is better (and responsible) to put the child parts in the *passenger seats* and invite a competent adult part to drive. We can all imagine what would happen if an unsupervised three-year-old drove a speeding train. I don't think any of us want our lives to be a train wreck.

I have found that re-parenting is initially challenging, but that, over time, it becomes habitual, like so many other life changes. It is a good change to make if you find yourself living with critical, internalized parents that manifest in belittling remarks toward yourself or in making poor decisions about your wellbeing.

My scenario looked very much like this. I would put myself down and mercilessly cut the tender skin of the little girl inside me who just wanted to be loved. I put myself in situations that were dangerous physically and emotionally, allowing myself to be run over by someone else's train, driven by their inner three-year-old. I allowed myself to be hurt by being in front of toxic people, not leaving until the situation became utterly intolerable. Still, I eat sometimes in ways that indicate that I am feeding an emotional need rather than a physical one. I find myself sometimes reaching for approval from people or places that cannot give it to me. I want someone to love me utterly and unconditionally when they cannot even love themselves. These are all signs of an active inner child part that needs attention.

The inner child is very real. As I have mentioned, in shamanism, it is believed that we carry all the ages we have ever been inside of us into this present moment unless something occurred somewhere along the way that keeps a part of us stuck in the past. This usually happens when there is some kind of overwhelming experience to the psyche. Called *trauma* in psychology, we say in shamanism that these moments of overwhelm can "freeze" us emotionally and energetically, causing considerable drain in our lives. It becomes the shaman's task to retrieve the part of us that is caught in an energetic web of trauma, freeing us to be one in the present.

Psychology mirrors this concept when we talk about integration of parts of self into wholeness. Integration is another word for healing, and healing is what is needed when a part of self is acting out of alignment with our optimal health and wellbeing. It is important to bring all parts of self into some sense of alignment with our larger Self, the mature, wise, and highly evolved core that some might call the "spiritual" Self. The more integrated we are, the fewer conflicts there are in the internal dialogue among our parts. Less inner conflict means moving forward in our lives with ease and grace.

Sometimes "moving forward" means leaving a part of ourselves behind because it is what is needed, as children, for our survival. The biological imperative to *live* wins in the end, and so we do what must be done in order to survive. A child who encounters intense abuse, for example, may dissociate in order to live through the experience. The cost of that temporary reprieve is that a part of the child is caught by the trauma of that moment and that part does not move in concert in maturation with the child as they age. Emotion may be stunted; the later adult may have an emotional literacy that is developed only to the age they were "frozen."

Many, many children are walking around in adult bodies. I know because I was raised by two, encounter them every day, and have even been one of them. Over twenty-five years of recovery work later, I am still uncovering parts of myself that were caught in the trauma of some violent moment in my life. I am blessed to have had excellent support and loving guidance in retrieving parts that wandered loose from my center: unparented, wild child parts, scared two- or five-year-old parts, or angry thirteen- or seventeen-year-old parts, all aspects of my psyche that hold important keys to my actualized life.

From the perspective of being on the other side of my technique, I can speak to the benefit of retrieval work, the integration of parts of self into a kind of central "Home in the Heart." I began calling these aspects of my psyche my "inner tribe" in 2004, and developed the Inner Tribe™ technique soon after.

I envision a large campfire around which the majority of my inner tribe sit, telling stories, talking and laughing, and holding council when necessary. When I notice that a part of my Self seems to be acting out in ways that are incongruent with my maturity level, I look beyond the circle around the fire to who is lurking at the dark edges. I will see a part of my Self with its back turned, a child who is crying or a symbol that represents a quality of my personality that is tied up in the traumatic net of the past. I am then called upon to be my biggest, best Self, my most compassionate and wise nature, to navigate bringing this lost part of Self home to the tribe.

Making Good Medicine Out of Bad Medicine

I am amazed by the ability of women who were abused by their mothers to reach deep into themselves to find the ideal mother so they do not pass on the wounding to their own children. Repeatedly, I am astounded by my women clients who have encountered heinous acts of violence and, somehow, have picked up the pieces of their broken psyches and healed themselves to the point that they can actually help others. Great Mother told me that *the yearning for mother creates a vacuum, a need inside of us; if we allow ourselves to feel that yearning, the universe will answer, sometimes through our own desire to be a good mother.*

There is something about how we, as women, can experience the worst that humanity has to offer and are able to transmute it through our very bodies into something that serves as medicine for the people, for the future generations. Naturally, I attract these kinds of women in my practice and as friends because this is who I am—absolutely, fiercely, passionately devoted to making good of my pain.

Inner Tribe™ work puts the best of our archetypal mothering into action as a healing tool. I have continued journaling to work with the parts of myself that need mothering.

My Inner Masculine, Age Fourteen

Inner Tribe™ Case Study

I became aware of a part of self that is like a teenaged boy; I could see him in my mind's eye, gangly, awkward. I found that he lived in my right shoulder/chest/back when I zeroed in on him. I had been having trouble with my right shoulder for over two years, exhibiting a "frozen shoulder," according to my physical practitioners.

I went inside to my body, in the center of the right shoulder. I saw him. He was bound tightly, wrapped and tied up with ropes. He said, "I can't move. Cut the ropes." I imagine coming forward with a knife to cut the ropes, and see that several other children of all ages are coming forward to help. They work diligently to free him. I get the impression that he is a respected part, kind of like a Peter Pan figure to the younger parts. We free him, and he stands up. He is glowering, his face angry and emotional. He says, "She killed me. She crucified me." He is so angry that he wants to hurt my mother for tying him up.

I empathize with him, saying, "Of course, you do. It makes sense that you feel that way."

Feeling my permission for how he feels, he breaks down, and I wrap my arms around him. "Why did she hate me so much?" he asks through his tears.

I tell him she hated herself, not him, and I just hold him. I tell him how remarkable he is, how strong and capable, and how the world is at his feet and that he has his whole life ahead of him. In my heart, I feel such compassion for him, and I call on Great Mother to help him heal, from the inside out. All of the others who came forward to help him get free jump up and down and clap with glee. I integrate him in, and I feel and hear a pop in the deep center of the right side of my chest, under my shoulder blade, and my shoulder swings free, freer than it has in more than two years.

Inner Tribe™ Technique

Inner Tribe™ work is subtle and based in love, and is therefore very powerful. I developed this technique first to heal myself, and upon realization of its complete effectiveness, to teach it to my clients with great success. It is very important to me to teach tools that empower individuals to heal themselves; I have found it effective in combination with other therapies, as well. I am an advocate for whatever works with our unique set of issues and psychology/neurobiology.

The basics of Inner Tribe™ work revolve around respect, compassion, and acknowledgment. Here are the steps to healing a part of self that has splintered off from your larger Core Self:

1. Acknowledge your feeling. Something is uncomfortable; what is it? Allow the feeling to emerge; be curious about it.

2. Notice the body. Is there a part of your body that feels different? Painful, achy, tight, spasms, cold or hot? Is there a place in your body that seems to be calling out to be seen?

3. Go within. Go into that part of the body and feel/see what is there. Visualize or sense that there is a part of self, which may be a child, person, object, color, or other symbol. Get as much information as possible and describe what you see/sense. If it is a child, for example, notice what they are wearing, if they are holding anything, the facial expression, if they are doing anything in particular, etc. Notice the landscape.

4. Have dialogue with your Inner Tribe™ member. You are interacting with a part of yourself, so do so respectfully and with love. Imagine that you are the greatest mother in the world, and your dialogue with the Inner Tribe™ member is informed by the great love and compassion of the mother's heart. Ask that part of you if they have anything they want to tell you or show you. Listen with non-judgment.

5. Establish trust. You are here to listen and heal a part of yourself that was diminished or traumatized in some past time of your life. This Inner Tribe™ member needs to feel that you are trustworthy to reveal why they split off from your wholeness in the first place. This takes incredible trust on their part. Your conversation with them needs to be loving and non-judgmental, and you need to actively send compassion from your heart during this important interaction. If the Inner Tribe™ member feels a whiff of unsafety, they will retreat. Do not despair if this occurs; it takes practice to be compassionate and non-judgmental with ourselves. The opportunity to heal this part will arise again.

6. Integrate the Inner Tribe ™ member. As the part of self unburdens its pain and secrets, it will become lighter and the interaction may change form. Ask the Inner Tribe™ member if it is all right for you to hug

them; get down on their level and genuinely beam love from your heart to them. This is the time when the part is most likely to melt into your body, *a signal that the part is now integrating into your wholeness.*

~ ~ ~

Everything in the physical universe happens in relationship. It is arrogant to believe that we do everything by ourselves. Try brushing your teeth without a toothbrush! Every single thing we do, create, or dream into being is done by the generous offerings of others. We are better and more than the sum of our parts, and this work to reclaim our Inner Tribe™ is a call to value relations between the aspects of ourselves in a coherent, cohesive way in order to be most effective in our lives.

My intention in sharing the basic steps of Inner Tribe™ work is *to empower you to heal yourself.* In a patriarchal culture, we are told we do not have the power to heal ourselves, or to speak to God directly, we cannot be trusted with such important matters, and must go to an authority. I reject this notion in principle, but believe in balance. As an experienced practitioner, I acknowledge that there are often exceptions to the rule due to our individual circumstances. I advocate a discerning eye toward healing ourselves, utilizing a professional at times, as well as working on our own behalf to heal. I have greatly benefitted from a balance of both.

The Trauma of Patriarchy

The more I worked with the parts of myself that were frozen in time somewhere in my psyche, the more I understood that the splitting off of parts of ourselves is a function of a culture that asks us to split off from our Core Self in order to survive. Just like in an abusive family, where a child must suffer the traumas and put the sensitive, wounded parts away in order to live through the abuses, we live in an abusive culture that demands that we put wounded, sensitive parts of ourselves away in order to be "good citizens." We live in a traumatic environment of hatred, bullying, bigotry, sexism, racism, religious intolerance, homophobia, and rejection of anything perceived as different, frightening, weak, . . . and feminine.

Many resources are available to study about feminist theory, so I won't expound into the mechanics of inequality and the origins of patriarchy here. What is important in the scope of this book is to understand that *mainstream culture teaches us to reject, rather than to include.* The archetypal Mother that I have encountered taught me to scoop up the errant parts of myself and love them back into my wholeness, and this is a microcosm of what is needed on our planet at a seemingly critical time in human history.

I realized that Inner Tribe™ work is the appropriate answer to the cry for wholeness and the perfect vehicle for healing with Great Mother energy. The missing parts of self suppressed by the patriarchal culture are essential to the return of feminine principles on our planet. Bringing these parts home is a way of embodying the Great Mother archetype in feminine style. This practical healing approach could heal the rifts in our brains, our genders, and our species, and even our eventual outcome on our planet.

Women are usually the initiators of healing. Almost always, the wife in a heterosexual marriage seeks marriage counseling; almost always, the village crone brought factions together to stop fighting (see the legends about White Buffalo Calf Woman, who brought the peace pipe to native plains peoples in the America); almost always it is a little girl on the playground, comforting a bullied or injured fellow student. Why is this? Why are women the bringers of connection and healing? Because we are built to do it.

Research suggests that our brains are different than men's brains; the corpus callosum (the bridge between our brain hemispheres) is thicker in women, enabling more connections between the empathic, emotional, intuitive regions in the right and the logical, deductive, and exclusive left hemispheres. Because we are more "whole-brained," we are able to see, feel, sense more communally then most men. Some research indicates that these physical differences in the brain are created by social conditioning. Recent research indicates we are both male and female in our brains, but that we are conditioned to bring forth certain areas of our brains by our environment.

I know from my life's experience that I have both masculine and feminine energy within me, and I have found parts in my Inner Tribe™ that are male and female, boys and girls. This has borne out in my work with women and men clients. Made of both feminine and masculine energy, we are indeed a complex, multi-gendered community inside of us.

Our culture of rejection is one of splitting us from ourselves. This is abusive to everyone. We are indeed recovering, as we see a mainstream groundswell of self-help, healing, and recovery movements; the rise of pop spirituality, while not particularly grounded or practical, indicates a reaching out for a larger intelligence that will help us. We seek and are indeed making motions toward wholeness, shown by the wave of truth-telling that has emerged in the last two years; I have seen much personal revelation about racism, sexism, homophobia, and all manners of hate.

We are healing ourselves of the trauma of patriarchy.

Part Three

Her Voice

Chapter 9: The Waters

To Thine Own Self Be True
Collage © 2010 Licia Berry

My Daughter,

As you come into your body, you will feel the waters within, waters that carry the feeling you have not allowed yourself to feel. For you, sweet one, this is sadness. Sadness is in your body, and it wants to move out. Allowing this motion of your inner waters is a key to your joy.

Allow the waters to flow. You have observed the waters of the Earth when they flow freely and when their flow is dammed or hampered. The waters must move freely in the body, just as they must move freely on the Earth. Impeded water can become stagnant and create pollution in the body.

Set the intention to allow the waters to flow within you. You will feel sad, yes. This is as it should be, for you have reason to feel this way and have not expressed it, as you should have been allowed to. You are safe now to express your sadness without being persecuted for it.

I am with you,
Great Mother

As Great Mother taught me, water is a messenger, a carrier of information. Water bears forth data that travel from one place to another, in the body of the Earth and in our own bodies. The sacred role of water includes being the bearer of news, whether good or bad. We would do well to heed the messenger, and not ignore or kill it.

Water carries memory and our voice of the deep feminine, the wisdom of the belly, the amniotic fluid of our creativity. We are made of mostly water, and water remembers the beginnings of life on this planet. To come home to the water is to come home to our genesis.

Heeding feelings (emotions) is heeding information and is inherently neutral in charge. Judgment, a human invention of the intellect in response to an internal emotion, gives value to the information as good or bad, but information in itself is neutral. The waters, like Earth, God, and the feminine, have been projected upon as a face of something mysterious and fearful, but water is a conduit. By itself, water is a divine carrier of data, not a frightening entity. It is the information in the waters that brings the message, not the water itself.

Memory travels in water. *The waters in your body carry the memory of all that has touched it*, Great Mother told me. Water retains an imprint of what it has been exposed to, according to a recent experiment by the Aerospace Institute of the University of Stuttgart in Germany. The research shows that water carries data from everything it touches: the participants in the experiments, flowers dropped into pitchers of water, even rivers and oceans. As the head scientist describes, our oceans are not simply great expanses that divide us, but bodies of memory that unite the land. Water is a conduit, alive with information.

When the waters are polluted with what is not life-affirming, it interferes with the data transported in the water. The memory is warped into something that is no longer life-affirming. As Japanese researcher Masaru Emoto showed in his water crystal experiments, water is impacted and transformed by our thoughts.

Feeling as the New Frontier

A lot of folks are feeling a swell of emotions right now. The world seems to be in chaos—gun and bomb massacres, climate change, political conflict, open hate for "others" in the form of racism, religious intolerance, homophobia, and, of course, sexism. It can be overwhelming to be present to so much stimuli that induces emotion. It can be tempting to shut down and comfort ourselves with whatever our addiction may be (food, technology, alcohol, drugs, shopping, exercise, sex, etc.) Feeling the reality of how bad things are can be unpleasant! But I maintain that running from our emotions is how we got here to begin with.

Looking at historical data, the human species began to move toward the intellect and reason at the same time that we learned to speak. The species became more left-brain oriented as we learned language, cultivated crops, and defended the territories that were created by the non-migration that cultivated life afforded. The Age of Reason created even further dependence on the faculties of the left brain, as we sought progress in medicine and the sciences. All of the developments of technology can be credited to the dominance of the left hemisphere of the brain.

The down side of the left-brain dominance is the dismissal and rejection of input from the right hemisphere of the brain: empathy, connection, understanding, imagination, intuition, and emotion. While all of that progress was being made, a whole lot of awful feelings were being ignored. Think for a moment about the genocide of millions of Jews, Native Americans, and women. If the powers that ordered those millions of souls snuffed out were in touch with their empathy, could they have executed so many?

The right hemisphere of the brain is the governor of the left side of the body, seen as "the feminine side" of the body in many medicinal philosophies. The feminine half of our brain has been dismissed for thousands of years, and the feminine half of the body has borne the brunt. In indigenous traditions, the connection to the Earth is through the feminine within our body. As babies, we are more whole-brain oriented, but are taught to become more left-brain oriented as we name objects and place things into categories. This, in itself, is not a bad thing if we also are taught to honor the input of the right brain, but the mainstream culture does not reward right-brain input.

If we relate to the world only through the left brain/right side of the body, we relate only in a masculine way, one of competition, separation, defense of boundaries, logic, and mathematical precision. We miss feeling, empathy, and emotion entirely.

My understanding from Great Mother is that the reemergence of the feminine in the collective psyche looks like folks FEELING their feelings, not just talking about them or conceptualizing them or thinking "positive thoughts." Positive thinking is wonderful, but not as an escape from things that need attention. My native family believes that the wave of "thinking positive" thoughts, when not balanced with self-honesty, is a form of mental illness that allows horrid things to occur on this planet. The reality of life is that there is hardship sometimes, and ignoring this truth is denying reality.

Once a woman called in to my radio show. She was a "Law of Attraction"-inspired coach in her day job, but she called in seeking some answers for a traumatic event in her life. Her son had committed suicide. She was driving herself crazy, trying to cope with this incredible, unnamable loss by "thinking positive thoughts" and looking for "spiritual" answers about it.

What I offered to her was swift and clear: "Honey, you need to allow yourself to grieve." What madness to believe she could "positive think" her way through the death of her precious child! She broke down on the air then wrote to me several months later that the permission I encouraged for her to FEEL changed her life.

I understand why intellect and thought are so attractive to us. Feeling is not logical in any way; it is the opposite of category, reason, or order. Feeling is the antithesis of putting things in a box so we can understand them. Feeling defies being domesticated, cultivated, or tamed. Feeling is wild, animal, messy, uncontrollable, heart, soul, dreams, and water. Feeling is the balance to the way humanity has lived for over five thousand years.

We are meant to feel. This is part of our design as human beings. We have physical, mental, spiritual, and EMOTIONAL capacities, all of which serve a purpose and have a critical function toward our being fully human.

The wonderful neuroscientist Jill Bolte Taylor explains that our body is designed to deal with emotions swiftly and efficiently. We go through a process: we think a thought, we have an emotional response to that thought, a corresponding chemical response in our brain flushes through our body, and then our chemistry comes back to stasis. *All of this occurs, from beginning to end, in ninety seconds.* She goes on to say that if we feel an emotion for longer than ninety seconds, it is because we keep thinking that thought! So assuredly, we can deal with an emotion without fear that we will become stuck in it forever as long as we deal with the initial wave right then and there and do not re-initiate the emotional cascade through thinking about it over and over again.

The trouble comes when we do not allow the emotion to flow through and out of our body, when we freeze it or suppress it, burying it in our cell structure. The chemicals that are meant to flow through and out of our body in the expression of the emotion remain in the cell, creating inflammation and toxic waste in the cells. Ahhh, the "pollution" referred to by Great Mother?

No wonder we periodically feel called to fasting or cleanses. If we have suppressed emotion for a length of time, we may have a backlog of emotional chemistry that needs help to flush out of our bodies.

But Don't We "Create Our Reality"?

Some people use the idea of "we create our own reality" to explain why they are in a particular situation. Frequently, these words have a slightly punishing spin on them.

I also hear people voice fear about feeling and expressing their emotions, afraid it could "create" something awful in their lives. "If I think about or feel what my mother did to me, won't I create more of it?", for example.

Here's the thing. *The emotions are in you, regardless of whether you allow yourself to feel them.* Before you became enamored with an intellectual idea about how you create your reality, you were a little girl who was sad because her mother was unkind to her. Those feelings are still inside you, somewhere in your body and psyche, and they are driving you to behave in ways that impact your life. You can live with those feelings, haunting you from some dark corner, or you can allow them to come to the surface and express, leaving you fresh and clean to feel, think, and live in a different way, in the present, free of your past.

I believe and experience that this idea of "we create our own reality" can be useful insofar as it reminds us of our responsibility and power to co-create with the rest of the universe. As far as I can tell, this life is a collaboration, so it makes sense to me that I need to realize my part in the way of things, to realize that I can step in and affect change. Our energy moves in an outward and generative spiral, so remembering my power encourages me to make change in my own best interest.

When this idea of "we create our own reality" is used to punish, or criticize, or to encourage me to stick with a situation—even if it feels wrong—just because I must have created it and therefore must need it, want it, etc., then the energy moves in an inward and destructive spiral and carries a harmful message directly to my inner being. If I am responsible for creating the situation with my mother, then I must have been one powerful little girl. In fact, I must have been ALL powerful that I could have caused my mother to behave the way she did!

It is truly unkind to take responsibility for the abuses we may have suffered as if we created them. Regardless of our spiritual beliefs or inclinations, it is irresponsible to the child we were to blame ourselves for what was done to us. Abuse is never the child's fault. Never.

Some people are concerned that if they let themselves feel what was done to them, they will never come out of it. They judge themselves for feeling small and weak, and then judge others who have the courage to talk about the abuses of childhood. We live in a victim-shaming culture.

Far from "wallowing in it," allowing ourselves to feel with the intention to free and heal ourselves is the opposite of weak. It is courageous, responsible, and in integrity—for ourselves and every life we touch. My experience shows me that the problems come when we judge ourselves for what we are feeling, or that we are feeling at all.

If you find yourself in tears more frequently lately or feeling a little chaotic on the inside, maybe even angry or depressed, I offer that you should not think you are going crazy or that something is wrong with you. I FEEL and am told that *feeling* is the next frontier in human consciousness and expansion/evolution. I think women will lead the way in learning how to BE this feeling state that we are entering—at least the women who have not internalized patriarchy so much that they are "men in skirts." We will have to allow this feeling to BE us. Then we will teach others, and then the world will truly change to that balanced state so many of us feel coming.

I have found healing, understanding, self-acceptance, and incredible love as a result of allowing myself to feel without judgment or conception. Just FEEL. When I allow the feelings, no matter how uncomfortable or painful to move through me, I come out the other side wiser, cleansed, and feeling whole.

I'm Not as Cheerful as I Thought

As we come into our feelings, allowing the inner waters to flow into our consciousness, we may be surprised by the nature of the emotions that we discover inside of us. We may not realize that there has been anger, grief, sadness, or despair underneath our daily smiles.

When I tapped into the wellspring of emotions that had been dammed up in my body, I was mortified at first to find rage. It took some years for the rage to express through art, writing, movement, healing therapies, activism, and other outlets that I found constructive.

As I wrote in *Soul Compost*, the "Anger Prescription" of making tantrum motions on my bed, kicking and flailing while shrieking, provided helpful releases. I found after doing this for just a few seconds that the rage relented to grief. I would then allow myself to cry and wail, making deep sounds in my throat and belly. It was productive to do this. It reconnected my mind and body, reorganized my nervous system into a more resilient, integrated state, and improved my health physically, emotionally, mentally, and spiritually as a result of giving my emotional body time and space to express, to put down its burden.

I came to the realization that I had explored my early

Near Liberated
Collage © 2010 Licia Berry

spirituality from a more masculine perspective of the elements of Air (visionary, mental, intellect, curiosity, futurist) and Fire (pioneer, expansion, determination, restlessness, impulsive). I had learned many valuable lessons during this exploration, but I was not very grounded. Once I "hit the ground" and came into the waters and the earth of my body, I realized I had been carrying emotions that I stuffed deep down inside me, divorced from my feelings and intuition, a pattern of survival from childhood. The anger I felt as I came back to my human, animal body was a shock. Having seen myself as "the good girl" who sought love and affirmation from women, I began to wonder if I was as cheerful a person as I thought.

Collective Emotion

As we dive in bravely to our bodies and feel our feelings, we may find that we come up against an internal threshold. As I practiced making friends with the waters—feeling my feelings, making space for them, not judging them, expressing them in constructive ways—I became familiar with my inner territories, something I called "The Frontier Inside." I learned to navigate rich landscapes, complete with obstacles, helpers, treasures and special powers. I became familiar with internal places that were helpful, easy. And others that were trials of initiation, tests of my strength. I was amazed to find that my Frontier Inside mirrored some external, real-world landscapes.

One day, I followed a trail of my feelings in my internal landscape and came over a hill to find a sea of women, a throng of billions that went to the horizon, as far as my eye could see. I was overcome by the sheer presence of the feminine principle and the power of so many women. They were of all historical eras of human experience, in all stages of life, many cultures, many languages, many ethnicities.

As I stood watching them, some raised their fists and wailed against the sky, some in anger, some in grief, some in warrior-like protest, similar to the Haka ritual of the Maori of New Zealand. Some danced in powerful native ways, some held and hugged each other, some were collapsed into themselves, and some simply looked at me with seriousness and intense focus, as if they waited for me to say or do something.

I asked the sea of women what they were doing in my internal landscape—not disrespectfully, but curiously, because I truly wanted to know. The information was clear. The collective emotion of women over thousands of years of injustice and persecution hit me like a tidal wave. This sea of women showed me the emotions of billions of women over time, a collective female experience of life on Earth. I was one of them; they were not separate from me. I realized that the feelings that I thought were mine alone were the feelings of women since the beginning of our oppression.

We may make space for feeling our personal emotions—and this is a vitally important step—but then we also may tap into grief and rage that is larger than our own life experience. We may realize that we are indeed connected to our human family, and to women through the ages. Women carry a layer and level of experience of the last several thousand years that is different and unique to us as females in a patriarchal era. The lack of safety, the crushing of our feminine power, and the burying of our innate wisdom so that it became invisible to even our daughters is a collective wound that gapes in the human psyche. My felt experience of this ancient truth mobilized me.

When we come into collective emotion, we realize what has been lost. We realize, too, how important it is that we stand up and act.

What an interesting evolution—that allowing myself to feel and express my personal emotions would then connect me with collective emotion and motivate me to act toward positive change in the world. No longer content to sit, meditating quietly on my cushion, judging something as "unspiritual" or "unnecessary drama," I chose to engage from the sidelines. I descended from my intellectual tower, rolled my sleeves up, and got dirty. This was the day that I joined the human race.

When we do not feel, we have no empathy for the suffering of others. We stand by and allow horrors to occur. When we do not feel, we miss the importance of standing in our power. When we do not feel, we get to the end of our lives and realize we have lived a mere shade of our existence. By then, it is too late.

When we do not feel, we miss the staggering beauty, the giddy joy, the sheer miracle and sacredness of life. If we do not feel the profound grief that inevitably comes from having our hearts deeply pierced, then we cannot experience love. How can we walk through life as a loving being if we do not feel the value of all life? How can we walk in love if we do not grieve?

Through our disconnection from our feeling, our inner waters, what has been lost is *our awareness of the sacredness of all life*. When we feel, we understand the great gifts we are given, and we motivate to protect them. We feel and we remember what is being given to us every day, the generosity of all life to keep us alive through the offerings of food, water, light, night. We rediscover that we are loved deeply. And that we are worthy of that love.

Crucifixion of the Feminine

One day, my son remarked to me how ruthless women are to one another.

"It's true," I told him. "It is one of the great tragedies of our world that women often tear each other down instead of lift each other up."

"Why," he asked? "Doesn't the world tear them down enough without doing it to each other?"

"Yes," I agreed. "It's the world that taught them not to trust each other, and in the end, not to trust themselves."

Gossip, backstabbing, competitive "tripping up" of other females—the unkind things that women do to one another is the stuff of wildlife documentaries. It is truly extraordinary how we have learned to take each other out in covert ways that we think cannot be traced. However, if you are a feeling, conscious, present person, you recognize that there are women who are actively taking you down, even if you cannot see them. You can feel it.

Women with an active (unhealed) Mother Wound often have what I term a "Rejection Repository." This is a place inside that was initially scarred by our mothers' rejection of us as children, but over time, the scarring is "added to" by rejections from other women. This makes us hyper-alert to the possibility of rejection, in which we anticipate it occurring. We actually look for the woman who dislikes us, passing over the ten women who like us just fine. Our brain created a neural pathway for the initial rejection from our mother, and each time it happens again, the neural pathway strengthens. It becomes a self-fulfilling prophecy; the "repository" fills a little more, and our Mother Wound is activated all over again. For women with active, unhealed Mother Wounds, this is a devastating cycle.

I see this most often in women who are baffled by why they seem to have trouble in relationships with other women. When our Mother Wound is unhealed, we may (unconsciously) seek out women who mirror our mothers' behaviors and with those women, we play the role as their daughters. Conversely, we may seek out women who can roleplay us as the daughters, so we can treat them as our own mother treated us. Difficulty in relationships and bonds with women is a hallmark of the Mother Wound.

Unfortunately, we are trained as youngsters to view each other with competitive eyes, not coincidentally, the eyes of unpartnered masculine energy. Instead of exalting the feminine energy within each other, we view it with suspicion and skepticism, or worse, downright offense. We respect other women culturally who have "manned up" and lead companies or are successful financially. But we prefer that women do not get ahead of us or gain something we have not gained for ourselves. Why is this?

Because we are mimicking the patriarchy. We crucify the feminine in each other just as the larger culture does. We echo what we saw as children, in the classroom that focuses on achievement and winning. We perpetuate what our mothers— they themselves victims of a dominant paradigm of unpartnered masculine—taught us about how to be women.

When we grow up in the care of women who do not love themselves and have not learned to stand in their feminine power, we cannot know how to care for another woman's heart, and so we are betrayed, and we betray other women's hearts, over and over again, until we heal ourselves.

The Consequence of the Feminist Movement that Unintentionally Undermines Women, and Everyone

I absolutely consider myself a feminist in the sense that I believe all should have equal opportunity. As my brother reminds me, I have actively voiced my opinion about the injustices toward women since I was a teenager. However, when I look back at my concerns from my current understanding, I see that what I was angry about was a deeper issue: *that the feminine principle is judged as inferior*.

I internalized a masculine world view in order to survive my parents, my family, and my culture. I considered the feminine within me, the connective, feeling, intuitive, imaginative (right-brain) side of me, to be weak. I disdained the left side of my body and exalted the masculine, right side as the stronger, clearer, active side. If I had a hole in my sock, it would go on the left foot because the left side was my feminine side. What a clear metaphor and mirror of our patriarchy as expressed by a teenaged girl!

The sacred role of mother, the bringer and nurturer of life, has been minimized. We have been programmed to believe that a career, or at least a job, is more important than mothering. Approximately one-third of children live in mother-only homes, and it is most often necessary for the mother to work outside the home whether she is single or with a committed partner. According to the U.S. Department of Health and Human Services, a number of studies have shown that separation in excess of twenty hours per week before a baby is one year old increases the risks of insecure attachment. We are taught that "quality-time" is what makes the difference, as though any amount of time the mother can spend with her baby is good enough as long as she is actually paying attention to the baby and is not just in the baby's presence.

Mothering is not the simple biological act of housing a developing baby and then popping it out into the world, like a playdough factory, to fend for itself. It is a lifetime commitment of connection, guidance, wisdom, discernment, nurturing, and letting go. *Mothering is a physical, emotional, mental, and spiritual offering, doing our part in the continuation of All Life in this universe.* It is my fervent prayer that my children are more evolved than I am, that my efforts and personal sacrifices launch them in such a way as to exceed my knowledge and ability, and that they then take the world further into love, justice, goodness.

And no, I don't suggest that mothering is for every woman. I believe powerfully in our free will and that we choose what we want to do with our lives. What I suggest here is that if we DO choose to be a mother, that we honor this role as the sacred role that it is, and honor women for their ability to do it.

The female body is the portal between the energetic, or spiritual, realm and the physical realm. We are the only beings strong enough to navigate unborn spirits onto this planet, and then to guide them in strength, truth, and beauty toward a greater life. So, why do we not treat motherhood as the sacred role it is?

Acceptance of the Feminine Means Connection

Accepting the feminine as important in others begins with *accepting the feminine in ourselves.* The principle of feminine qualities is centered on connection; and we cannot dominate, compete, and appropriate *if we feel our connectedness* with All Things.

If we feel our connection, we take care of that connection. Tending to what we care about demonstrates where we feel love; tending to what we care about illuminates what we feel loved by.

From late pregnancy through the second year of life, the human brain experiences a critical, accelerated period of increased focus on right-brain development. The right brain is deeply connected to both the sympathetic and parasympathetic nervous systems, which control vital functions that support survival and cope with stress, as well as the limbic system of the brain, which includes the hippocampus and the amygdala. The limbic system is the neurological seat of emotions; the hippocampus and the amygdala are closely tied to memory and the regulation of emotions, including aggression. What has emerged in brain research is mounting evidence that stress and trauma impair optimal brain development while healthy attachment promotes it.

"Limbic resonance" is the theory that the capacity for sharing deep emotional states arises from the brain's limbic system; this means that our brain chemistry and nervous systems are measurably affected by those closest to us. Limbic resonance refers to the capacity for empathy and non-verbal connection that is present in mammals and that forms the basis of our social connections, as well as the foundation for various modes of therapy and healing. This is the biological/psychological basis for attachment theory and attachment parenting, the belief that the mother-child bond is the essential and primary force in infant development, and thus forms the basis of coping, negotiation of relationships, and personality development.

Our systems synchronize with one another in a way that has profound implications for personality and lifelong emotional health. Our nervous systems are not self-contained, but rather demonstrably attuned to those around us with whom we share a close connection.

Our right and limbic brain urges us to stop when we have the potential to hurt someone through our words or actions. It is the part in each of us that attempts to communicate in subtle, non-verbal, and intuitive signals, guiding us in our lives. It is a part of us that we have learned to dismiss because the culture dismisses it. Sometimes this "voice" of our right brain/limbic brain suggests something that is in contrast with what we think we want. I equate this to the child/parent or ego/spirit conversation. Our little self wants ice cream before dinner, but our larger Self reminds us that we need to eat our broccoli first. I have trained people for years how to access their larger guidance through the right brain because the input of our right brain can lead to a much smoother life. My family has avoided catastrophe multiple times by listening to these subtle communications. My regular use of the input of my right brain is also how I began to be a conduit for the voice of Great Mother.

When we are not shown caring by our mothers, we learn a broken sense of connection with others. As adults, we yearn for their love, especially the love and regard of other women, yet always have an ear to the ground for the inevitable rejection.

When it comes, it devastates us. "She doesn't like me" reverberates in our hearts, an old childhood refrain. The Mother Wound activates yet again, and we fall into the rabbit hole of our old despair.

Healing the Mother Wound means that when other women reject us (which is inevitable—not everybody will like or agree with us), we no longer go into the rabbit hole. We see clearly that they may be operating from their own woundedness, and it has nothing to do with us. We do not move through the world, actively looking for the next rejection. We can feel and appreciate the positive affirmation of women who love us.

If we need to be accepted and affirmed by others in order to feel good about ourselves all of the time, we can be reasonably certain we have not healed our childhood wounds. The rejection of a daughter by a mother is an issue I see rampant in women who seek to be affirmed in the masculine world, through business, through competition, through fame and celebrity. As they push to excel and to be acknowledged for more masculine pursuits, I wonder about their relationships with their mothers. Were they loved and affirmed for simply being?

When I learned to take responsibility for my own mind, I could recognize when I had thoughts about another woman that were unkind, and instead of gossiping about her, I could say "I'm not attracted to her," or "I'm not drawn to her work," or "We are not a match for one another." I could take responsibility for my feelings about her without tearing her down or making her "evil." Women throw dark projections on each other in our culture. When we become conscious, we begin to see how those projections are untrue. We begin to see one another's light.

When Great Mother taught me to take responsibility for my own heart, I could examine the ways in which I held myself apart from other women for fear that I would do to them what my mother did to me—the active, aggression of ripping me to shreds which hurt me so badly as a girl and young woman. I wanted so much not to hurt other women that my distance wound up hurting them in another way.

I am issuing a call to women to choose to treat each other differently, to support and lift one another up. If we cannot be friends, then we can at least respect one another by taking responsibility for how we speak of one another, ceasing our dark projections onto each other and bearing ourselves up with dignity and integrity as we walk in the world. *Let us be beacons, showing the world how to treat us by how we treat one another*, as if we were raising one another as the precious daughters that we are.

Great Mother's Voice

Each time my feet touched the Earth I knew my Mother was there with me. I knew this body was not mine alone, but a living continuation of my Mother and all of my ancestors. These feet that I saw as "my" feet were actually "our" feet. Together, my mother and I were leaving footprints in the damp soil.
–Thich Nhat Hanh in "No Death, No Fear"

My process has led me to remember my childhood awareness of Nature as the teacher. In my work with others, I am always reminded to follow the seasons in honoring our body and in our psyche. Nature does not jump divine timing, does not push the river. As Great Mother has reminded me, *there is a Larger Logic to allowing things to unfold as they are ready.*

In ourselves, we are Nature, too. We are subject to the same mysterious laws that grow corn or roses out of the ground. We are creatures of the Earth, of Her body, and are organic in the ways we grow. Healing happens at the rate that we can withstand, and no more. If we try to push ahead of our timing, we inevitably will be forced back to what is sustainable in our lives. We cannot outwit or exceed our readiness. The way to health and wholeness is to *trust the process.*

When doing Inner Tribe™ work, for example, we might be tempted to push and dig and ferret out parts of ourselves that are disenfranchised, but there is no need. Inner Tribe™ work is gentle and relies on the laws of Nature to reveal a part of self when it is the correct time. Parts come forward when we are ready to address them—and when THEY are ready to be seen and to "come home" to our Core Self.

For my Inner Tribe™ members to come forward for healing, they need me to prove that I can be trusted to make good decisions for them. I have to integrate and solidify and become stronger and more dependable for the parts to believe they are safe to come home. *In other words, I have to be a good mother to them.* The archetypal Mother that I found taught me how to be just that.

This Night Will Pass
Collage, © 2010 Licia Berry

Our biological mothers may not have known to love all the parts of us, to accept us unconditionally and embrace us as we are. But Great Mother does. Once we let go of needing our human mothers to love us this way, we can feel the support of the archetypal Mother under our very feet. We are daughters of the Earth, the ground, the dirt.

As I came more into my own wholeness, I felt the love of Great Mother in the Earth. While I had let go of my biological mother when I was adopted, I realized that I was still expecting a human mother to quench my thirst for mother love. My thirst was too great for any one woman to slake. My quest to be mothered took me to the land and the waters, where I found the river of compassion I had been seeking. Then I could really let go of the expectation of being mothered in the ways I needed by anyone except Great Mother.

As one client said of a little girl part in her Inner Tribe™, "She has to know that my decision-making is sound before she trusts me enough to let go of her wish/belief/fantasy that my mother will turn around and love her."

As a result of learning how to honor the feelings of my wounded parts of self, to allow the waters to flow, I became the kind of mother (to my children, to my community, and to myself) that I wished I had.

Chapter 10: The Ancestors and the Body

Remember Your Power
Collage © 2010 Licia Berry

Our Ancestors

Souls come forth on Earth to execute the work of their ancestors.

— The Book of the Dead

The Earth is awake. She is a living being, with intelligence and memory in her iron ore heart, at her core. We are Her children, and our Ancestors are part of Her. We emerge into form as physical bodies from Her memory, the lives of all who lived before us.

We are part of the Earth, as our indigenous ancestors lived and breathed. I became aware of this when I was pregnant with my first son, Jess. The mountains spoke through me while I carried him inside of me, the desert making his little body through the air I breathed, the water I drank, the food I ate. I felt the spirits of the land around me and the creatures of the air blessing me. This child was not mine alone, but belonged to the Earth. I was the vessel that bridged spirit and the physical, the conduit through which Nature created a new life. I was the collaborator in bringing forth the Earth's dream of a being, a man who would someday answer Her need for a medicine bringer for Her deserts and their special beauty.

Our Ancestors Are With Us

Traditionally people say that our male ancestors—the great-grandfathers, our grandfathers, our fathers, our uncles, our brothers—stand behind us on the right side, and our female ancestors—the great-grandmother, the grandmother, the sister, the aunt—stand behind us on the left side. And they say, "Oh, maybe this one will be the one who will bring forward the good, true and beautiful from all the past generation and the generations to come. Maybe this one will be the one that will bring the end to all the harmful family patterns, maybe this one will be the one."

— Angeles Arrien

My grandmother Ruby (my mother's mother) held me in her own womb when I was a fully formed egg in my mother's growing infant body. I am of my grandmother as much as I am of my mother. Perhaps this line between grandmother and granddaughter is a way that feminine wisdom is passed on, Great Mother's lineage that holds women together in an unbroken chain.

I am her and she is me. When I was adopted by my biological aunt, the umbilical cord experience we had "transferred" me to Wendy as my mother, but kept me within the lineage, preserving my grandmother's line within me. There are important issues that I carry as her descendant that I am called to resolve.

My Grandmother Ruby, age nineteen

Ruby is important in my life's memory; she is the most present to me of all of my grandparents, standing out as a kind of light in comparison to the others. She is the one who stopped drinking when she realized she had scared us children, and she is the one who sought psychotherapy to dive into her psyche for the cause of her unhappiness. In the company of other adults—people made of smoke and mirrors who seemed not to care very much about their responsibility to their younger generation or to know what drove them to drink or behave insanely—she felt solid. She saw me clearly, as a child and as a woman. I provided some kind of mirror for her, and she did for me. In some ways, I am like her. We share some similar healing opportunities. I hope to catch the issues in the ancestral lineage that she was meant to resolve, but could not, so that my descendants are free.

Great Mother in Her wisdom has shown us where our ancestors' hurts lie and has provided us an opportunity to heal them.

Our Family Heritage

We come from a long, long line of Earth's children. Her expressions are many-colored and multi-hued, resulting in an infinite number of combinations. Nature has cooperated by arranging factors in the most life-affirming ways, ensuring the survival of All Creation.

We used to know that we come from our ancestors and gave honor to those who came before us, paving the way for the existence of our lives, our joy, our offspring. We gave thanks and felt them all around us, supporting us and loving us as life went on.

If you go back in time to the very beginning of life, you will find that we are related to one another. We are indeed family, distant cousins from the star-born relatives of our past. The grandmothers and mothers of the ages are responsible for bringing us forth. Women are uniquely able to embody the imprints and memories of those who traveled before us. Men look to spirit, to the grandfathers and fathers for guidance, but *women need not look anywhere but inside themselves.*

A woman's body does greatest service to the human race: to continue the species, to nurture it to its fruition. I feel that we, both men and women, have lost the understanding of this service. If we did recognize it, wouldn't we respect and hold women and their bodies as holy? How much we disdain this sacred sacrifice.

The Earth understands the gravity of this service. I heard the voice of the Earth say, "Men are to revere the woman, the carrier of the line of humans, the vessel through which humans continue. Women are to know their power, to know their divinity, their sacred place."

My people tell me that we have lost our way; current cultural norms are such that we do not walk in connection or in deference to the planet that we call Earth, nor to the millions of relatives who walk the Earth in our given path as we occupy space.

Our body is made of the ancestors. We are literally a walking patchwork quilt of our ancestors, including the food, the waters, the air, the fire, everything on the Earth. We have traveled a long chain of intelligence that has kept the human species alive, that has resulted in this current time, this present moment, and our bodies. When I realized this, REALLY got it, I fell on my knees in gratitude, as well as in shame for my previous lack of understanding of the profound gift of life, all that has brought forth seed in support of an anticipated future in order to make existence possible for me to be here. The loss of this awareness, our disconnection from All Creation that has lovingly borne us through time to this moment, is the greatest tragedy and greatest insanity that I can fathom.

Many of us do not realize that we have lost this connection. We feel we are alone and living our lives according to our whims and desires, but we are part of a lengthy chain of those who came before we arrived. We are the result of so much love from the very beginning.

Our ancestors stand behind us
And every day they say
And they say
Maybe this one
Will be the one
To bring forward the true, the good, the beautiful in us
Maybe this one
Will be the one
Who will break the harmful patterns we allowed to continue
Maybe this one
Will be the one
To change the culture through courage, vision, love
Maybe this one

Will be the one
To allow a new world to emerge through her and her
descendants
At the urgent request of life's unfolding.

Taking Our Bodies Backward in Time

A labyrinth is a geometrically designed structure that creates a defined sacred space, used for personal, psychological, and spiritual transformation. Labyrinths are thought to enhance right-brain activity, our connection to all things beyond the concrete, physical present. The earliest known labyrinths date to the Bronze Age (see image, below); they are seen in many major cultures, including Native American, Greek, Celtic, and Mayan.

A labyrinth is built around a core, or center, with a spiral path inward and outward again. The center of the labyrinth is the destination, the pause point, the walk symbolic of the journey to the treasure at the center. The center of the psyche is potent, full of ancestral information, similar to the Earth's core, where She stores her memory, and so it is mirrored in the structure of the labyrinth. The experience of walking the labyrinth is one of walking backward into our past, back to the

womb, and back to the beginning of humanity—even back to the beginning of the cosmos.

A simple but powerful ritual created by Miriam Theresa MacGillis called "The Cosmic Walk" is a way of bringing our knowledge of the fourteen-billion-year development of the universe from our heads to our hearts. A spiral representing the entire almost fourteen billion years of the cosmic and evolutionary journey is laid out on the floor or ground. The first station, located at the very center of the spiral, represents the emergence of the universe from its Womb. (There is a "Cosmic Finger Walk" spiral based on this ritual, as listed in the Additional Resources section.)

We can talk to our ancestors at the center of a labyrinth. I have experienced the power of meeting an ancestor face-to-face as if the long walk into the core erected walls between me and present day, allowing me free range in the halls of time. Walking inward to the center is a parallel journey to walking inward to the Core Self. I often use labyrinths in Inner Tribe™ work, as well, because it is an easy way to interact with tribe members who might be reluctant to integrate. I had one such experience on the beach while at a retreat.

The Little Boy in the Labyrinth

I looked forward to the time I would have at the retreat with nothing to do except pay attention to my needs and inner life. I advocate for time to retreat for everyone. It does wonders for the body, mind, and soul to tend to the inner garden in a safe container, with no pressures to attend to service to others.

I was relaxed and happy, and went out on the beach that sunny morning to do some intuitive movement and breath work. As I listened and deepened my inner awareness, I noticed that in my body's experience and my inner vision, I picked up myself as a little girl, and she whispered in my ear, "You are such a good mom." This delighted me to no end, as I have had a tough time convincing her that I would be a good mother to her! I smiled and allowed this lovely experience to permeate me. Then I felt the prompt to walk the labyrinth.

As I stood at the opening, I prayed to experience my inherent wholeness. I was in a very happy place and did not feel the need to initiate any healing process as per my usual stance. As I walked, I hummed to myself as I felt my inner little girl integrating into me even more than she had before. When "we" got to the center, I waited in silence for several minutes. I could not discern anything in particular in terms of a course of action or intention, so I just paused there. I definitely felt I was at the center of some womb space, far from the outer world of the beach and sun and sound of the surf. The insulated quality of being inside the labyrinth was reflected in my mind and heart as I listened deeply for any sign of message or instruction.

I did not feel anything in particular except great, great joy, so began to move out of the labyrinth. I had taken a few steps when I noticed in my mind's eye a little lump of a person behind me in the center of the labyrinth. I continued to walk forward, not thinking much about it, when I felt distinctly I was to STOP. (I have learned, when I get a strong "STOP" message, to do it on a dime!) I paused, and as I listened, I was told to go back to the center and "pick him up."

Him? When I looked back at what had been a little lump of a person, I saw now that there was a dejected-looking boy, perhaps three or four years of age. He looked sad and lifeless, like he had no energy in him at all. I was puzzled, but my maternal instinct took over, and I walked back into the labyrinth's center to be with this mysterious boy.

I sat with him for a while, me next to him on the sand. He did not look at me except occasionally, a sideways glance out of the corner of his eyes. He made no contact and did not speak in any way to me. As I sat, I had the distinct feeling that I was to pick him up and carry him out of the labyrinth. I still did not understand who he was or why I was to help him, but I lifted his limp body into my arms and carried him out of the labyrinth into my life with me.

I have carried this little boy with me ever since. Since that day when I was so puzzled about his arrival, I have learned that he is a personification of my inner masculine. Thwarted very early in my life from expressing my power and will, this aspect of myself was arrested and has been in a de-powered state ever since.

In his de-powered but frightened stance, he would sometimes hold up his fists, perceiving the whole world to be a threat, and other times he would just lie about and do nothing. Another symptom of his immaturity was to force things when, instead, some quiet stillness or discernment was needed. My tendency to push myself relentlessly, as well as to analyze with my head were both out-workings of this immature masculine within.

His anger was palpable; his rage at having his legs cut out from under him, being belittled and made to be still for unspeakable atrocities made him a very mad little boy. The fact that I did not know to acknowledge him within myself for all of these years might have added to his feelings of being alone in the world. So focused on my womanliness and my embodiment of the Divine Feminine, I did not see that what was even more broken inside of me was my own inner masculine.

As the weeks after the retreat went by, he began to show signs of life. The more I got to know him and acknowledge him, the perkier and more animated he became. Eventually, he looked at me, and occasionally talked to me, too. I worked with "him" every day, listening for guidance about how to support him, to heal him, to help him grow up. My dreams of tiny babies, just inches long, being lost in my pocket or in a drawer, evolved into dreams of laughing baby boys who were able to morph into full-grown teenagers, with awareness of and delight in their remarkable evolutionary process. My dreams, messages from my subconscious, were telling me he was healing.

The pain I felt as I opened this door into my consciousness was very real and very intense. There were days when I hurt inside so much it felt like leaving the house was too much. I doubted my sanity; in all the years I have done this hard work to reach into and heal the darkness within me, I had always been able to hold myself above the swirling dark waters of my feelings of rage and powerlessness—a dip into the madness here and there, but never complete immersion . . . a coping mechanism, to be sure. I kept reminding myself that I would not be feeling the intensity of the pain if I were not strong enough to do so.

Looking back at this important juncture of my life, I see the larger logic of my developmental phases. It was required that my embodiment of the feminine come first in order to then heal my inner masculine. Because of the connective nature of the feminine principle, she paves the way for the masculine to come home to center, and into union.

This broken masculine's intense pain was what was under the surface of my life, all along. It was the feminine guidance to make friends with the waters and to dive deep into my psyche and ancestral consciousness that opened up this well of pain, generations deep. Like the rabbit hole in Alice in Wonderland, it was the shamanic entry into other worlds of understanding and experience.

Pain is a Message

The generations now are in danger of forgetting completely the origin of their pain, the result of imbalance or harmful actions of their ancestors. We hide behind our computer screens and electronic devices, avoid the rigorous growth that intimacy with other human beings provides, self-medicate in the form of drugs, food, sex, and other addictions, even form "spiritual" philosophies that injure through judgment, condemnation, and separation—all of this to avoid feeling pain, our inheritance.

There is a reason we feel the pain we do; *it is because we are here to transform it.*

Personal pain is a message about what needs healing. It points the way to our personal healing, of course. But *our personal pain is also a message about what needs healing collectively, for our ancestral lineage and future generations.*

In a culture that is pain-denying and death-defying, we seem to be told in not-so-subtle ways that we should ignore the pain. Pop-"spiritual" approaches even advocate pretending pain is not there. We are trained to "rise above it," RUN from pain, to bury it, suppress it, "fake it till you make it." Let's think positive and maybe it will all go away. . . .

I agree that we should not dwell or wallow in our pain because this is imbalanced. We can lose sight of far too much good in life when we are stuck in our pain. However, *we miss an opportunity to give back to the world when we do not acknowledge and face our pain.* In feeling our pain, we are compelled to do something to change. Only people who are unsettled or unhappy with things the way they are will create world change.

What if the agitation and discomfort we feel is the key to who we truly are, at a SOUL and HEART level? What if, in All Creation's great wisdom, we are expressing the answer to one of the world's ills through our own lives? Could it really be an accident that we feel this way? What if our individual, unique pain is a key to our brilliance and a solution to many people's problems?

I have found my highest calling through my willingness to dive headfirst into my pain. If it is true that we have a "divine assignment," a mission or purpose in this life, then we discover it through our willingness to make our mark on the world. And we have the courage and the gall to do that *through feeling our unrest, our wish that things be different than they are.* We can then offer our unique expression of service to our people.

My calling is the transformation of the Mother Wound. I became a full-time student of the Voice of Nature Intelligence and Mother Earth—and once I owned this, I ceased being confused or distracted by other paths or possibilities. My choice to accept this calling was in proportion to my willing sacrifice to the pain inborn, to embrace my most terrifying fears. I dove deep into this pain and discovered my true destiny. Not the most conventional route, it's true. But it is what I was born to do.

I challenge you to embrace your greatest pain. In it lay a treasure greater than anything that could be gained by avoiding it or running from it. Transform lead into gold! Turn bad medicine into good medicine. Make compost of the crap! Reclaim the positive side of your pain as the thing that happened to you which made you into who you are meant to be. The world needs us to express the healing of our wounds so that the wounds of others can be healed, too. Our pain is our prize.

The Pain Isn't Only Ours

Personal pain can be our ancestors' pain, too. Each of us is a walking physical record of our ancestors' memories, so the waters (emotions) swirling around inside of us carry our DNA's information into our lives. As a result, we can unconsciously perpetuate unresolved ancestral issues; we may feel we were born at the wrong time, or feel a strong pull to a particular era in history or place on the globe. We may have patterns in our subconscious that our ancestors evolved in order to survive, and they may not be relevant to our particular situation. However, because we carry them in our being, we may recreate the situation that matches the unresolved issues and survival patterning. We may intentionally or unintentionally manifest issues in our lives, throwbacks to ancestors we may not even know.

In my family lineage, the Mother Wound goes back several generations, back to my great-great grandmother, Ruby's grandmother. Ruby remembered her as a very "manly woman," expressing as busy, grumpy, constantly active, and intolerant of the feminine side. With a short fuse and a quick temper, my great-great grandmother was the source of the wound of burying the feminine in my maternal lineage. To learn more about how this occurred, I was guided to look back in time at her experiences as a child and young woman. I was given information that was later corroborated by living ancestors, information that revealed the cause of her pain.

She was originally a very intuitive girl. She had the gifts of clairsentience and claircognizance, powerful divine sources of knowing. Over her life, her gifts were frightening to people. She eventually diminished her gifts in an effort to be accepted by others.

The perils of being a messenger for the invisible force that binds the universe are well-documented. Burnings, witch trials, beheadings, drownings, torture—an unending list of persecution for women who embodied the feminine (or right-brain) principles were good reason to abandon her gifts, as well as the terror of religious persecution. I understood that she was forced to convert from her way of life into a Christian religion, one that condemned women like her. She became despondent, angry, and eventually a perpetuator of the very religion that suppressed her true spirit. She abandoned the feminine. It was through this that she created a lasting Mother Wound in my family line. My role was to heal this.

Learning of her life's pain, I could understand mine: the mistrust of the church yet the call to investigate the good in Christianity, the fear of being persecuted for my gifts yet the strong mandate to utilize them, my masculine expression earlier in my life yet the yearning for the feminine embrace. I was living her pain; I therefore could heal the pain from a physical, emotional, mental, and spiritual perspective. I was in a perfect position to end the cycle due to my consciousness of the wound and my knowledge about how to heal the ancestral line. My body remembered her even if my brain did not. The most recent epigenetics reveals that ancestral trauma is passed on to descendants through DNA. No wonder we know our ancestors' pain, yearnings, and hopes.

What is planted in each person's soul will sprout.
— Rumi

Listen to the Ancestors
Collage © 2010 Licia Berry

Recognizing that our ancestors are indeed part of us, I was guided to develop a technique similar to the Inner Tribe™ work to heal the unresolved wounding in the ancestral lineage. Through this holy work, I do what the medicine people of old did when a member of the tribe or village passed on, except that it is done now, and is "retroactive" to the source of the ancestral wound. Accessing the Great Mystery through the help of deep spiritual knowledge and the relationships developed over time with spirit helpers in other realms, I initiate healing for issues perpetuated through family lines for multiple generations and through various permutations.

In my family lineage, we have seen several unique expressions of the Mother Wound. We have seen the devouring, abusive, and abandoning mother, and we have seen the over-protective, controlling, smothering mother, and everything in between. Each ancestor touched by the Mother Wound can be a carrier, similar to how we can be a carrier for disease in our genes. Even when a carrier recognizes that they have been damaged by their experiences of the wound, the carrier can be a perpetuator of the wound. If they do not actively heal it, the wound will find a home in subsequent descendants. For me, the conflict of opposites, internally and externally, showed me where I had ancestral wounding asking to be healed.

I had perpetuated the Mother Wound by trying to be the opposite of my biological mother. Although I did not identify myself as an over-protective, somewhat controlling worrier, that is what I became because it seemed to be the opposite of what my mother was. In fact, it was the other side of the shadow mother, the unhealed wounded daughter who tries to heal herself through being a different kind of mother. Only when I healed my Mother Wound did I see this truth clearly. Then I began to make haste in healing this pattern with my children. I did not want them to unconsciously perpetuate the Mother Wound to their descendants.

My mother issues had been a direct manifestation of a conflict in my great-great grandmother. Her unresolved pain lived through each of her descendants, expressing in a unique way to their own life. My call to the San Luis Valley answered a request from generations before me to have a wound healed. I later learned that, after fleeing Eastern Europe for fear of being reduced to ashes, the woman who abandoned her faith and her gifts had lived in the same vicinity of southern Colorado that we had. She lived in Colorado, married to a shepherd who was my great-great grandfather, and became a Mennonite with him. My great-great grandfather had been a calm, nurturing, soulful, and feeling man, like my husband.

Was this why I felt the need to go there in the first place? I knew nothing of this woman's history. I never heard a story about her or the shepherd or any tie to Colorado. And I was living the persecution she was so afraid to experience . . . in the very same area of Colorado! How had I come to relive her life in ways I could not realize?

Healing of Opposites

My paternal ancestry carried a major wound, as well. My father's ancestors were white Europeans and Native American Indians. I uncovered a need for healing that went back more than five hundred years, a rift between the Caucasian and the native people of his bloodline, one that continues even to this present time. My grandfather and his two sons, as well as my grandmother, carried a prejudice that they vocalized frequently; my black friends were referred to in the common derogatory manner and the gay men of the planet were a scourge.

When my Aunt Grace whispered conspiratorially that we had Indian ancestry, she was taking a risk. Our people were white, from England, and had been on the Outer Banks since the beginning, or so went the family mythology. Thousands of years of Native American ancestry had been deleted from the family history book. Exposing the truth opened up an entire side of my ancestry that had been locked behind closed gates. Those gates had been rattling incessantly for me and got louder as my understanding of ancestral healing and peaceful reconciliation grew. My entire Native American line of ancestors sought to be acknowledged, to tell their story, to be brought back into the consciousness of their descendants.

As I discovered in the labyrinth, healing the broken or emasculated masculine in myself and my family line is also part of my ancestral calling. The Mother Wound, or abandonment of the feminine in the Caucasian, European cultures, created the need to colonize and eradicate the Native American side of my ancestral lineage, eventually stripping away even the cultural identity of the ancestry, whitewashing it of any native history, despite thousands of years of heritage.

Over the years of doing this work, I have seen a Native American standing at my right who has evolved from a forlorn, angry man, spitting at being so dishonored, to a trusted guide and elder, who feels more seen by me. I made him (and all who stand behind him) a promise that I would write their stories down (the inspiration for my book *Blue-eyed Indian*), and he is pleased with that promise. There is no more knowledge in living oral record of the traditions of the Carolina Algonkian. The only historical evidence is from the archaeological digs in the vicinity and journals of the early European settlers, with record of the language, ways of life, and drawings of the indigenous people and their villages—and in the genetic memory of our DNA, our connection to the intelligence of our ancestors.

Our Helping Ancestors

If we carry intergenerational trauma (and we do), then we also carry intergenerational wisdom. It's in our genes and in our DNA.

— Kazu Haga

The ancestors who care about the continuation of their lineage (and therefore the human species) are lined up to help us make good decisions toward sustainability, life-affirming choices that benefit our lives.

I experience that there are wise, kind, and eager ancestors awaiting our call to support us and our human descendants (as well as the Earth and All Creation). It makes sense that if our predecessors fought hard to survive and to pave the way for their lineage to succeed, they would seek opportunities to assist us. The harmful and unconscious behavior of recent generations does not negate the goodwill of thousands of generations that struggled and sacrificed and evolved the human family.

We can go to our ancestral lineage for healing, guidance, and wisdom. In our cells, we carry memory. The memory can be useful to direct our lineage in good ways, ways that change the outcome for the lineage.

So much good is available to us. The last seven generations in my ancestry have lost their way. Before these ancestors became so lost, many of my ancestors followed the discerning road of taking care of the planet and themselves. They knew they were part of the Earth and felt Her alive under their feet. They knew they were part of something bigger than themselves and that love was the glue that held them together. We are a result of this long line of love.

Some ancestors may have made bad decisions and taken hurtful action toward us. We may not trust them to act on our behalf, and that may be wise. But we do not have to let this truth prevent us from accessing the wealth of love and support that is available to us. Before those generations who acted from unconsciousness, thousands of generations before knew how to tend one another, understood how to care for the tribe. *In the body of our ancestry, there is so much more health than there is dysfunction.* We can rely on this strength, health, and goodness when we undertake the necessary work of healing the unhealthy patterns of our recent ancestry.

Ancestral Trauma

Many aboriginal cultures understood that when a person walks on (dies), it is necessary to bring to resolution all things left unresolved in that person's life. This is done for the purpose of helping the deceased move on in freedom, but perhaps even more importantly, to free the descendants from carrying the burden of that person's unresolved life into future generations.

The medicine keeper in the tribe or village was responsible for this task, and shamanic rites were enacted to clean up any leftover issues from illness to emotional distress. All manner of things were up for examination. Did the person avoid healing trauma that had occurred? Was there unexpressed grief, rage, depression? Were there unhealthy patterns of behavior, such as addiction? Were there habits of thought that were not life-affirming? Any part of the person's life was up for review if it meant the subsequent generations would suffer as a result of leaving it in place in the lineage. For the subsequent generations to live as was their birthright, the previous generation had the responsibility to clean up anything messy, unresolved.

Today, no one talks or thinks of subsequent generations unless they are forced. The focus on acquisition and gratification has moved us from *we* to *me*, and our descendants are paying the price. Climate and environmental issues are a primary symptom of this unconsciousness. Individually, we see a rise in the nervous system and brain disorders, such as autism.

Given the inheritance of trauma suggested by epigenetics, we now see the natural consequences of our ancestors' oversight in resolving their issues. The ground we walk on is the same ground our ancestors walked. Home is where we feel our resonance with the land and with our community. We are made of the land, and our bodies carry the land's voice. It follows, then, that our bodies are mirrors of the Earth and that our bodies speak of the Earth's challenges. We carry trauma in our bodies, and we manifest illness when the trauma is not healed. How we feel is an indication of how the land feels. The rise in anxiety and depression, in cancers, in autism, in fear, in obesity, in gun violence, in suppression of truth—these are all manifestations of unresolved trauma. Our only salvation is to heal the wounds. Our home is our body, just as much as Earth is, and our tribe is each other.

The loss of the feminine, of the right brain's inherent understanding of connectivity and empathy, and of the awareness of indigenous ways of life are the reasons we face possible extermination as a species. **The Mother Wound, so much deeper than the relationship we have with our biological mom, is the core of the imbalance of the Earth today.** In women's bodies, we can see a closer mirror to the Earth. We can see the need for healing this wound in the relationship we have with women's bodies as well as with the planet. If a woman is meant to be used as a resource, harvested, to lay down and take it, to remain dumb and mute while her precious nature is ravaged and denied, can we not see that we do the same to our home?

The ancestral wound of unmothered daughters is the reason this book sought to be written: women who are told their body, connection to the Earth, or inner guidance is crazy, false, or evil; women who are taught they are less in the eyes of the Divine; women who victimize other women because they believe women are dirty; women who hurt themselves because they are told they are unworthy; women who become men in order to survive.

Our ancestors speak loudly about injustice. The issues we care about are informed by the pain our ancestors carry, based on the experiences that touched their lives. One by one, I have met my ancestors in their pain, eyeball to eyeball, heart to heart, my ear bent to their whispers.

Through this, I know that ancestors are present in our daily machinations, savoring the foods we eat, enjoying the physical sensations of a hot spring or sex, reading a book and enjoying the story. The social injustices are a platform for unanswered pain to be healed for so many generations. We engage in activism for the present and for the future, but the past yearns for healing, too. We are the answers to their prayers.

Healing Our Ancestral Lineage

Our lives can feel overly burdensome at times, and this may have nothing to do with what is current in our experience. We may be carrying forth pain that we are not responsible for, nor meant to transform.

I have sometimes felt angry at my ancestors who did not heal their traumas and therefore passed them on to subsequent generations. I have made it my purpose to clean up my lineage so that my children and grandchildren do not have to carry the pain that I experienced. It has not been easy. I can relate to Shakespeare's Hamlet when he rails, "O curs'd spite, That ever I was born to set it right!"

This has been especially difficult because my living ancestors do not acknowledge that there is a problem or that they have a responsibility to resolve it. I have felt that I, like Poseidon, am holding the two walls of the Strait of Messina apart, making safe passage for my children, grandchildren, and descendants to sail the middle course into their future without straying into the rocks, in an attempt to free them from pain that is not theirs to carry. I feel alone sometimes in my awareness, and I need to remember that I chose this life path.

It is a rare individual today who knows the extent of our connection to our ancestors. Many of us do not realize we have lost this connection or our responsibility to our ancestral lineage and our descendants. As a whole, we are not aware of this truth; it has been taught out of us. The voices of my ancestors ask that I bring it back to our attention, not only to be remembered for their contributions and sacrifices to bring us here, but for the purposes of ensuring the continuation of the human species.

Sometimes I go about pitying myself, and all along, my soul is being blown by great winds across the sky.

— Ojibwe saying

Her Voice in the Wind

Sometimes the ancestors speak to us from unexpected sources. The complexity of the Web of Life is revealed when we suddenly become privy to secrets from our ancestral heritage.

I went recently to my home state of North Carolina, into the mountains on Lake Nantahala to write. There I experienced such a presence of native people as to be almost overwhelmed by it. I was guided to connect with the lake in an old way, perhaps as the aboriginal people did before connection to the spirit of the land was lost.

I found myself surrounded by many indigenous spirits who seemed to be connected to the lake. I asked, "Who are these people?" and heard that there were "Indians in the lake." I was shown an image that led me to understand that the lake had become a kind of repository for native spirits, that the water actually carried their spirits. I was unsure what this meant or why it was important that I have this information; however, I agreed to be of service in assisting those who were ready to move on.

I was seemingly thanked with an immediate rise in the wind; a tremendous gust blew across my cheek, shaking the tops of the trees. I heard, "We are grateful, and we have a story to tell. The ancestors in the lake are trapped there through their grief about being chased from their homeland."

I did not understand what this meant exactly, but chose to open to the spirits that wished to move on to their next plane. They thanked me as they left, evaporating as if into smoke. The days that I spent there were rich in the presence of old knowledge. As I walked on the mountain hills, I felt old songs ask to be sung in a language I did not understand. It reminded me of my years in Asheville when the land had asked me to open my belly to the feminine in the Earth.

So I sang into the fabric of time and space, imagining I was walking this ancient land before the colonization of my native ancestors. The land seemed to respond to me, as if it recognized the songs. A dark indigo snake, three and a half feet long, slithered across my path, stopping as if to block my way. Remembering the years of learning snake medicine and that the snake is a symbol for the feminine, with its belly to the Earth, I bent to connect with the spirit of the snake. It "told" me that the land was very happy that I had returned after so many years, and that I had ancestry there from an ancient time. I was puzzled; I knew of no ancestry in the mountains there.

The next day I went into Andrews, the town closest to the east of Lake Nantahala. There I found a history book about the area and learned that the lake had been made by covering native settlements. Entire villages were covered with water from the river, all for making electricity for the towns nearby. In addition to this, I learned that the Cherokee people were relocated from their land and rounded up in Andrews, the starting point for The Long Walk, or the Trail of Tears.

I was stunned to know this history and began to understand the grief I had felt in the waters of the lake. It was not until later that I learned that some Cherokee ran into the hills to hide, thus avoiding The Long Walk, and remained in hiding or moved east to the lower coast of North Carolina. There, they married into the local populations and survived to be assimilated into the people who are there today. The old families of the coast were not only Algonkian, but Cherokee. Oh, the tangled webs we weave.

Chapter 11: The Earth

The Life Giver
Collage © 2006 Licia Berry

Earth Mother,
I enter your body
Earth Mother,
I enter your bones
Earth Mother,
I sing to your memory
Earth Mother,
I sing to your stones
Ahwey ahwey ahweya
Ahwey ahwey ahweya
Ahwey ahwey ahweya
Ahwey ahwey ahweya

— **Author Unknown**

~ ~ ~

My Daughter,

How great thou art! The daughter of the center of the universe!

You came from the stars. And to the stars you will return, but you are here, in the world of physical nature. You are here, having the experience of Earth's planetary movement and your own evolution, and it is no accident that you are of the Earth, in a physical body made of Her. Your body is your mini-Earth. Take care of Her within you, and you will take care of the planet.

Great Mother

~ ~ ~

We do indeed come from the stars, as science tells us. The dust of billions of years of the universe's movements and machinations is in our bodies, the water, the soil. The universe is not separate from us, and we are an integral part of the universe. The dust that has traveled across time and space to become this planet and our bodies started as something non-physical, as not-matter, as subtle energy. The black void of space contains the secrets of how the physical universe came into being from the field of pure potential.

Walking Where Our Ancestors Walked

I walked the land in Colorado with ears in the bottoms of my feet, something I had begun in Asheville. Listening to the voice of the area geology became a common request of the spirit of the land. The land told me of its history, of its beginnings in fire, then of ice and water, then fire again. What a dynamic process it had lived through! Changed and transformed and reduced to its basic nature over many millennia, the land spoke of the ultimate truth, that everything is temporary.

By walking the land with the intent to listen, I embodied feminine energy, an old practice before patriarchy covered the feminine with its smothering presence. Great Mother said to me that this is what was done for all of human existence, and it would be done again. Never having died out, the embodiment of the feminine would regain a foothold, bringing balance to the power dynamic on the planet.

I learned about faces of the Sacred Feminine since the beginning of art-making in our species. Far from gone, She is alive and well, if not a little tarnished from Her thousands of years buried in the deep unconscious of the collective psyche.

I became prolific in my art-making and my writing as I opened this conduit. By listening to the stories the land told me, I was able to learn about the history of the San Luis Valley and the native people who lived there before they were driven out. This became an impulse to record the stories, the inspiration for my book *Blue-eyed Indian – Stories the Land Told Me*.

Long Lost Queen
Collage © 2008 Licia Berry

"She was found lying face down in a pile of rubble, but her hairstyle and headdress marked her as royalty."
– National Geographic, November 2006

This is also where I first learned about my great-great grandfather, the shepherd (referred to on page 347), whom I had known nothing about. The land of southern Colorado held such a heart-stirring awe for me in daily waking life and spoke to me in my dreams at night. I sometimes awoke with my hand on my heart and tears in my eyes, with an intense feeling of loss. Another time, Jewish religious scholars surrounded me, gesturing insistently with their hands as if trying to tell me something.

The role of shepherd is also an interesting metaphor for a refugee fleeing persecution to find religious freedom. Shepherds are associated with the Pan, God of Nature, the Wild, Shepherds, Flocks, Goats, and of Mountain Wilds. Humble shepherds—not kings, priests, or dignitaries—were the first to receive tidings of the birth of Yeshua, to be given the message of the impending messiah. What did the connection with the land have to do with this great spiritual message being delivered to rugged people of the wilds? At that time, the religious leaders maligned the shepherds, banning the pasturing of sheep and goats in Israel, except on desert plains. Is it possible that the original heralding of the birth of a balanced feminine/masculine boy was given to the lowly shepherds because they were the truer, more spiritual recipients of this news?

I had been connected with sheep since I was young, being drawn to their sweetness and docility, but also mysteriously as a herd to lead. I had fantasies for most of my adulthood of owning a sheep farm. The connection with the land was such that I felt a calling to do what the lowly shepherd did, and my spiritual connection was similar in that I felt cast out from the religious institution, forced to find my own route to Spirit. How did ancestral memory form the strange paths my life has taken? My little family and I had been drawn mysteriously to the wild and rural San Luis Valley, a remote land of indigenous history and awe-inspiring natural landscape, perhaps to answer the call of a forgotten ancestor asking to be acknowledged.

We Are Indigenous People

indigenous (adj.) – from Latin indigena "sprung from the land, native," literally "in-born," from Old Latin indu (prep.) "in, within" + gignere (perfective genui) "beget."

A shift is occurring on our beloved planet that brings a new beginning for humanity, one that will bring us closer to the Earth. We are in a transitional period between the full seating of the incoming Aquarian Era and the out-going Piscean Era, experiencing the typical confusion, activity, and upheaval that comes during a "changing of the guard." The more we allow ourselves to breathe in the new dynamic, releasing and surrendering the old world to the new world that is most surely manifesting, the less resistance, fear, and uncertainty we will experience as the Aquarian Dynamic fully seats into our lives. The shift that is occurring is akin to when a baby moves from crawling to learning how to walk. It as a bridge time, an in-between or threshold, a time of potential to truly change the trajectory of our species.

In my 2008 book *Love Letter – A Message of Comfort, Self Care and Sanity in Stimulating Times,* I wrote of the great wisdom (and need) to ground deeply into the Earth, the way a tree does to avoid toppling over in the times of great winds. The developmental phase that humanity is experiencing is a powerful window, and change is not easy while the sweetest breeze blows. "Getting down in our foxhole" is one way to weather the shift without being blown to bits.

We come from the land. We are born of it, just as surely as we are born of our mothers. Aboriginal cultures across the globe speak of their peoples' beginnings as "sprung from the land" or emerged from a hole in the Earth. The Hopi speak of the Grand Canyon as the womb from which they emerged, a great yoni of the Earth. A *sipapu* is a hole in the floor of a Pueblo Indian kiva, symbolizing the place where the mythical tribal ancestors first emerged from the primordial underworld regions into the earthly realm. Our ancestors understood that our physical lives came from the planet and are inseparable from it. Sciences confirm we are made of the elements of our planet. In a very real way, the Earth begat us. We are indigenous.

The need to *ground deeply into the Earth*, a necessity of life that was understood and practiced by indigenous cultures prior to the worship of intellect and ensuing left-brain dominance, is being given new attention. Spiritual practice (in multiple traditions) touts the need to "get grounded," and it has even become common vernacular to speak of an "ungrounded" expectation, belief, or person. While we lived in Colorado, one of my lessons from Great Mother was to practice grounding. She taught me that I needed to touch all the way into the core of the Earth. A couple of inches below the surface was not deep enough.

The Memory of the Earth

One of the techniques I learned from direct experience to ground into the planet is **The Down Breath** (see Additional Resources section). I regularly set the intention to ground fully into the Earth, all the way to its iron, magnetic core. Sometimes I will "hear" the deep clunk like the sound of my black cast iron pan making contact with another surface, or I will taste iron in my mouth. This is an energetic awareness and my signal that I have made contact with the iron ore sphere at the Earth's core, the planet's great magnetic heart. The black ore at the center of the Earth is a memory keeper, a dense historical record of all that has occurred on this planet. The intelligence there is clear when we bother to listen.

In Tibetan Bon, the indigenous tradition of Tibet that pre-dates Buddhism by sixteen thousand years, as well as many other ancient traditions of thought and spiritual practice, it is understood that, in the beginning, "everything came from nothing." I was taught that the black void of space, the "dark matter" (*dark mater*=dark mother) was indeed the field of potential from which all solid matter emerged. In a very practical, yet mysterious way, the Beginning of All Things is Great Mother.

The non-physical (therefore spiritual?) spark traveled from pure potential across time and space, tumbling and infusing with other sparks, forming agreements between molecules, becoming denser as it slowed down, came into contact with gravitational fields, forming into the physical life we know. Moving from non-physical into physical density means more gravity and, therefore, the possibility of friction. Friction means atoms rubbing together. Atoms rubbing together means exchanging information and memory. The relationship between atoms that come into contact with one another means evolution of the universe.

In the movement from non-physical (subtle energy) into physical, the rules change. We are subject to physical laws. We are born, we touch each other, we experience joy and pain, we die. Physical life is a gift, a miracle, but over time in the grip of the Piscean Era, the separation of spirituality from our daily life and the subjugation of the feminine (in women, in our collective psyche, and in the Earth), we have been taught that we are "born in sin," that physical life is a punishment that must be endured until we get to our reward (after our bodies die).

Salvationist religions (I include "New Age" philosophy in this category), in which we must perform various acts in order to transcend our physical nature and be "spiritual," have stepped in and interceded between our unique personal relationship with God and our birthright connection to the planet we live on. We have been taught to fear Nature, cultures that connect spiritually with the Earth, the darkness, and the feminine. It is no wonder that many of us are unaware, even reluctant to ground deeply into the Earth.

Our mothers birthed us, held us, nurtured us, just as the planet does. If we had a mother who was not present to us as children, we may mistrust the support under our bodies as constant, everlasting, or present. The relationship we have with Earth is reflected in our relationship with women, which is informed by our relationship with our mother and Great Mother, the feminine principle. My understanding is that we ground deeply into the Earth when we feel safe and we "pull up anchor" when we feel unstable.

The years-long odyssey we took after leaving our Asheville "forever home" left me unrooted, ungrounded. This resulted (for example) in a level of discomfort with gardening, as well as a lack of success after years of a prolific "green thumb." My old relationship with the dirt was that I could evoke the mystery of producing food from a seed, with tender attention, water, and sunlight. Now, I could not grow vegetables with any solid ability; it was as if I had lost my relationship with the land because we were mobile for seven years. I forgot how to evoke a response from the soil, in the form of my successful, abundant garden.

I felt called to women, but in a way that was unconscious. I felt drawn to some women who were very damaged in their psyche. This frightened me, and I pulled away when I realized how unhealed they were. My running away from them, a survival instinct that I developed in my relationship with my family of origin, was another avoidance pattern that is typical of unmothered women and men.

I saw this ungroundedness in relationships, too. As ungrounded as I was, so did I attract. I began an account on Facebook in 2007, in tandem with my growing web presence, and had a high ol' time making "friends" with folks of similar "spiritual nature," until one such "friend" stabbed me in the metaphorical back. It was a painful part of the deep mother work that was to come and prepared me for more of the same. My ankle break came at the perfect juncture to bring me back down to the planet after trying to float above the surface for a few years. My path was not to be one of the "new spirituality" people. My path is to speak of old medicine, the memory of the Earth.

Resonance and Leadership

Earth teaches lessons on resonance all of the time. Resonance has many definitions depending on the discipline, but they all have a common thread—*a quality of evoking response*—so we see resonance in Nature regularly. The sun sends out waves of radiation that evoke life to grow. The epicenter of an earthquake sends out waves that evoke a response of moving land or water. The waves of the uterus evoke the movement of our baby from our womb. If we look, we see the concept of resonance everywhere, especially when we look at people.

We feel drawn to people and do not know why, or they seem to be familiar to us yet we have never met them before. Sometimes, there is a genuine heart connection that is beyond our understanding. More often, we are in the grip of resonance. We respond to one another subconsciously, sensing the emanation of that person's true state, regardless of the image they project.

I find it an interesting experiment to watch the responses of people around me as I intentionally change my state. The days I am less conscious of my internal dialogue, I may experience unconscious people in my path. The days I am centered and grounded, I tend to experience more joy and seem to draw people I enjoy interacting with. *Unconscious* simply means we are not fully present; our state of being emanates from us whether we are aware of it or not, and we broadcast our state out into the world. I find that the more present I am, the more I have control over my state of being, navigating in a world that mirrors my consciousness.

I have had fun closing my eyes and feeling the energy of another person. After looking at them with my eyes, I might have one idea of how they are, but when I feel with my eyes closed, the energy can be quite different. Our eyes see the image we are conditioned to see by our cultural training. Depending on the acuity of our felt senses, we can get quite a different truth about someone's internal state than the one they portray with their image. Resonance is a response to the truth; it is an accurate mirror.

I have noticed that the most turbulent times in my life have held the most disappointing relationships. Conversely, the times when I enjoy a stable, grounded, and joyful existence, my relationships deepen and grow in positive ways.

Also, the more grounded I am, the more I exhibit positive leadership qualities. Leadership is an opportunity to experiment with resonance. I am in the position of leadership with frequency, as a speaker and an author. People look to me as a leader because I have some expertise, as well as because I have made my work a vital aspect of my life. The choices I have made put me in a position of authority, whether I like it or not. My responsibility, then, is to manage my internal state so that I evoke the response I truly want. My course *Leading by Being* teaches people how to manage our internal state toward a resonance goal we have in the world.

The Toning of the Temples

In the beginning, the Great Heart of the universe pulsed, and its rhythm evoked the response of universal creation. Other "hearts" formed, patterned after the First Heart. The relationship between that Beginning of All Things, and all "hearts" that came after—our Central Sun, the lesser Suns, our immediate Sun, the heart of the Earth, our human heart, the heart of the cell (the nucleus), and the heart of the atom (the neutron, which is the basic building block of everything in physical form)—is an accurate reflection of *Leading by Being*.

From top to bottom, cosmologically to atomically, the Center of All Things sets the tone through a pulsing vibration, and then the tone is carried out farther as the next proximate suns resonate with that pulsing. Then the next immediate suns pick up the pulse, and so on, until our human heart responds by picking up the pulse. The nuclei in our cells do the same. With each pulse, the Heart of the Universe (in fact, every heart) *reminds* us of the way to live, to move forward. This way we are all in resonance. Since the beginning of time, this lifting of the vibration has occurred in perfect order, exactly when the universe could hold the next level of vibration.

We have had an intense ride lately because we are getting so much energy from the Great Central Heart, and this "waking up" of the human heart is a symptom of coming into resonance with the pulsing of the next level up in our evolution. Light pulsates from the Central Suns in a rhythm like a heartbeat. We can think of our own heartbeat as a smaller and individual version of the galactic heartbeat. I sometimes envision my heart as a blazing sun in my chest. This is how we are designed and an example of the holographic nature of creation. We are being asked to live from our hearts in way that we have not before now.

I was taught by one of my Tibetan Bon teachers about a tradition he referred to as the "Toning of the Temples." The main temple in Lhasa (the "heart" of that spiritual tradition) sets the tone for the bells in the other temples around Tibet. The temple in Lhasa chooses the tone with which all of the other temples resonate. Starting with the temple in Lhasa and emerging in concentric circles, like a ripple effect, the other temples match their bells with the tone of the Lhasa temple. This way, an aligned resonance is carried throughout all of the temples. This unified resonance over a large geographical area lifts the vibration of Tibet and creates a strong "container" within which seemingly miraculous things can occur.

In a similar manner, the center of the Earth vibrates and sends "messages" from the "heart" or core of the planet. Great Mother taught me that Earth is intelligent and that the planet is evolving, just as we are. The throes of developmental process that this larger intelligence goes through are experienced by us as extensions of the planet. Human beings, as well as every other speck of life on this "rock" we call home, are intimately connected with Earth's evolution and are deeply impacted by everything that happens to the intelligence of this planet.

Remembering that we are made of the elements (earth, air, fire, water, and space in the Tibetan tradition), we are vibrating along with the elements present in the Earth—not separate, not isolated. We can pretend all we like that we are in dominion over the Earth, but the truth is that She is in dominion over us. The physical world (of which we are a part and an expression) is the evocation of response to the intelligent resonance of the Earth's core.

By grounding deeply into the Earth's core, I feel the connection with this historical intelligence, as well as the present-moment experience of the immense process the Earth is undergoing. I also feel more stable as She undergoes Her waves of transformation. Feeling anchored and moored to Her center, I am less likely to be negatively impacted as She goes through the necessary changes as She evolves. Intentionally grounding deep into the Earth is good for me and for all of Her creatures. By doing this, we remember that we are connected with this planet and Her lands.

In this sense, we are truly indigenous. We *are all indigenous because we are all "of the land."* We are indigenous to the Earth, and we are indigenous to the geographic location we come from. We are being reminded now to reclaim our indigenous relationship with the Earth and to connect to the land where our bodies formed in utero (and perhaps where we were born), because we are made of the elements of that geography. We must go beyond what we have been shown about the Earth as a resource and see Her as a biological entity that changes and evolves, just as we do. We must connect to Her intelligent heart (the core) in order to know how to support Her (and therefore support all that live on this planet.)

The land remembers us because we carry the elements of that place in our bodies—and the land remembers itself, through us. We touch ground in our home state, or we eat food of our ancestral homeland, and we are moved to tears. The land meets and recognizes the land inside of us, and it is joyful in its reunion with parts of itself, just as we are joyful when we unite with parts of our psyche in Inner Tribe™ work.

The memory inherent in the land also remembers all who walked there. Our ancestors are held in remembrance of the atoms of the ground we walk upon. In a very real way, we are made of the land our mothers walked, ate of, bathed of, drank of. The air she breathed contained microbes from the soil, and she exchanged atoms with the trees that she touched as she walked by. Our bodies formed in the dark of her womb, built of the gifts of the Earth.

The Land of Our Ancestors

My shamanic traditions teach that old wisdom is passed on by land, and the mountains are the repository of that area's history. The mountains appreciate when someone wants to listen to their stories and will call to us to learn from them. The memory in the mountains is localized, but I have discovered that the mountain ranges of the world know about and speak to each other. This is because they communicate through Earth's intelligence, a network of electrical impulses that flow through all of Earth's creations. Akin to the Web of Life described by indigenous peoples, this circuitry that connects everything is the perfect communication switchboard, allowing all inhabitants of the planet access to the flow of intelligence here.

Our cultures can prevent us from hearing the voices of the Earth. Busy and loud, constant distraction makes a deeper logic and active intelligence in the Earth seem impossible. The planet can appear dumb, mute, and animalistic to our left-brain, capitalist eyes and ears.

My ankle break in 2009 and its forced quiet reminded me that a rhythm we do not often hear is under our feet and all around us. The rhythm is not unlike a drumbeat or the beating of a great heart. We can feel it in our bones. The rocks and mountains also feel it. With each beat, the layers of memory vibrate into cohesion with the next moment of data. Yes, we are adding to the memory of the Earth every moment, building Her memory banks like a great library. What we perceive as other lives may in fact be the memory of the Earth calling to us through our ancestors. Every experience and thought is recorded.

The bones of our bodies are like the stones of the Earth, carrying experiential record of our lives, and are a repository for old memory. The denser the vibration, the more experiential records something has. Our body and the Earth are mirrors for one another, so the likeness of bones and stones is not the only parallel. The waters of the Earth and the waters in our bodies are also similar in that water is a carrier of data from one place to another. Over time, water wears down rock and carries the memory to another place on the planet. In this way, memory moves through water to new lands, and the people of the new land can access this information and know of peoples and histories that they have never experienced. Our current world culture and our ability to move waters from place to place has ensured that the memory in a particular geographic location can be accessed by completely different cultures and from completely different locations. Just ask someone in New York if they can taste the minerals in their bottle of spring water from the French Alps. It is no accident that aboriginal people speak of the waters as the blood of the mother, our planet.

I have experienced the wind as a carrier of memory, as well. Remembering the voice of the wind in Nantahala as it told me the story of the "Indians in the lake," I think of the movement of winds similar to the movements of water across the face of the globe. The temperature, waters, and resonance of the core of the planet contribute to induce the movement of the air, therefore enlisting the winds as transport agents of memory. Hurricanes are an example of the movement of emotional memory with a tight central spiral that dissipates over the passage of land. The land is the repository, soaking up the waters, being caressed by the fingers of the winds.

The Ultimate Truth

Our bodies are real; they are of the land, and the land is an amalgam of everything that has occurred, a miracle of life created by an orchestra of the efforts of quadrillions of atoms dancing in partnership and joy. Our bodies, the waters, the air, the elements of All Creation come together to make life possible. The fact that there is *life* is completely amazing and generous, an act of love. Our aboriginal ancestors knew that everything is infused with the creative life force of the universe, and that everything is related, connected. The indigenous awareness of the co-creative nature of reality is that there is no separation. We are participating together with All Creation to construct reality, and we can participate together to create a new one if we do not like the current one. But that means we have to agree.

We can decide to change reality in a moment, and in some realms of vibrational density, that can happen easily, such as in the realm of spirit and of thought. Other realms take longer to affect change, such as the emotional and physical realities. We may wish we could heal a broken bone in a moment, but it is not probable that physical reality will bend to our desire, unless it is supported by the co-creation of All Things. Our feelings are A Truth, OUR Truth, but perhaps not Ultimate Truth, the Truth that is congruent with the Larger Truth of All Things.

I have spent much of my life seeking ultimate truth, perhaps because I doubted my truth. I learned that my truth was not real to my mother, and so I learned that my feelings, thoughts, and experiences must not be real. It has been quite a journey for me to give myself permission to feel, think, and trust my experience.

It is my belief and understanding that there are many roads to the end destination, whatever that may be. It is my understanding that all roads are valid, too. I do not believe that there is any one right way to do things, but I do believe that honoring oneself as a source of wisdom is an honorable and truthful way to go. I do not believe in doing things or thinking things or believing things just because we are told to, or expected to. To me, everything in all of existence is up for self-examination, perhaps because my truth changed as I changed. And our wisdom deepens as we evolve.

I have found that our ultimate truth as physical beings is the reality of our body, which limits us and can even stop us no matter what other kinds of truths we may experience, such as intellectual or spiritual or emotional truths. As long as we are in physical form, the body is the practical, regulating factor in our earthly existence. This is the truth of being in a physical body, but is there an ultimate truth that is NOT physical?

It depends on where you look. Every reality is real to the consciousness that is experiencing it. The waters tell the truth. They carry information, so the data are just data, such as in the situation of crying tears; the tears carry the toxic chemicals of emotion from our bodies. The chemicals are data; the emotions that induced them are truth to the person crying those tears. Thoughts become ultimate truth to the person who thinks them repeatedly, thus forming beliefs. For them, their beliefs ARE ultimate truth. And spiritual truth varies per the tradition or culture that practices them, yet they form a kind of ultimate truth for the practitioner.

To find an ultimate truth that was not tied to us as human beings with thoughts, beliefs, and emotions, I had to go beyond us to the larger intelligence. To the depths of space and the beginnings of the Omniverse, I went in my earnest quest for Ultimate Truth, the answers to my questions, provided by Great Mother. And this is what She taught me:

While you are physical, that is an Ultimate Truth. Your physical body is subject to physical truths.

While you are emotional, that is an Ultimate Truth. Your emotional body is subject to emotional truths.

While you believe and form thoughts, that is an Ultimate Truth, and it is given to you according to your beliefs.

While you are spirit, that is an Ultimate Truth, and you belong to the Ultimate Truth in this universe and beyond.

Our physical body is a third-dimensional form created by the elements of the Earth, formed by Nature according to instructions from an "architectural blueprint" designed by our genetic code. Our physical body must be honored because it is the marriage of spirit and matter. The ultimate truth? That's easy; the body is the temple. The recognition of this honors ALL of the Ultimate Truths. It also helps us appreciate another ultimate truth—that the body dies. We can trust this truth. The body is honest; it will tell us its needs and desires unfalteringly. We choose to listen or ignore the body, and it is with ourselves that we must live in the end.

Making peace with the fact that there are many truths, as many as there are intelligences, is a key to making peace in general. It is like making peace with our internal parts. Even the different truths of the land express through places, much like our personalities. Making peace between our body and the Earth, between our mind and our body, and between our spirit and our mind is a good start to healing the rifts we experience with our fellow humans.

As we rest in our relationship with the Earth, we begin to calm. I observe that the epidemic of anxiety, addiction, violence, and depression are a symptom of being out of relationship with the Earth, and this epidemic is only growing. Separation of spirit from grounded reality results in soul loss and mental illness. The limbic brain relaxes when we are supported and safe, and we emanate a peaceful, joyful resonance, one that helps others feel at peace.

Earth is our closest, most immediate, most consistently present and supportive face of Great Mother. How we treat the Earth is a reflection of that relationship. How each of us treats our body is a reflection of our relationship with Great Mother, as well. And of course, that is determined by our relationship with our physical mother.

In the 2015 climate talks, the indigenous elders of many tribes of Earth reminded us to honor our Mother, the planet.

They are correct to say that our fate is tied intimately with Earth's health and wellbeing. Much can be done to remember our deep connection. I am not joking when I say that healing the Mother Wound is what will save our species from destroying itself.

The reclamation of our relationship with the Earth is taking back what has been stolen, a redistribution of power and correct relationship with one another. We step into being fully human, what my Inuit Grandmother called True Human. We recognize the sacredness of All Life and our body. My observation of the interest in older aboriginal cultures and shamanism is that we are seeking to balance our relationship and recognition of the importance of our planet. If we are interested in the continuation of our species, then we must take back what belongs to us. We must become fully present in our bodies and reground to the core of the Earth; this is where our true power lies.

The intelligence of Earth is like Great Mother. She runs through everything, underneath our noses, in all things. There is nowhere that She is not. Because She is in everything, it is, therefore, easy *not* to see Her. Like the fish, when asked how it likes breathing water, replies in confusion, "What water?", She is invisible until we make her visible, until we evoke Her presence in our daily lives. This intelligence is what everything stands upon and expresses from; it is the order of the universe and is, therefore, the Ultimate Truth. But like the all-powerful Mother that She is, She stands back and lets her children take the credit.

I Am Her Daughter

Great Mother brought me love in the form of many faces, and I now can give this gift to others. I am a daughter of the universe, hooked into the greatest love there is. As I wrote about the obstacles I have faced in my life and the process I have undergone to love myself, I wondered if I was adding to the sorrow in the world. I am a voice of joy and light, after all. Great Mother tells me that telling the truth IS love. She taught me that giving permission for hard stuff to surface, to FEEL what is REAL, and to speak about it frees others to do the same. Loving ourselves like Great Mother loves us, that is real love. This is all She wants for us. To allow ourselves to be subsumed in her deep and immense embrace.

At the Gulf of Mexico, when I sat in the RV in 2004, gazing out over the expanse of wild water, I was afraid of so much. I was afraid to surrender to the vast reaches of love that hold me, hold all of us. I was afraid of my own unconscious, so full of wisdom and treasure. I was afraid of the raw power that gives so much and then takes it away. I was afraid of MY power as a woman and a seer. Here is what I now know: let go and trust.

We must live into dying every day, and to accept, to love, to trust, to keep showing up while knowing, at any moment, our lives can change for better or worse. We must step into the deep waters and allow them to carry us home, to the nature of the feminine. We must remember that We Are Her Daughter.

Epilogue

As I edited *I Am Her Daughter* in the winter of 2015, I sat witness for Tinka as she went through her death process.

Tink, introduced in Chapter 4, is our beloved family cat, the one who found us in Albuquerque, New Mexico, and became the glue that held our focus in love while we transformed our family. Her service to our family and her cycle of life complete, she began a new journey.

The ultimate truth of our bodies is that we are subject to the laws of nature and will return to the Earth. Our bodies, made of the borrowed elements—we surrender them as we move to other realms, adventures, and experiences.

I had just returned from a trip to Tucson, Arizona, that winter to be with Mama Wendy for an intensive mother/daughter retreat. We attended an End of Life Conference, ostensibly for our future work together in creating an organization that reconnects people of Earth with the Web of Life (and the memory contained there). I was being prepared for the deaths that I would midwife in my life, as well as my own someday.

As I watched our cat move through the natural phases of life's end, I was taught that all things are temporary and that the compassion we feel for one another makes our short sojourn on this planet one of a good life. Even in death, we can bring compassion to bear witness and foster a "good death."

Tinka lay on the ground outside, where she sought to be. Her frail body, unwilling to bear her up to continue, seemed to seek the shade of a cool overhang. Her legs splayed out as her heart made direct contact with the ground, the Earth, and she seemed to melt in its embrace. Under my watchful eye, she returned to the Mother from whence we all came.

In my grief, I turned to Great Mother for comfort. She said to me:

> *Daughter, you will return home to me someday, too, and it is true that your body will go back to the Earth and you will cease to exist. But you will become one again with the tides and the stars and the whispers of your ancestors. You will live on in memory and in the hearts of those you love and who love you and who speak of your words.*

It reminded me that we will all return to our Mother as we complete our life cycles. We, too, will melt into Her embrace as She welcomes us home.

Additional Resources

Recommended Reading

A Whole New Mind, by Daniel H. Pink

Half the Sky: Turning Oppression into Opportunity for Women Worldwide, by Nicholas Kristof and Sheryl WuDunn

Molecules of Emotion, by Candace B. Pert, Ph.D.

Navigating Midlife: Women Becoming Themselves, by Robyn Vickers-Willis

Our Stories Remember, by Joseph Bruchac

Possessing the Secret of Joy, by Alice Walker

Revolution from Within, by Gloria Steinem

Soul Compost: Transforming Adversity into Spiritual Growth, by Licia Berry

Stalking the Soul - Emotional Abuse and the Erosion of Identity, by Marie-France Hirigoyen

The Body Keeps Score, by Bessel Van Der Kolk, M.D.

The Body Never Lies, by Alice Miller

The Celestine Prophecy, by James Redfield

The Down Breath, as described in *Love Letter – A Message of Comfort, Self Care and Sanity in Stimulating Times*, by Licia Berry

The Gnostic Gospels: www.gnosis.org/library.html

The Science of Parenting, by Margot Sunderland

The Tibetan Book of Living and Dying, by Sogyal Rinpoche

Tools

She Is My Mother – Meditations for Experiencing the Archetypal Mother: see liciaberry.com.

Thought Record (referred to in Chapter 7):
http://media.psychology.tools/worksheets/english_us/simpl e_thought_record_en-us.pdf

Classical Labyrinth Drawing (referred to in Chapter 10):
https://labyrinthsociety.org/download-a-labyrinth

Blog Links for Further Reading

All blog posts can be found at the URLs provided and can also be located on my website at www.IAmHerDaughter.com or www.liciaberry.com/blog/. Locate the "Search my blog" box and enter the blog article title.

Learning How to Walk, May 7, 2009
www.liciaberry.com/2009/05/07/learning-how-to-walk/

The Little Boy in the Labyrinth, November 10, 2009
www.liciaberry.com/2009/11/10/the-boy-in-the-labyrinth/

Epiphanies on Epiphany. January 7, 2010
www.liciaberry.com/2010/01/07/epiphanies-on-epiphany/

My Jess, January 26, 2010
www.liciaberry.com/2010/01/26/my-jess/

...and the Balanced Defender, October 7, 2010
www.liciaberry.com/2010/10/07/and-the-balanced-defender/

Mothering and Allowing, January 17, 2011
www.liciaberry.com/2011/01/17/mothering-and-allowing/

The 5 Stages of Healing from Trauma, February 18, 2013
www.liciaberry.com/2013/02/18/the-5-stages-of-healing/

A New Definition of Allowing, March 27, 2013
www.liciaberry.com/2013/03/27/a-new-definition-of-allowing/

On the 7th Day, She Rested, March 31, 2013
www.liciaberry.com/2013/03/31/on-the-7th-day-she-rested/

Intruder in the Night (the Little Rock Incident), July 25, 2013
www.liciaberry.com/2013/07/25/intruder-in-the-night/

Looking for a New Dream – Women and Midlife Rebirth,
August 27, 2013
www.liciaberry.com/2013/08/27/looking-for-a-new-dream/

The Wanted Daughter, November 12, 2013
www.liciaberry.com/2013/11/12/the-wanted-daughter/

Bibliography

Auerbach, David. 2015. A child born today may live to see
humanity's end, unless . . . Reuters.
http://blogs.reuters.com/great-debate/2015/06/18/a-
child-born-today-may-live-to-see-humanitys-end-unless/.

Be, Lisa. n.d. Scientists From Germany Show That Water Has
Memory. This Video Blows My Mind. {Life}Buzz.
http://www.lifebuzz.com/water-theory/.

Burney, Robert. 2004. Inner Child Healing.
http://joy2meu.com/Innerchildhealing.html.

Colin, Virginia L. June 28, 1991. Infant Attachment: What We
Know Now. U.S. Department of Health and Human
Services. https://aspe.hhs.gov/basic-report/infant-
attachment-what-we-know-now.

Edwards, Lin. 2010. Humans will be extinct in 100 years says
eminent scientist. PhysOrg.com.
http://phys.org/news/2010-06-humans-extinct-years-
eminent-scientist.html.

Emoto, Masaru. 2010. What is the Photograph of Frozen
Water Crystals? Office Masaru Emoto.
http://www.masaru-emoto.net/english/water-
crystal.html.

Estes, Dr. Clarissa Pinkola. n.d. "Simple Prayer for
Remembering the Motherlode."
https://www.facebook.com/pages/Dr-Clarissa-Pinkola-
Estes/29996683634

Giversen, Soren and Birger A. Pearson (translators). n.d. The Testimony of Truth. The Nag Hammadi Library, The Gnostic Society Library. http://gnosis.org/naghamm/testruth.html.

Goldman, Jill, Marsha K. Salus, with Deborah Wolcott and Kristie Y. Kennedy. 2003. *A Coordinated Response to Child Abuse and Neglect: The Foundation for Practice.* U.S. Department of Health and Human Services, Administration for Children and Families, Administration on Children, Youth and Families, Children's Bureau, Office on Child Abuse and Neglect.

Kristof, Nicholas and Sheryl WuDunn. 2009. *Half the Sky: Turning Oppression into Opportunity for Women Worldwide.* Alfred A. Knopf, New York.

MacRae, George W. (translator). n.d. The Thunder, Perfect Mind. The Nag Hammadi Library, The Gnostic Society Library. http://gnosis.org/naghamm/thunder.html. *Note*: the translation by MacRae presented herein was edited, modified and formatted for use in the Gnostic Society Library. Original translation of this text was prepared by members of the Coptic Gnostic Library Project of the Institute for Antiquity and Christianity, Claremont Graduate School. The Coptic Gnostic Library Project was funded by UNESCO, the National Endowment for the Humanities, and other Institutions. E. J. Brill has asserted copyright on texts published by the Coptic Gnostic Library Project.

National Park Service. n.d. Padre Island National Seashore, Texas. http://www.nps.gov/pais/index.htm.

Rich, Adrienne. 1975. "Reforming the Crystal" from *Poems: Selected and New*. W.W. Norton & Company, Inc., New York.

Rogers, Fred. 2003. *The World According to Mister Rogers: Important Things to Remember*. Hyperion, New York.

Scotland.com 2003a. Scotland Discussion Forum. Thread: where does the name "Wendy" come from? http://www.scotland.com/forums/235655-post2.html.

Scotland.com 2003b. Scotland Discussion Forum. Thread: where does the name "Wendy" come from? http://www.scotland.com/forums/language/15689-where-does-name-wendy-come.html#post235655.

Steinem, Gloria. 2014. Speech at the Wisdom Sharing Retreat at Ghost Ranch, Abiquiú, New Mexico.

Took, Thalia. 2004–2013. "Sekhmet" and "Sedna" on A-Muse-ing Grace Gallery. http://www.thaliatook.com/AMGG/sekhmet.php and http://www.thaliatook.com/AMGG/sedna.php.

Values in World Thought. December 1999 and 2002, Interview with Angeles Arrien. http://values.mountmadonnaschool.org/interview_data/transcript/arrien02.html.

Vatican. Universal Prayer, Confessions of Sins and Asking of Forgiveness. http://www.vatican.va/news_services/liturgy/documents/ns_lit_doc_20000312_prayer-day-pardon_en.html. See Parts IV through VII, and Concluding Prayer.

Women's Health Australia. 2016. Australian Longitudinal
    Study on Women's Health. http://www.alswh.org.au/.

World Health Organization. 2012. "Understanding and
    addressing violence against women."
    http://apps.who.int/iris/bitstream/10665/77433/1/WHO
    _RHR_12.35_eng.pdf.

To continue the journey with Licia Berry into your True Power and inherent Sacredness as a Woman, please see the following.

I Am Her Daughter Facebook page:
www.facebook.com/IAmHerDaughter

Join the community; receive special communications from Licia by email. Go to: IAmHerDaughter.com.

She Is My Mother – Meditations for Experiencing the Archetypal Mother: see liciaberry.com.

I Am Her Daughter Handbook (includes processes/ dialogue/case studies to work with the inner tribe, creative arts approaches), available 2017

Illumined Hearts Radio (you can listen for free to many topics about the feminine emergence), for example:

- I examined the need for Sacred Boundaries, http://www.blogtalkradio.com/liciaberry/2013 /02/02/the-need-for-boundaries
- And made the case for Women stepping into their unique power, http://www.blogtalkradio.com/liciaberry/2013 /09/18/women-power-and-the-true-self

Inner Tribe™ Work and Certification with Licia Berry

Learn the mysteries of Women's Wisdom in empowering Ecourses on my website

Read for free, years of blog articles on my website

Athena's Alliance, my mentoring program for intelligent women of heart who seek to lead the world in new/old ways

Customized VISION QUESTS and creative/spirituality retreats for women to claim their voice. Contact Licia to create yours!

Learn more about the BERRY TRIP: The adventures we had and the deep transformation we each encountered individually, as well as in our marriage and family as a whole, are something I am still writing about; a book and screenplay are in the works. Peter and I teach about our experiences in workshops and retreats, and we speak to audiences about our epic pilgrimage that utterly changed our lives. We want to support people in their relationships, marriages and families to come home to what's truly important ... each other. Berry Trip: www.berrytrip.us

More resources will be available soon!

Acknowledgments

I owe a deep bow of gratitude to so many as a thanks for their support. Even those who taught me through pain deserve some thanks, because I did indeed learn from them. But I am especially grateful to those who taught me through their love:

To my editor Gina Hogan Edwards, whose gentle and deeply wise observations and guidance midwifed me and this book into being. (www.AroundTheWritersTable.com)

To my friend Gail Dixon, for her beautiful foreword in this book, and for encouraging me in my momentary lapses of belief in the importance of my work and mission on this Earth.

To Aunt Wendy, who claimed me early, scooped me back up in my forties and eventually became my adopted mother, and Uncle Zach, who had the great idea and became my adopted father. Thank Godde for you both for changing my life at a critical time.

To Great Uncle Ernie, who saw my tender heart and was gentle, kind, and encouraging.

To Grandmother Ruby, who showed me that we have the power to make choices, and who saw me clearly in the end.

To other teachers who saw me and encouraged me in my life: Mrs. Mooney in first grade, Mrs. Lancaster in fourth grade, my sixth-grade honors teacher (whose name I have lost but who showed me a woman in her power), my high school homeroom teacher Ms. Hagewood (a smiling face every day during a tumultuous time), and women teachers in college who met me with their power because they respected mine.

To Alice Walker, Gloria Steinem, Dr. Chung Hyun Kyung, and other role models/teachers/mentors in my adult life, for lighting the way.

To friends who graciously offered the Jensen Beach house and the Nantahala Lake house, patrons of this writer by offering their exquisite homes by the water for me to write, and where miraculous visitations of Great Mother occurred to oversee this project.

To friends/peers who have seen/supported me, not been intimidated by my power or depth of seeing and, as a result, parented me through their acceptance and respect.

Friends and family and peers who rejected me, I owe you thanks, too, for helping me to understand that the Mother Wound is something all women face, but not all are willing to heal it.

And to those countless people (and other aspects of All Creation), who in their myriad and mysterious ways encouraged me to use my voice.

In addition, I deeply thank my dear life partner, my beloved Peter, for making it safe for me to heal by loving me—no matter what. Great Mother worked Her mysteries through his constancy and steadfast love for me. My dearest, you will never know the gift you have given to me.

I thank my sons, Jess and Aidan, for showing me what is possible when children grow up in a home that loves and values them for who they are, and for being the conduit through which Great Mother has taught me so many lessons. You two are remarkable young men and the reason I have hope for this world.

I thank all of my mothers, physical and not.

I thank my passionate, warrior heart, for its unending desire and determination for healing and integration, not just for me, but for humanity and the Earth. Its fierce will has guided my steps.

To my birth mother, whom I honor for building my body within her body and for being the vessel through which I traveled into this life, thank you. You drove me into the arms of Great Mother and, as a result, drew forth a fiery need to bring Her back to this world. Even after everything, I love you.

And I owe all thanks to Great Mother, the exquisite and infinite Mother of us all. Without Her, we are not human, not physical, not even in existence.

About the Author

Licia Berry

Author, artist, speaker, and women's advocate, Licia (pronounced LEE-SHA) Berry is known worldwide as **The Woman's Guide to the Frontier Inside**™. Licia is an agent of change through her writing, art, speaking, and facilitation.

She has a passionate belief in women's innate resilience and is on an incessant quest to nurture women's empowerment, leading her to teach other women to claim their unique life song. Leading by example, Licia works to show women how to transcend their experiences to achieve physical, emotional, mental, and spiritual wholeness. Her primary work is in accessing ancestral memory for the purposes of healing ancestral trauma, creatively, shamanically, and neuro-biologically. Writing on juicy themes of women's issues, resilience, consciousness, divinity, and creative approaches to a balanced, grounded, and inspirited life, her words have impacted seekers of wholeness around the globe.

Licia has a twenty-five-plus-year career in education, spanning public schools, state agencies, non-profits, and private practice internationally. In group settings and one-on-one, she mentors women in awakening to their innate wisdom. Additionally, she speaks nationwide and offers live events including Vision Quests and retreats, as well as teleclasses and an online curriculum library.

Learn more about Licia Berry on her website www.liciaberry.com, Facebook, Twitter, LinkedIn, and YouTube. To book Licia to speak, please contact her at Licia@LiciaBerry.com or 850-661-9370.

Other Books by Licia Berry
All available at www.LiciaBerry.com

Love Letter – A Message of Comfort, Self Care and Sanity in Stimulating Times (2008)

The **Woman, Awake** series

Soul Compost: Transforming Adversity into Spiritual Growth (2012)

I Am Her Daughter: The Healing Path to a Woman's Power (2016)

Unearth: the Re-Emergence of the Sacred Feminine (Part of The 81, in process)

Hallowed Sun: the Return of Great Father and the Divine Masculine (Part of The 81, in process)

Sacred Systems: Union and Partnership in the Aquarian Era (Part of the 81, in process)

and

Road Trip to the Heart: A Family Love Story (in process)

Blue-eyed Indian – Stories the Land Told Me (in process)

The Aquarian Gospels (in process)

Curriculum/Courses
PEMS – Personal Energy Mechanics System
The Frontier Inside: A Woman's Path to Personal Power

Leading by Being: a Whole-Brain, Yin/Yang Women's Leadership Model
I Am My Own Daughter: Mothering the Self
Peace with the Parts: Mentoring the Inner Tribe™
Faces of Her – Embodying the Feminine
Faces of Him – Healing the Masculine
Sacred Systems – Living the Aquarian Gospels

Athena's Alliance *Resource, Education and Mentorship Program*

Made in the USA
Lexington, KY
12 February 2017